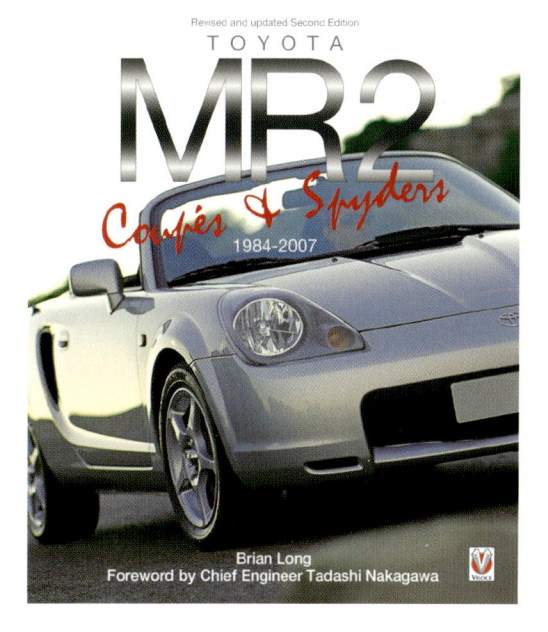

Revised and updated Second Edition
TOYOTA
MR2
Coupés & Spyders
1984-2007

Brian Long
Foreword by Chief Engineer Tadashi Nakagawa

Some other great books from Veloce:

Those Were The Days … Series

Alpine Trials & Rallies 1910-1973 (Pfundner)
American 'Independent' Automakers – AMC to Willys 1945 to 1960 (Mort)
American Station Wagons – The Golden Era 1950-1975 (Mort)
American Trucks of the 1950s (Mort)
American Trucks of the 1960s (Mort)
American Woodies 1928-1953 (Mort)
Anglo-American Cars from the 1930s to the 1970s (Mort)
Austins, The last real (Peck)
Don Hayter's MGB Story – The birth of the MGB in MG's Abingdon Design & Development Office (Hayter)
Drag Bike Racing in Britain – From the mid '60s to the mid '80s (Lee)
Dune Buggy Phenomenon, The (Hale)
Dune Buggy Phenomenon Volume 2, The (Hale)
Endurance Racing at Silverstone in the 1970s & 1980s (Parker)
Hot Rod & Stock Car Racing in Britain in the 1980s (Neil)
Last Real Austins 1946-1959, The (Peck)
Mercedes-Benz Trucks (Peck)
MG's Abingdon Factory (Moylan)
Motor Racing at Brands Hatch in the Seventies (Parker)
Motor Racing at Brands Hatch in the Eighties (Parker)
Motor Racing at Crystal Palace (Collins)
Motor Racing at Goodwood in the Sixties (Gardiner)
Motor Racing at Nassau in the 1950s & 1960s (O'Neil)
Motor Racing at Oulton Park in the 1960s (McFadyen)
Motor Racing at Oulton Park in the 1970s (McFadyen)
Motor Racing at Thruxton in the 1970s (Grant-Braham)
Motor Racing at Thruxton in the 1980s (Grant-Braham)
Superprix – The Story of Birmingham Motor Race (Page & Collins)
Three Wheelers (Bobbitt)

General

11/2-litre GP Racing 1961-1965 (Whitelock)
AC Two-litre Saloons & Buckland Sports cars (Archibald)
Alfa Romeo 155/156/147 Competition Touring Cars (Collins)
Alfa Romeo Giulia Coupé GT & GTA (Tipler)
Alfa Romeo Montreal – The dream car that came true (Taylor)
Alfa Romeo Montreal – The Essential Companion (Classic Reprint of 500 copies) (Taylor)
Alfa Tipo 33 (McDonough & Collins)
Alpine & Renault – The Development of the Revolutionary Turbo F1 Car 1968 to 1979 (Smith)
Alpine & Renault – The Sports Prototypes 1963 to 1969 (Smith)
Alpine & Renault – The Sports Prototypes 1973 to 1978 (Smith)
Anatomy of the Works Minis (Moylan)
Armstrong-Siddeley (Smith)
Art Deco and British Car Design (Down)
Autodrome (Collins & Ireland)
Autodrome 2 (Collins & Ireland)
Automotive A-Z, Lane's Dictionary of Automotive Terms (Lane)
Bahamas Speed Weeks, The (O'Neil)
Bentley Continental, Corniche and Azure (Bennett)
Bentley MkVI, Rolls-Royce Silver Wraith, Dawn & Cloud/Bentley R & S-Series (Nutland)
Bluebird CN7 (Stevens)
BMC Competitions Department Secrets (Turner, Chambers & Browning)
BMW 5-Series (Cranswick)
BMW Z-Cars (Taylor)
BMW Boxer Twins 1970-1995 Bible, The (Falloon)
BMW – The Power of M (Vivian)
Bonjour – Is this Italy? (Turner)
BRM – A Mechanic's Tale (Salmon)
BRM V16 (Ludvigsen)
Bugatti Type 40 (Price)
Bugatti 46/50 Updated Edition (Price & Arbey)
Bugatti T44 & T49 (Price & Arbey)
Bugatti 57 2nd Edition (Price)
Bugatti Type 57 Grand Prix – A Celebration (Tomlinson)
Carrera Panamericana, La (Tipler)
Chrysler 300 – America's Most Powerful Car 2nd Edition (Ackerson)
Chrysler PT Cruiser (Ackerson)
Citroën DS (Bobbitt)
Cobra – The Real Thing! (Legate)
Competition Car Aerodynamics 3rd Edition (McBeath)
Concept Cars, How to illustrate and design (Dewey)
Cortina – Ford's Bestseller (Robson)
Coventry Climax Racing Engines (Hammill)
Daily Mirror 1970 World Cup Rally 40, The (Robson)
Daimler SP250 New Edition (Long)
Datsun Fairlady Roadster to 280ZX – The Z-Car Story (Long)
Dino – The V6 Ferrari (Long)
Dodge Challenger & Plymouth Barracuda (Grist)
Dodge Charger – Enduring Thunder (Ackerson)
Dodge Dynamite! (Grist)
Dorset from the Sea – The Jurassic Coast from Lyme Regis to Old Harry Rocks photographed from its best viewpoint (Belasco)
Drive on the Wild Side, A – 20 Extreme Driving Adventures From Around the World (Weaver)
Dune Buggy, Building A – The Essential Manual (Shakespeare)
Dune Buggy Files (Hale)
Dune Buggy Handbook (Hale)
East German Motor Vehicles in Pictures (Suhr/Weinreich)
Fast Ladies – Female Racing Drivers 1888 to 1970 (Bouzanquet)
Fate of the Sleeping Beauties, The (op de Weegh/Hottendorff/op de Weegh)
Ferrari 288 GTO, The Book of the (Sackey)
Ferrari 333 SP (O'Neil)
Fiat & Abarth 124 Spider & Coupé (Tipler)
Fiat & Abarth 500 & 600 – 2nd Edition (Bobbitt)
Ford Cleveland 335-Series V8 engine 1970 to 1982 – The Essential Source Book (Hammill)
Ford F100/F150 Pick-up 1948-1996 (Ackerson)
Ford F150 Pick-up 1997-2005 (Ackerson)
Ford GT – Then, and Now (Streather)
Ford GT40 (Legate)
Ford Model Y (Roberts)
Ford Small Block V8 Racing Engines 1962-1970 – The Essential Source Book (Hammill)
Ford Thunderbird From 1954, The Book of the (Long)
Formula 5000 Motor Racing, Back then … and back now (Lawson)
Forza Minardi! (Vigar)
France: the essential guide for car enthusiasts – 200 things for the car enthusiast to see and do (Parish)
From Crystal Palace to Red Square – A Hapless Biker's Road to Russia (Turner)
Grand Prix Ferrari – The Years of Enzo Ferrari's Power, 1948-1980 (Pritchard)
Grand Prix Ford – DFV-powered Formula 1 Cars (Robson)
GT – The World's Best GT Cars 1953-73 (Dawson)
Hillclimbing & Sprinting – The Essential Manual (Short & Wilkinson)
Honda NSX (Long)
Inside the Rolls-Royce & Bentley Styling Department – 1971 to 2001 (Hull)
Intermeccanica – The Story of the Prancing Bull (McCredie & Reisner)
Jaguar, The Rise of (Price)
Jaguar XJ 220 – The Inside Story (Moreton)
Jaguar XJ-S, The Book of the (Long)
Jeep CJ (Ackerson)
Jeep Wrangler (Ackerson)
Karmann-Ghia Coupé & Convertible (Bobbitt)
Kawasaki Z1 Story, The (Sheehan)
Kris Meeke – Intercontinental Rally Challenge Champion (McBride)
Lamborghini Miura Bible, The (Sackey)
Lamborghini Urraco, The Book of the (Landsem)
Lancia 037 (Collins)
Lancia Delta HF Integrale (Blaettel & Wagner)
Land Rover Series III Reborn (Porter)
Land Rover, The Half-ton Military (Cook)
Laverda Twins & Triples Bible 1968-1986 (Falloon)
Lea-Francis Story, The (Price)
Le Mans Panoramic (Ireland)
Lexus Story, The (Long)
Little book of microcars, the (Quellin)
Little book of smart, the – New Edition (Jackson)
Little book of trikes, the (Quellin)
Lola – The Illustrated History (1957-1977) (Starkey)
Lola – All the Sports Racing & Single-seater Racing Cars 1978-1997 (Starkey)
Lola T70 – The Racing History & Individual Chassis Record – 4th Edition (Starkey)
Lotus 49 (Oliver)
Marketingmobiles, The Wonderful Wacky World of (Hale)
Maserati 250F In Focus (Pritchard)
Mazda MX-5/Miata 1.6 Enthusiast's Workshop Manual (Grainger & Shoemark)
Mazda MX-5/Miata 1.8 Enthusiast's Workshop Manual (Grainger & Shoemark)
The book of the Mazda MX-5 Miata – The 'Mk1' NA-series 1988 to 1997 (Long)
Mazda MX-5 Miata Roadster (Long)
Maximum Mini (Booij)
Meet the English (Bowie)
Mercedes-Benz SL – R230 series 2001 to 2011 (Long)
Mercedes-Benz SL – W113-series 1963-1971 (Long)
Mercedes-Benz SL & SLC – 107-series 1971-1989 (Long)
Mercedes-Benz SLK – R170 series 1996-2004 (Long)
Mercedes-Benz SLK – R171 series 2004-2011 (Long)
Mercedes-Benz W123-series – All models 1976 to 1986 (Long)
MGA (Price Williams)
MGB & MGB GT– Expert Guide (Auto-doc Series) (Williams)
MGB Electrical Systems Updated & Revised Edition (Astley)
Micro Trucks (Mort)
Mini Cooper – The Real Thing! (Tipler)
Mini Minor to Asia Minor (West)
Mitsubishi Lancer Evo, The Road Car & WRC Story (Long)
Montlhéry, The Story of the Paris Autodrome (Boddy)
Morgan Maverick (Lawrence)
Morgan 3 Wheeler – back to the future!, The (Dron)
Morris Minor, 60 Years on the Road (Newell)
Moto Guzzi Sport & Le Mans Bible, The (Falloon)
Motor Movies – The Posters! (Veysey)
Motor Racing – Reflections of a Lost Era (Carter)
Motor Racing – The Pursuit of Victory 1930-1962 (Carter)
Motor Racing – The Pursuit of Victory 1963-1972 (Wyatt/Sears)
Motor Racing Heroes – The Stories of 100 Greats (Newman)
Motorsport in colour, 1950s (Wainwright)
MV Agusta Fours, The book of the classic (Falloon)
N.A.R.T. – A concise history of the North American Racing Team 1957 to 1983 (O'Neil)
Nissan 300ZX & 350Z – The Z-Car Story (Long)
Nissan GT-R Supercar: Born to race (Gorodji)
Northeast American Sports Car Races 1950-1959 (O'Neil)
Nothing Runs – Misadventures in the Classic, Collectable & Exotic Car Biz (Slutsky)
Off-Road Giants! (Volume 1) – Heroes of 1960s Motorcycle Sport (Westlake)
Off-Road Giants! (Volume 2) – Heroes of 1960s Motorcycle Sport (Westlake)
Off-Road Giants! (volume 3) – Heroes of 1960s Motorcycle Sport (Westlake)
Pass the Theory and Practical Driving Tests (Gibson & Hoole)
Peking to Paris 2007 (Young)
Pontiac Firebird (Cranswick)
Porsche Boxster (Long)
Porsche 356 (2nd Edition) (Long)
Porsche 908 (Födisch, Neßhöver, Roßbach, Schwarz & Roßbach)
Porsche 911 Carrera – The Last of the Evolution (Corlett)
Porsche 911R, RS & RSR, 4th Edition (Starkey)
Porsche 911, The Book of the (Long)
Porsche 911SC 'Super Carrera' – The Essential Companion (Streather)
Porsche 914 & 914-6: The Definitive History of the Road & Competition Cars (Long)
Porsche 924 (Long)
The Porsche 924 Carreras – evolution to excellence (Smith)
Porsche 928 (Long)
Porsche 944 (Long)
Porsche 993 'King Of Porsche' – The Essential Companion (Streather)
Porsche 996 'Supreme Porsche' – The Essential Companion (Streather)
Porsche Racing Cars – 1953 to 1975 (Long)
Porsche Racing Cars – 1976 to 2005 (Long)
Porsche – The Rally Story (Meredith)
Porsche: Three Generations of Genius (Meredith)
Preston Tucker & Others (Linde)
RAC Rally Action! (Gardiner)
RACING COLOURS – MOTOR RACING COMPOSITIONS 1908-2009 (Newman)
Racing Line – British motorcycle racing in the golden age of the big single (Guntrip)
Rallye Sport Fords: The Inside Story (Moreton)
Renewable Energy Home Handbook, The (Porter)
Rolls-Royce Silver Shadow/Bentley T Series Corniche & Camargue – Revised & Enlarged Edition (Bobbitt)
Rolls-Royce Silver Spirit, Silver Spur & Bentley Mulsanne 2nd Edition (Bobbitt)
Runways & Racers (O'Neil)
Russian Motor Vehicles – Soviet Limousines 1930-2003 (Kelly)
Russian Motor Vehicles – The Czarist Period 1784 to 1917 (Kelly)
RX-7 – Mazda's Rotary Engine Sports car (Updated & Revised New Edition) (Long)
Scooters & Microcars, The A-Z of Popular (Dan)
Scooter Lifestyle (Grainger)
Singer Story: Cars, Commercial Vehicles, Bicycles & Motorcycle (Atkinson)
Sleeping Beauties USA – abandoned classic cars & trucks (Marek)
SM – Citroën's Maserati-engined Supercar (Long & Claverol)
Speedway – Auto racing's ghost tracks (Collins & Ireland)
Sprite Caravans, The Story of (Jenkinson)
Standard Motor Company, The Book of the
Subaru Impreza: The Road Car And WRC Story (Long)
Supercar, How to Build your own (Thompson)
Tales from the Toolbox (Oliver)
Tatra – The Legacy of Hans Ledwinka, Updated & Enlarged Collector's Edition of 1500 copies (Margolius & Henry)
Toleman Story, The (Hilton)
Toyota Celica & Supra, The Book of Toyota's Sports Coupés (Long)
Toyota MR2 Coupés & Spyders (Long)
Triumph Tiger Cub Bible (Estall)
Triumph Trophy Bible (Woolridge)
Triumph TR6 (Kimberley)
Two Summers – The Mercedes-Benz W196R Racing Car (Ackerson)
TWR Story, The – Group A (Hughes & Scott)
Unraced (Collins)
Velocette Motorcycles – MSS to Thruxton – New Third Edition (Burris)
Vespa – The Story of a Cult Classic in Pictures (Uhlig)
Volkswagen Bus Book, The (Bobbitt)
Volkswagen Bus or Van to Camper, How to Convert (Porter)
Volkswagens of the World (Glen)
VW Beetle Cabriolet – The full story of the convertible Beetle (Bobbitt)
VW Beetle – The Car of the 20th Century (Copping)
VW Bus – 40 Years of Splitties, Bays & Wedges (Copping)
VW Bus Book, The (Bobbitt)
VW Golf: Five Generations of Fun (Copping & Cservenka)
VW – The Air-cooled Era (Copping)
VW T5 Camper Conversion Manual (Porter)
VW Campers (Copping)
You & Your Jaguar XK8/XKR – Buying, Enjoying, Maintaining, Modifying – New Edition (Thorley)
Which Oil? – Choosing the right oils & greases for your antique, vintage, veteran, classic or collector car (Michell)
Works Minis, The Last (Purves & Brenchley)
Works Rally Mechanic (Moylan)

For post publication news, updates and amendments relating to this book please visit www.velocebooks.com/books/V5062

Also available … eBook Download now from www.digital.veloce.co.uk

Also available … Apps Download now from www.digital.veloce.co.uk

Hubble & Hattie

BATTLE CRY!

www.velocebooks.com

First published in 2002 by Veloce Publishing Limited, Veloce House, Parkway Farm Business Park, Middle Farm Way, Poundbury, Dorchester DT1 3AR, England. Fax 01305 250479 / e-mail info@veloce.co.uk / web www.veloce.co.uk or www.velocebooks.com. ISBN: 978-1-787110-62-5; UPC 6-36847-01062-1. This second edition published January 2017.
© 2002 and 2017 Brian Long and Veloce Publishing Ltd. All rights reserved. With the exception of quoting brief passages for the purpose of review, no part of this publication may be recorded, reproduced or transmitted by any means, including photocopying, without the written permission of Veloce Publishing Ltd. Throughout this book logos, model names and designations, etc, have been used for the purposes of identification, illustration and decoration. Such names are the property of the trademark holder as this is not an official publication. Readers with ideas for automotive books, or books on other transport or related hobby subjects, are invited to write to the editorial director of Veloce Publishing at the above address.
British Library Cataloguing in Publication Data – A catalogue record for this book is available from the British Library. Typesetting, design and page make-up all by Veloce Publishing Ltd on Apple Mac. Printed in India by Replika Press.

Revised and updated Second Edition

TOYOTA
MR2
Coupés & Spyders
1984-2007

Brian Long
Foreword by Chief Engineer Tadashi Nakagawa

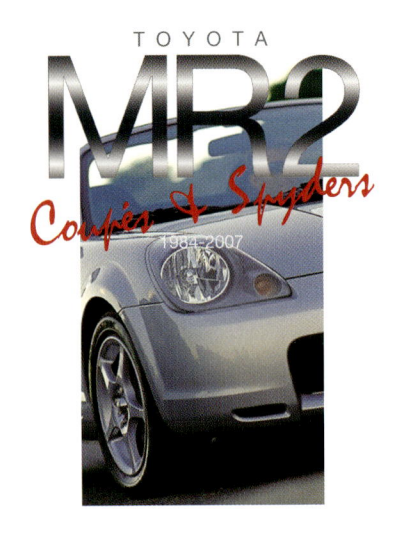

CONTENTS

Introduction & acknowledgements 6

Foreword 7

Chapter 1 The Toyota Story 9
    Birth of an Empire 9
    Toyota after WWII 11
    A new beginning 11
    Continued growth 12
    A fresh image 16

Chapter 2 A Midship Runabout 19
    Toyota's 'Middy' 19
    The 1983 Tokyo Show 23
    The home market 31
    The new car in Britain 39
    The MR2 reaches America 47
    Minor changes 50
    Competition news 55
    A new Celica, a new Supra 55
    The T-bar roof 56
    A supercharged model 57
    UK news 59
    The US 1987 model year 63
    Minor changes 64
    1988 model year in America 65
    News from the Antipodes 67
    More minor changes! 68
    Bowing out from the States 69
    News from Europe 71

Chapter 3 The Concept Matures 72
    The range in Japan 89
    The new MR2 In Britain 96
    Reaching American shores 100
    News from Australia 104
    The 1991 model year proper 104
    Limited editions 106
    1992 Stateside 106
    Minor changes 106
    Changes for the UK 110

America's 'New Car'	112
UK update	116
The MR2 In competition	116
Other Toyota sports cars	116
The 1994 model year	119
More changes for Europe	120
News from America	125
News from Japan	126
Bowing out from America	126
The 31st Tokyo Show	126
UK news round-up	132
The JGTC	133
The Technocraft MR Spider	134
The TRD 2000GT	138
The UK market for 1997	138
The MR2 story continues	138
The model's finale	139

Chapter 4 A New Direction 143

The 32nd Tokyo Show	145
The MR-S development story	146
The dream becomes reality	157
The home market	161
The new car in the UK	162
The MR2's return in America	166
MR-S Specials	170
Japanese update	174
News from Australia	176
Europe in 2001	177
The US 2001 & 2002 model years	179
A minor change	179
The US market	182
Rhd export markets	184
Another change	187
Christmas present	188

Appendix I Specifications 191

Appendix II Production Figures 196

Index 199

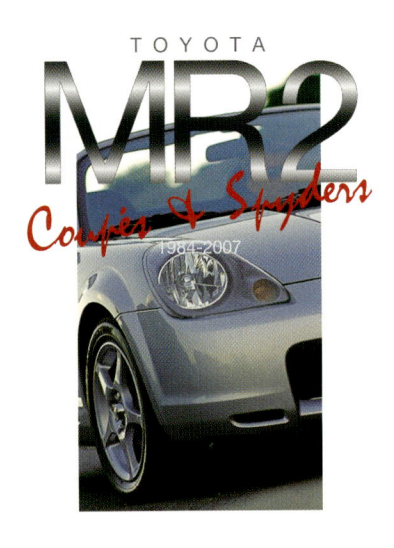

INTRODUCTION & ACKNOWLEDGEMENTS

Introduction
The MR2 was a landmark Japanese car, up there with the legendary Toyota 2000GT, the Datsun 240Z, and Mazda's RX-7 and MX-5. It was the first mid-engined production model to come from the Land of the Rising Sun, and will always have a special place in the hearts of enthusiasts all over the world.

The MR2 started life as the SV-3 concept car, introduced at the 1983 Tokyo Show. By the middle of the following year, the first production models were filtering into Japanese showrooms, but they didn't stay there for long: the MR2 was an instant hit, and demand soon outstripped supply. It was a similar situation in export markets when it went on sale during the early part of 1985.

For 1987, the T-bar roof option gave the little Toyota wider appeal, and there was a supercharged engine for Japanese buyers, and later, American ones, too. However, time was running out for the First Generation model and its replacement was duly introduced at the 1989 Tokyo Show.

The Second Generation MR2 was an altogether different beast; more Grand Tourer than lightweight sports. With a turbocharged or naturally-aspirated power unit, initial reactions were mixed, but the concept quickly matured and gained worldwide critical acclaim. Sadly, by 1996, only Japanese, European and Australian enthusiasts were able to buy one as, for various reasons, the model was prematurely killed off in the United States.

The 1995 Tokyo Show saw the debut of the MRJ, leading everyone to assume it was the latest incarnation of the MR breed. However, it was the MR-S concept car of 1997 vintage that was destined to provide the basis for the next production model. This lightweight open roadster was eventually launched in Japan at the end of 1999 (as the MR-S), making its way into the European and American export markets, badged respectively as the MR2 Roadster and MR2 Spyder, shortly after.

Acknowledgements
Tammie Kanda was a fantastic help in the States, as was the Tokyo Design Office and the Public Relations Department in Japan; I would particularly like to single out Masumi Akihiro, who looks after the photographic side. She responded quickly and efficiently to my many requests, and this book is all the better for her efforts. Thanks also to Anna Nishiwaki and Sonomi Aikawa.

Apart from the official sources of material, I am very fortunate to have some good friends in Japan whose work, reproduced here by kind permission, has enhanced the quality of this book no end. Yoshihiro Inomoto (aka the 'Cutaway King') let me use his superb artwork, and fellow RJC member, Hideo Aoki, once again provided a number of his valuable photographs. I am extremely grateful to both of these true gentlemen.

My wife, Miho, did her usual sterling job translating various articles and interviews for me. One day, I really must get round to paying her! Meanwhile, I hope a big 'thank you' will suffice ... Finally, I would like to extend my appreciation to Tadashi Nakagawa, the man behind many important Toyota sports car projects, for taking the time to write the Foreword for me. Many thanks.

Brian Long
Chiba City, Japan

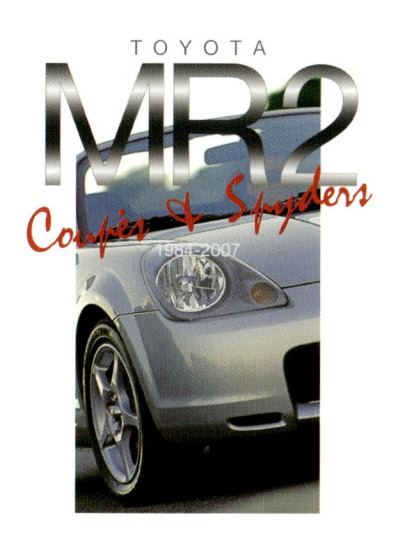

FOREWORD

I first met Brian Long at the 1995 Tokyo Show. I was explaining the new MRJ concept model to journalists, and can clearly remember being approached by him and his charming wife. My overwhelming impression from that first meeting was of a real enthusiast, with a passion for sporting machinery. I often instruct members of my staff to be like him – a person who combines professional, technical knowledge with an undying enthusiasm for driving and all things motoring. If he were a TMC worker, he would be my ideal partner in developing sports cars.

When I took over the MR2 project in 1992, it was a very difficult time for Japanese sports car manufacturers. The economy, which had been riding on an exceptional high, suddenly fell apart – the bubble had burst. As a result, unfortunately, sales of the Second Generation MR2 were pitifully small. Not surprisingly, the management took a dim view of the model, and decided that this lack of support would almost certainly signal the end of the MR2. It was a strange situation, however. Although I was now the MR2 Chief Engineer, there had been no official news regarding this decision from my predecessor and, indeed, no direct word from the Board regarding the vehicle's future, only a lot of rumours from within the company and in the press.

Undeterred, I naturally set about my new task – how to make the Third Generation MR2 a better machine. Several key points were established: originality and character were absolute necessities in a car of this type, its packaging had to be more efficient, and it had to fit in with the expectations of the new century.

Eventually, after a great deal of research, I decided to go for a lightweight sports car with a longer wheelbase. Common sense would seem to rule out the long wheelbase, as handling is ultimately compromised due to the added weight necessary to make the monocoque rigid and strong. However, my theory was that if the body could be kept light, handling would be enhanced, and the vehicle's packaging much better than that of a traditional mid-engined sports car. I managed to prove this through simulation, but no-one believed me. Fortunately, I found support in the Technician Group, who said they would happily build a prototype for me as "a form of training." It was an ideal project for these craftsmen to undertake, but, in reality, it was a somewhat shady way of getting my car built!

We took an MR2, cut it through the middle, and added 150mm (5.9in) in the wheelbase. In addition, we took out as much poundage as possible in order to reduce the overall weight to just 1100kg (2420lb), and then changed the two-litre 180bhp engine for a lighter 1.8-litre 125bhp unit to reduce the weight still further. Although this prototype was lacking the power of the original, when I took it to a circuit for testing, it felt quicker than the normal MR2. More importantly, its handling was confidence inspiring, and it was great fun to drive. So much so, I just kept going round and round, and lost all track of time.

I duly showed the vehicle to the head of the Technical Departments. He scolded me verbally for having built this "outrageous" machine, but, after the initial grim-looking face, I could sense in his eyes a far warmer reception than his first reaction had suggested, and I was convinced he was more than a little interested in the project deep down. At last, even though not officially, I had

Tadashi Nakagawa has loved cars all his life. He joined Toyota in April 1969 after graduating from Tokyo University Graduate School master's course. He started his career in the Experimental Department, specializing in drivetrains, before a spell in Europe founding Toyota's European R&D section. On his return to Japan, he became involved in Production Planning for some 20 years, ten of which were spent as a Chief Engineer. He was based in Brussels as a Chief Executive Engineer and Board Member of TMME at the time of writing this Foreword, but has now retired from the motor industry.

found someone that went along with my theory.

It was around this time that Toyota asked for ideas for the 1995 Tokyo Show concept cars. The timing was perfect – I put forward my proposal for a strange little sports car with a long wheelbase and variable 2+2 seating. It was duly accepted as an interesting design, and appeared on the company's stand as the MRJ. Thankfully, the car found favour with the public but, as usual, the critics were quick to find fault. A few said the 2+2 seating took away some of the car's sportiness, while others questioned whether it could be built so light as a production model – if it was over 1000kg (2200lb), was it really a lightweight sports car?

All of this quibbling simply fuelled my desire still further to build a true LWS. I took in people's comments, analysed them, and subtly changed my plans until I was sure I had the ultimate Third Generation MR2 in my mind. Even then, people in the company still doubted whether I could build an open car weighing in at under 1000kg (2200lb).

I approached Akihiro Wada (the top of the Technical Departments and an Executive Director), a world-famous authority on body engineering, and explained over several months my goals and problems. Eventually, he gave me his full support, but I still had to convince the rest of the management. Fortunately, the project was given a green light, much to the surprise of a number of people. I remember after the first car came off the line, one member of staff said to me he didn't think it was possible to build the vehicle as I wanted it, and that my insistence that it could be built to my specifications was simply a case of me blowing my own trumpet!

Of course, the project went far from smoothly. All members involved were asked to find at least 20 places per person where they could save a few grammes. It was incredibly difficult to do this whilst retaining quality and meeting regulations, but I used the threat that if the car was over 1000kg (2200lb), it would not go into production, and the name of the group which failed to reduce the weight enough would be posted throughout the company! We were fortunately able to reduce weight both on paper (at the planning stage), and as the prototypes were developed.

Naturally, handling is a number one priority with a sports car. As the project progressed, I had the pleasure of personally being able to check the prototypes at each stage to ensure the Third Generation model was capable of fulfilling my dreams, and up to my expectations as an engineer. Every time we encountered a problem, we would quickly assemble underneath the vehicle, and put forward a decision on how we could cure it. I must go on record stating my appreciation for the effort everyone put into the new MR2. Sports car projects seem to bring out the best in people and, very often, members went without food – and occasionally sleep as well – in order to get the job done. As a result, the vehicle's handling far exceeds our greatest hopes.

At the same time as work on the Third Generation MR2 progressed, I was developing the Seventh Generation Celica – another car designed for enthusiasts. But while the future of the Celica was assured, the mid-engined model was rather like a hobby project – a personal aspiration. As time passed, the company shifted its stance on the MR2, and gave me the funding to make my dream a reality. As such, I feel as if Toyota loaned me several hundred million dollars to fulfil my ambition. Now I have to work hard in Europe to repay them!

Sports cars provide the purest form of driving enjoyment, and this volume traces the entire history of Toyota's mid-engined sporting line. Like the MR2 itself, I truly believe this book will be fun for enthusiasts and followers of motoring lore.

**Tadashi Nakagawa
Brussels, Belgium**

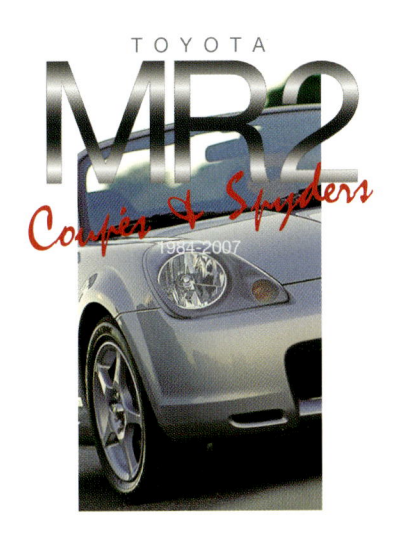

Kiichiro Toyoda, founder of the Toyota Motor Company.

1
THE TOYOTA STORY

The Toyoda Automatic Loom Works Limited was established in 1926 in Kariya, near Nagoya. Sakichi Toyoda, who founded the company, duly introduced a number of improvements in weaving machinery, and made a small fortune granting the patent rights to a firm in England. As a motoring enthusiast, Sakichi earmarked a substantial amount of this money to enable his son, Kiichiro, to set up a car building department.

Japan was a long way behind the automobile-producing countries of Europe and America. Indeed, it wasn't until 1907 that the first petrol-engined Japanese car was produced. Even then, much of the chassis technology employed on the Yoshida Type 3 (better known by its nickname, the 'Takuri') had been borrowed from French manufacturers, and two of the ten built were powered by twin-cylinder units imported from the States.

However, by the time of the First World War, the fledgling Japanese industry was starting to find its feet. Shintaro Yoshida, the man behind the Takuri, had introduced a series of vehicles under the auspices of the Tokyo Automobile Works, including his country's first four-cylinder model, which appeared in 1911.

It was in 1911 that Masujiro Hashimoto founded the Kaishinsha Motor Car Works – the origin of the Datsun marque; later, a merger led to the formation of the Nissan Motor Company. Meanwhile, in 1912, Ohta was established in Tokyo, and, a few years after, the first Mitsubishi was built.

Despite this period of growth, there were still very few cars in Japan, even during the 1920s. In fact, a survey conducted in 1923 showed there to be less than 13,000 vehicles on the road at the time, and almost all of these were American, initially brought into the country to get it mobile again following the massive Kanto Earthquake of that year. A few more manufacturers joined the ranks, such as Ishikawajima (the forerunner of Isuzu) and Otomo, but, by the end of the decade, Ford, General Motors and Chrysler all had a strong foothold. Such was their dominance in the Japanese market that Ford and GM established their own assembly plants, in Yokohama and Osaka respectively.

It was against this backdrop that Kiichiro Toyoda joined the motor industry. Born in June 1894, Kiichiro had studied mechanical engineering at the Tokyo Imperial University, and also visited a number of American and European car manufacturers before commencing his career. His first project, which he started in 1930, was the construction of a 4bhp two-cylinder engine. Based on a Smith power unit from America, this fairly modest beginning signified the birth of the Toyota automobile empire.

Birth of an Empire
Toyoda's first car, a 1932 prototype built in conjunction with the Okuma-Nippon Sharyo concern, and named the Atsuta after a famous local Shinto shrine, was not a great success. However,

9

with advice and encouragement from his friends in the growing industry he persevered.

Towards the end of 1933, a proper automobile department was set up, Toyoda declaring that: "Instead of avoiding competition with Ford and Chevrolet, we will develop and mass-produce a car that incorporates the strong points of both, and that can rival foreign cars in performance and price."

In the spring of 1935, the Model A-1 prototype was completed. It featured a Chrysler Airflow-style body mounted on a Chevrolet-based chassis, and was powered by a 65bhp copy of the six-cylinder, 3.4-litre ohv Chevrolet engine. This proved far more satisfactory, and limited production of the Toyoda Model AA (a direct development of the A-1) began in April 1936.

The Toyota Motor Company Limited was formed on 28th August 1937 with a capital equivalent to $35,000. All future vehicles would be given the Toyota name rather than Toyoda: firstly, because it was easier to pronounce and, secondly, it had a 'lucky' number of strokes when written in Japanese *katakana* (eight strokes, instead of the ten required for Toyoda).

The birth of Toyota happened to coincide with a new sense of nationalism. The Japanese government – at that time run by the military – was alarmed at the amount of cash leaving the country, with the balance of trade stacked firmly in favour of the United States. A number of restrictions and tariffs were imposed on imported vehicles and, with the introduction of the 1936 Motorcar Manufacturing Enterprise Law, foreign manufacturers were eventually driven out. Although only Toyota, Nissan and Isuzu complied with the 1936 act, the government did everything within its power to encourage domestic producers.

The 1936 Toyoda Model AA Sedan, Toyota's first production car. A drophead version, designated the Model AB and powered by the same 3389cc, six-cylinder engine, was also available.

The recently-acquired Koromo factory site was expanded, late in 1938, with production increasing rapidly thereafter from around 100 cars per

The BA and BB appeared in 1940, taking styling hints from the contemporary Volvo (the BA was a four-light saloon, while the BB was a drophead prototype). This, the 1944 BC sedan, powered by an 85bhp six, is another model that failed to make it into production because of the war.

The Toyopet Model SA of 1947. Designed by Masao Morimoto, it was powered by a four-cylinder, 995cc, side-valve engine. It was in 1947 that Toyota's cumulative production reached 100,000 units. At the end of October 1949, SCAP finally granted Japanese manufacturers permission to produce cars without restrictions, but had it not been for military orders received at the outbreak of the Korean War, Toyota could have been in serious financial difficulties.

month in 1936 to roughly 2000 a month following the expansion programme. The town of Koromo was later renamed Toyota City, incidentally.

By now, cars, trucks and buses were being produced. In an effort to become more self-sufficient, the company also formed the Toyoda Machine Tool Works, the Aichi Steel Works, and two firms dealing with body pressings. However, for many years, steel was still being imported from America.

Just as Toyota was getting into its stride, Japan entered the Second World War. As the conflict in the Pacific escalated, production was turned over exclusively to military requirements and, as a result, a number of promising prototypes, such as the Model B saloon, were destined never to reach the showroom.

Toyota after WWII

It wasn't until 1947 that Toyota resumed car production. The first vehicle was a 4x4 model, which was the ancestor of the famous Land Cruiser line, although the SA, which appeared in the same year, was perhaps the most important – it was significant in a number of ways.

Kiichiro Toyoda was quite unusual for a Japanese industrialist during this period because he was interested not only in utility, but design as well. The 27bhp Toyopet SA was styled by Masao Morimoto, and demonstrated Toyoda's willingness to accept bolder, European-type profiles. Morimoto had joined Toyota as a stylist in 1940 but, owing to the war, this was his first design to reach the marketplace. Over the years that followed, he would pen the lines for a number of other monumental cars.

As well as advanced styling, the compact S series were the first Toyotas to feature small and efficient engines. They were designed to compete in a market sector below that of the big American machines, since few people in Japan could afford to run such cars in the immediate post-war years. However, in line with the directives issued by SCAP (the Supreme Commander for the Allied Powers), output was limited, and the SA was never allowed to fulfil its undoubted potential. Nevertheless, employment within Toyota kept rising; Nippondenso was established to produce electrical items, while the Toyoda Spinning & Weaving Company manufactured cloth and thread for use in both the automotive and domestic fields.

With such expansion, combined with low production, cashflow soon became a serious problem. The workforce, which had stood at 8000 in 1949, was cut back to 6000. In response, the remaining workers went on an eight week strike – the only one in the company's history. Subsequently, Kiichiro Toyoda resigned, with Taizo Ishida taking his place at the head of the business; Kiichiro died two years later, in 1952. However, his cousin, Eiji Toyoda, in the role of Managing Director, maintained the family link, and eventually became Chairman.

A new beginning

Eiji Toyoda had visited Ford in America, along with Shoichi Saito, a member of his management team, to study the latest ideas in car production. He stayed there for several weeks and, as a result, within a decade Toyota had totally transformed its working practices, increasing productivity and becoming one of the most efficient factories in Japan in the process. Much of this metamorphosis can be attributed to the 'suggestion system,' whereby the company invited workers to suggest ways of improving production. This system is still in use today. In 1993, for instance, more than 900,000 ideas were submitted, with almost all of them being adopted!

The Korean War of 1950-53 had also helped the Toyota Company, as it received a number of large military orders from the Allied forces. Mr Toyoda later said that "the orders were Toyota's salvation." At this time, of course, Japan was still under the Allied Occupation Authority following the Second World War, the Allies (largely Americans) not pulling out until 1952.

Toyota Motor Sales had been formed in 1950, thereby splitting the manufacturing and marketing organisations. TMS had the inspired idea of teaching more people to drive; this was a great success and, in the long term, sales increased beyond all expectations. In 1955, car production stood at 700 units a month; by 1962 the company had completed its one millionth automobile, and by 1965

11

The first Crown (the Model RS) was introduced in January 1955.

Toyota was building a staggering 25,000 cars a month, as well as a similar number of commercial vehicles.

In 1954, the company underwent a massive reorganisation in the way its products were designed. Clay modelling was introduced, along with the system of allocating different teams to the various projects. The First Generation Crown of 1955 vintage was the first to benefit and, from a styling point of view, proved to be a very important model.

Morimoto was subsequently sent to an American art school to learn automotive design, as well as Western tastes and styles. A proper Design Section was established on his return and, by 1966, it was the biggest and by far the most modern styling centre in Japan.

Japan's motor industry, still largely reliant on European technology at this stage, was not considered a threat by any of the established car-producing countries. When Renault complained to the French government that Hino had not been paying royalties on 4CVs built under licence, the response was that it was "hardly fair to pick on this poor little country which has such a task to feed hundreds of thousands of inhabitants."

Shotaro Kamiya was the motive force behind Toyota's entry into the US market – the influential President took the decision in mid-1957 following a visit to the country. The Crown was the first Toyota sent to America, two of the 1.5-litre machines arriving in Los Angeles (accompanied by Miss Japan) in August 1957. Toyota Motor Sales Inc. was founded two months later, although, at this time, Japanese cars and the requirements of American buyers were poles apart, and this initial attempt at establishing a market in the States was something of a failure. Donald Frey of Ford even went as far as to say that the first Crown he saw was "a heap of junk." Nonetheless, many lessons were learnt.

Continued growth

Taiichi Ohno (later Toyota's Vice-President) helped to increase productivity by the introduction of new work practices, and was the man behind the 'Just-in-Time' system, now employed throughout the motor industry.

During 1959, Toyota opened the Motomachi plant – the first Toyota factory dedicated solely to car manufacture. The Corona was already in production, having been introduced in May 1957, and was soon followed by the 1000 UP10, which was later developed into the Starlet. Interestingly, the Corona name was already in use in Japan; Nissan had a small coach called the Corona but, instead of trying to stop Toyota from using the appellation when the announcement was made, Nissan rang the Nagoya concern to thank it for advertising the little bus! The business of selling cars was certainly a more genteel affair back then.

Meanwhile, with sales picking up in the States, thanks largely to a bigger 1.9-litre engine being employed for the Crown, there was even talk of Toyota joining forces with Ford to produce the Publica economy car in the US. By 1963, the Japanese marque had begun its export drive and, having introduced an all-new Crown the previous year, was now in a position to supply America with the vehicles it needed. The company next set its sights on Europe.

Toyota's Corona series made its debut in May 1957, and was to become one of its most successful lines. This is a Second Generation (ST20) model dating from 1960, and pictured with Tokyo Tower in the background. With all the high-rise buildings surrounding the Tower nowadays, it has become extremely difficult to get a clear view of this famous landmark.

The diminutive Sports 800: Toyota's first lightweight sports car.

Exports went up from less than 6500 units in 1960 to nearly 43,000 for 1964, the year in which Japan was admitted to the Organisation for

The Sports 800 made quite a name for itself on Japan's race tracks; Togiro Ukiya and Shiomi Hosoya were leading exponents.

13

Japan's first true Grand Tourer, the Toyota 2000GT, at the 1967 Tokyo Show. Powered by the six-cylinder Crown engine, a 200bhp competition model was also available.

Economic Co-Operation & Development – an international group for advanced industrial nations. By 1967, exports had topped the 150,000 vehicles per annum mark and, within two years of this, Toyota had become the second largest exporter to the States, exceeded only by Volkswagen.

The 1.1-litre Corolla had been introduced in November 1966, and became Japan's best-selling model almost overnight. The larger, immensely popular Cressida followed a couple of years later. The range was by now quite extensive, and included everything from two-cylinder economy cars to V8 limousines.

In the meantime, Toyota had briefly entered the sports car market with its tiny Sports 800 (or UP15) for the 1965 season. First shown at the 1962 Tokyo Show as a concept car, it was just too advanced to go on sale, with features like a roll-back canopy instead of doors. Nonetheless, penned by Shozo Sato (the man behind the chassis of the Nissan 110 and first two generations of the Bluebird), it was a very accomplished design, based on the Publica.

It was displayed at the 1964 Tokyo Show in slightly more conservative form, powered by a 697cc engine, but went on sale six months later with a front-mounted, 790cc flat-twin. In addition, by the time the 'Yotohachi' went into production, to save weight it had gained an aluminium roof, boot and doors – remarkably, the Sports 800 tipped the scales at less than 600kg (1320lb)!

Launched at a very reasonable 592,000 yen, the price remained almost the same throughout its entire run. To put this into perspective, the Honda S600 was 653,000 yen in 1966, while the 1.6-litre Datsun Fairlady was around half as much again.

Sadly, despite excellent fuel consumption figures and a capability of 96mph (154kph) due to its light weight, it was not a car suitable for foreign markets – it was simply too small. Some fine results on Japan's race

An American promotional brochure for the 2000GT. Sadly, despite rave reviews from the motoring press, it made little impact on the US market, mainly because of a high price tag.

14

Advertising showing the 2000GT on its record-breaking run in October 1966.

tracks afforded it some kudos, but it was never destined to be a commercial success. By the time it was taken off the market in October 1969, just 3131 had been built, and very few of these were exported: only two are known to have made it to British shores.

The legendary 2000GT was launched at the Tokyo Motor Show in October 1965, created by Jiro Kawano and built for Toyota by Yamaha. Although perhaps better known for its links with music equipment and motorcycles, for a number of years, the Hamamatsu-based company had been developing sports car prototypes for outside concerns, and had been working on a similar one for Nissan at the same time (the forerunner of the 240Z).

The body was beautiful; in the mould of a classic European sports car; the only criticism being the large number of openings for maintenance access. With the vehicle being so low, pop-up headlights were used to comply with minimum height regulations in America. The engine was a dohc straight-six of 1988cc, developing 150bhp in standard form, or up to 200 in racing trim. A five-speed, all-synchromesh gearbox was used, the top ratio being overdriven for good fuel economy and comfortable cruising. Top

Japanese advertising for the Corona 1900SL, dating from 1972. Note the use of European models: a popular trend in Japan at the time, typified by Nissan's famous twosome, Ken and Mary.

speed was put at 143mph (229kph) for the production model, just 13mph (21kph) short of the lightweight racing machines.

Following racing practice, both the front and rear suspension was via double-wishbones, with discs all-round for the brakes. As *Classic Cars* noted in 1975: "It seemed perfectly balanced and as neutral as you can expect a front-engined car to be. A four-wheel drift could be induced easily through either steering or throttle control."

In May 1966, the 2000GT made its second public appearance, this time at the Japanese Grand Prix. Toyota

Stylish advertising for the immensely popular Celica, linking the past, present and future. Later, the original coupé was joined by a Liftback version which further broadened the appeal of the model.

entered two lightweight versions, with one finishing third behind two works Prince R380 mid-engined prototypes, although the sister car had qualified second on the grid.

At the Suzuka 1000km Race in June, the two cars came home in one-two formation, thus proving both the speed and reliability of the new Toyota. The final proof came when a 2000GT broke three world records and no less than 13 international records for speed and endurance in October, averaging 128.76mph (206kph) over 72 hours.

In the USA, three cars were turned over to Carroll Shelby and his team to be used for SCCA C-Production racing. Driven by Dave Jordan and Scooter Patrick (the third car was purely for development purposes), they were honed into 250bhp race winners by the end of 1968, but then, sadly, the 2000GT project came to an end.

This particular Toyota is now one of the most collectable of all Japanese cars. At the time, though, it sold in very small numbers; in fact, just 351 were built. However, it did at least pave the way for a more sporting and upmarket image to be adopted.

Meanwhile, during the late-1960s, Toyota acquired Hino and Daihatsu, bringing the former's car producing days to an end. (Toyota did not take complete control of Daihatsu until the latter half of 1998, incidentally.) At a time when others were making deals with the Big Three in America, purely to establish themselves in the world's largest market, Toyota not only stayed independent, but adopted an even more aggressive marketing and expansion policy, especially during the 1973 Arab Oil Crisis when its economy cars were in great demand.

In 1969, Toyota was the world's fifth biggest car producer, way behind General Motors and Ford, but not far behind Volkswagen and Chrysler figures. By 1972 – thanks, in no small part, to the huge success of the Corolla at home and abroad – Toyota had moved into third place.

A fresh image

The contemporary Corona (in Mark II form by September 1968) was already a proven winner, voted 'Imported Car of the Year' for 1969 by the American magazine *Road Test*. The decision to market the Celica coupé in the first place, however, was a bold one for

With regard to sales, the Corolla was undoubtedly the car of the 1970s. It was also a pretty useful rally car, as can be seen in this picture taken at the Arctic Rally in Finland. Almost seven million Corollas were sold during the decade.

a conservative company like Toyota, but was made at a time when Japan's economy was running at an all-time high. The public was starting to spend more money on leisure activities, and there was a notable swing towards Western trends.

Based on the EX-I (a concept car shown at the 1969 Tokyo Show), the new Celica was above all "a car for the seventies" – perfectly in tune with the changing times, but, perhaps more importantly, perfect for the American market. Announced in September 1970, the Celica joined a new breed of cars, such as the Mitsubishi Galant GTO, Mazda RX-2 and Datsun's 240Z and Bluebird-U, as perfect examples of modern Japanese sports cars, combining good looks with driving pleasure, economy and reliability.

Writing for *Motor* magazine in England, Paul Frère, the ex-Ferrari F1 driver turned journalist, noted: "In my opinion, this is the best Toyota yet ... It handles well, has a very good gearbox and quite a torquey engine ..."

The first Celica arrived in the UK in mid-1971. A couple of years later, the home market received the Celica Liftback, although this series wasn't exported until 1976. In the meantime, the First Generation Celica had attained some very favourable competition results, both in Japan and abroad. Win Percy was declared the winner of the 1600 Class of the British Saloon Car Championship (the forerunner of the BTCC) in 1975 and 1976, whilst in the World Rally Championship, Ove Andersson took second place in the 1976 Rally of Portugal, and Hannu Mikkola clinched second place in the 1977 RAC Rally.

The Second Generation Celicas. Again, a Liftback version was made available, and also a luxury GT with a straight-six engine, known as the Celica Supra, for the USA. At home, the larger model was known as the Celica XX.

The Third Generation Celica range had sharper lines and another Supra (seen here in British guise). This series of Celicas established Toyota as a serious competitor in the mass-produced sports and GT market.

Over one million First Generation cars had been sold by the time they were replaced in the summer of 1977. Once again, the Celica was available as a coupé or a Liftback model, and there were a large number of engine, transmission and trim options. Shortly after, the first Celica XX (or Celica Supra in export markets) made its debut – a Celica Liftback with a longer nose and a 2.6-litre, straight-six powerplant.

Although the Crown was no longer available in America, the Cressida (or Mark II as it was known in Japan) proved worthy of shouldering the former's mantle, and the new model, introduced in 1978, perfectly combined luxury with affordability and reliability. All Celicas were updated for the 1980 model year and, in August, the XX version acquired a more powerful 2.8-litre engine. Shortly after, the engine size of American Celicas increased from 2.2 to 2.4 litres.

It was all part of Toyota's plan to enhance the image of the brand abroad. Unfavourable exchange rates would soon make Japanese exports more expensive, and therefore harder to sell. In the early days of the Celica and the Datsun Z, the value of the yen made American imports extremely good value for money, but times had changed: cars now sold on their merits and not just their sticker price. Nonetheless, in 1980, Japan produced seven million vehicles during the year, becoming the world's number one car producer.

In July 1981, the Third Generation Celicas were announced, along with an attractive Second Generation Celica Supra, using the same formula as the previous model – a larger, six-cylinder power unit and an extended nose section. A number of interesting models came out of this series, especially those linked with Toyota's attack on the WRC. The Chief Engineer, incidentally, was Akihiro Wada, who would later become the company's Vice-President.

On the first day of July 1982, the Toyota manufacturing and sales organisations were brought together again under the presidency of Shoichiro Toyoda, Kiichiro's son. He was more receptive to fresh ideas than his predecessors, and the first completely new car to appear after this move was the mid-engined MR2.

Displayed at the 1983 Tokyo Motor Show under the SV-3 banner (its original codename), the MR2 further enchanced Toyota's new-found sporting image.

TOYOTA MR2
Coupés & Spyders
1984-2007

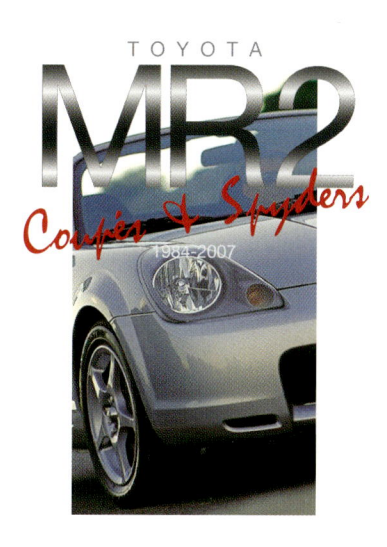

2
A MIDSHIP RUNABOUT

The Porsche 914 series was the first successful attempt at mass-producing a mid-engined road car, the layout having previously been the reserve of exotic vehicles built in limited numbers – and usually at very high cost!

Of course, Lotus had launched the modestly-priced Europa but, with less than 10,000 built in the best part of a decade, this was hardly mass-production. The French Matra concern had also sold a mid-engined machine – the M530 – but escalating costs forced prices up, thus reducing demand. Despite great hopes for the model, sales figures were ultimately similar to those of the Lotus.

So, the Porsche (actually a joint project with Volkswagen), with sales amounting to almost 120,000 units from September 1969 to June 1976, remained the only commercial success with this layout up to this point in time. Interestingly, though, Porsche abandoned the mid-engine concept for road cars until the advent of the Boxster almost two decades later.

In the meantime, just as it looked as if the days of the affordable mid-engined coupé were numbered, Fiat introduced the X1/9. The Bertone-styled machine made its debut in 1972, and had surpassed the Porsche in terms of sales figures by the early 1980s, by which time, the Fiat name had been dropped and production moved to Bertone. The X1/9 was eventually phased out in 1989, with around 180,000 units having been built.

Lancia introduced the Beta Montecarlo to the public at the 1975 Geneva Show but, like so many middies, it was destined to sell in small numbers (actually, less than 8000 were sold). In the same year as the Lancia made its debut, Nissan exhibited a small, mid-engined car known as the AD-1 at the Tokyo Show, but, sadly, nothing was to come of this interesting project.

However, as *What Car?* pointed out in a promotional brochure produced for Toyota GB: "Just as commentators were dismissing the idea of an affordably-priced, mid-engined sports car as a hopeless fantasy, Toyota went out and built one."

Toyota's 'Middy'

Toyota's mid-engined sports car project was originally started in 1976, but quickly relegated to the 'pending' file in the wake of the fuel crisis, as attention naturally turned towards economy models. By 1979, however, it had been revived, with Seiichi Yamauchi selected as Chief Designer.

As with all the cars produced by Toyota nowadays, the MR2 passed through three main stages of design: research, development and production considerations. During its research, the team of planners, designers and engineers behind the new car, headed by Akio Yoshida (who had joined the company in 1958), decided on a lightweight, sporty machine, that was first and foremost fun to drive, appealing to a wide range of people from young office girls to retired gentlemen.

The initial results of this research led to the aptly named 'Mid-Engine Sports Car' prototype, not all that different to the eventual production car, but slightly longer and heavier-looking. At this stage, there were definite shades of the Triumph TR7 in its profile, the X1/9 in its window graphics, and a strong suggestion of the contemporary Pontiac Firebird around the nose.

An early design study displaying heavily-flared wheelarches and a full-width rear light. The reduced height below the waistline goes a long way towards making the car appear lower. Yamauchi wanted to carry this feature through to production, but had to compromise in the end because of the use of so many parts from other Toyota models.

A front-wheel drive 'Sporty Commuter Car' followed, but, after building the full-size model, it became obvious that it was just too *avant garde* for a conservative car-buying public. Besides, after numerous studies involving new high-performance powerplants with FF (front engine, front-wheel drive) and FR (front engine, rear-wheel drive) drivetrains were assessed, considered and dismissed, the development team returned to the mid-engined concept, further refining it with a view to volume production.

In the meantime, the car's market position was established by Shiro Sasaki and his team, giving the designers something of a headache, as one of the main objectives was to sell the proposed new model at a price somewhere between the Levin Trueno and Carina Coupé, whilst providing a level of sportiness above that of the Fiat X1/9. In effect, Toyota was looking to produce a modern version of the Sports 800; ie a sports car that people could enjoy without having to be rich to buy one, or run one, for that matter.

Thus, the seeds were sown for Japan's first mass-produced, mid-engined vehicle. This seemed like an inspired move though, in reality, Toyota had simply spotted the vast expansion of the personal car market in America – the timing was right for such a vehicle.

Public preference had moved away from muscle-bound sports cars during the 1970s, when one fuel crisis followed another. However, the desire for fun at the wheel never diminished, it was just that few manufacturers felt there was a future in open roadsters after Federal proposals threatened to outlaw the soft-top (ironically, the threat was never carried through, but the damage was already done), and affordable, reliable, lightweight sports coupés were decidedly thin on the ground.

Although the aim of the exercise was to put Toyota ahead of the competition in Japan – perhaps the only country capable of such a project at the time, with Britain's industry in turmoil, Germany's currency too strong, and America seemingly incapable of making good small cars – it was sensible to keep the vehicle as practical as possible, otherwise many

A second very early sketch showing a decidedly muscular form.

The 'Mid-Engine Sports Car' – the origin of the MR2.

20

Left, top: A clay model of a later proposal. This picture has a curved glass panel covering the mid-mounted engine, but this particular idea was ultimately rejected as it caused a great deal of problems with heat and noise insulation. However, the front wing already has familiar looking lines, inspired by the Japanese katana, and most of the other leading features would be refined and included in the SA-X prototype.

Left, middle: Another early sketch, but already the final design is starting to show through. At this stage, however, the full-width rear combination light is still in place.

Left, bottom: Interiors started off being quite futuristic, with LED displays and a minimalistic approach to switchgear. Fortunately, Toyota designers managed to retain the feeling of individual cockpits.

potential buyers would dismiss it as a useless proposition for everyday use. As a result, it was suggested that the rear boot be designed to hold two golf bags, while the body would have to allow easy access to the cabin.

After being given the go-ahead by Kiyoshi Matsumoto, work began in earnest in 1980. The original 'Mid-Engine Sports Car' prototype was duly developed into the SA-X, which, in turn, was refined through a series of models, the final result being the SV-3. Dimensions had changed somewhat during this process, the length now being 3925mm (154.5in) compared to 3835mm (150.1in) of the red prototype, whilst the width also increased; at 1665mm (65.5in), it was 45mm (1.8in) wider than the red car. Likewise, the 1250mm (49.2in) height and 2320mm (91.3in) wheelbase measurements were respectively 75mm and 40mm (2.9in and 1.6in) more than the earlier version. The height was chosen to give the best compromise between easy entry and egress without ruining the car's sporting lines.

Regarding the styling, which was all done in-house, Seiichi Yamauchi (born in 1940 and Styling Room No 2 chief) said he ignored contemporary trends and, instead, took inspiration from uniquely Japanese items, such as the beauty of a *katana* (a traditional curved sword) and the simplicity of *noh*

As work progressed on the mid-engined project, the rear lights were changed, and the wheelarches became a more subtle styling feature.

masks (used in plays); the atmosphere inside the cockpit was reminiscent of that of a tea ceremony room! However, inspiration for the front mask came about when Yamauchi spotted a diminutive X1/9 surrounded by trucks on the highway: while aerodynamics were given priority, he knew straight away that the new Toyota had to have a certain amount of strength and mass at the front end for it to look as though it could survive in urban traffic.

Although Japan has the ability to produce a new model design quicker than any other car-building nation, drivetrains and other components were sourced largely from the corporate parts bin, thus saving on lengthy and expensive development costs. A number of mid-engined cars were inspected during this development period (the Japanese company bought as many examples as it could find for evaluation), and enthusiasm was running high. Toyota's people working on the project even gave up their summer holiday to further refine the

Another design proposal, with sharper lines and a strong styling feature around the sill area allowing the body to appear lither. Note the aperture under the front bumper, providing air to the front-mounted radiator, and the addition of a rear spoiler.

One of the earliest MR2 prototypes, this particular example is the SA-X, now an exhibit at the excellent Toyota Automobile Museum. Note the styling around the nose and rear pillar.

Another view of the SA-X. (Courtesy Hideo Aoki)

The MR2 taking shape, at least on paper. A series of full-size models followed, allowing Seiichi Yamauchi and his team of designers to create the final shape.

The final stages of development were conducted through three full-size prototypes. This white car displays a smoother nose, but very sharp lines around the roof and pillars.

mid-engined car at a test track near Fuji, the team having first received some expert high-performance driving tuition from Shiomi Hosoya, Toyota's Test Driver and an ex-Japanese Grand Prix entrant.

After some final detail changes, the car was almost ready to be shown to the world when potential disaster struck – news of the forthcoming Pontiac Fiero, which was to be built in the States, filtered through the grapevine. The first mid-engined production car to come from America, it duly arrived in time for the 1984 model year with a body made from Enduraflex plastic.

Fortunately, at least for Toyota, even though the Pontiac was very cheap (the base model was introduced at only $7999), sales soon slowed down after a brisk first couple of seasons. But the Japanese company was not to know this, and decided that the only way to reduce the threat was to exhibit the SV-3 prototype at the forthcoming Tokyo Show in order to create awareness of the project.

This silver car shows some of the features found on the higher-specification production models, such as the rear spoiler coming off the roofline; the final rear lighting arrangement can be clearly seen.

The 1983 Tokyo Show
At the 25th Tokyo Show, placed on a brightly-lit turntable, the SV-3 was

23

A mock-up of the interior. The dashboard was designed in such a way that very little change was needed to make the car either left- or right-hand drive.

At one point it was hoped that picnic tables could be incorporated into the seatbacks, providing a handy flat surface when the seat was folded forwards.

This red prototype could almost be a home market 1500S or 1600. Although the rear lights were rejected in favour of those on the earlier model, the narrow rubber safety strip on the leading edge of the pop-up headlights (put there to prevent children getting their fingers trapped) was adopted for production.

one of the stars of the Toyota stand. Finished in white with a light grey lower body and fine yellow waistline stripe, and displayed alongside such special vehicles as the futuristic FX-1 concept car, it caused quite a stir when the exhibition opened at Harumi on October 28th.

The styling was very modern and compact, featuring a low, sharply raked bonnet with retractable halogen headlights (quick enough in action to allow the driver to 'flash' oncoming traffic), integrated wraparound, foam-

One of the last sketches made before the MR2 dream became reality.

Akio Yoshida – the man in charge of the MR2 project, pictured at the time of its launch. It is interesting to note that Yoshida had spent a couple of years in Los Angeles just before the mid-engined car was given the go-ahead, giving him a good idea of what Americans wanted.

At the time of the Tokyo Show, the MR2 was known as the SV-3. The SV-3 featured a T-bar roof, something that would eventually be offered on the production model.

The SV-3 at the 1983 Tokyo Show. (Courtesy Hideo Aoki)

A single-page brochure introduced Toyota's new mid-engined sports car. This shot, with the background suitably retouched, was used as the main picture.

filled urethane bumpers, and crisp lines at the rear. The back end was, in fact, the only aspect of the design that caused any adverse comment, a number of journalists commenting that the car looked "unhappy" from the rear three-quarter aspect. In common with a lot of other mid-engined vehicles, flying buttresses were used to soften the profile, as the glass behind the driver was almost vertical.

A transverse-mounted, four-cylinder, twin-cam engine was employed (although the SV-3 was fitted with a 1.6-litre unit, there was talk of a 1.8 for America at this stage), situated between the driver and the rear axle for almost ideal weight distribution; a special mounting was used to cut noise and vibration to a minimum.

Drive was taken to the rear wheels through a hydraulically-operated clutch to a five-speed manual gearbox (the linkage being by twin cables), while the option of a four-speed automatic transmission was made available in some markets.

The independent suspension (christened Pegasus to represent Precision Engineered Geometrically Advanced Suspension) was derived from

The rather colourful interior of the SV-3, complete with intercom system.

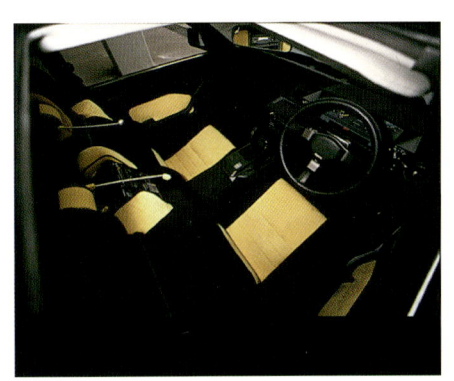

Another view of the cockpit, this angle clearly showing the fascia.

25

A front three-quarter shot of the SV-3 with its lights raised (the headlight mechanism was borrowed from the Third Generation Celica, incidentally). It will be noted that the overly-fashionable NACA duct was avoided in favour of a simple air intake for the engine. In fact, stylists wanted to position the opening lower, but had to settle for a higher location after they found it was too easy for mud and water to enter the intake.

The stunning, high-tech FX-1 concept car was another exhibit at the 1983 Tokyo Show. Interestingly, the Chief Engineer was Sumio Ono, who was also in charge of the Century limousine. Just two FX-1s were built.

that of the Corolla, via MacPherson struts with low-pressure gas dampers all-round, with a dual-link strut set-up at the back. An anti-roll bar was standard at the front only in Japan, attached by ball-joints for added efficiency, although most markets received a rear one as well.

It is well-known that Lotus had helped enhance the suspension on the Supra (Toyota initially acquired a 16.5% stake in the British company in mid-1983, after thoughts of a takeover were quashed – the MG marque was also considered as a potential purchase, incidentally!), but the Japanese were quick to emphasise that the MR2's anti-dive, anti-lift and anti-squat geometry was their own work, a product of the Higashifuji Test & Research Centre.

For production models, rack-and-pinion steering – PAS was not available, by the way – and servo-assisted disc brakes all-round (ventilated at the front of the 1.6-litre cars) completed the mechanical specification. Disc diameters were listed at 244mm (9.6in) at the front, and 241mm (9.5in) at the rear, the handbrake working on the latter, incidentally.

Inside, it was obvious that the functional cockpit, effectively split into two individual cells by the high central tunnel, was designed for the driver. The driving position was good, thanks to supportive sports seats, and the pedals were laid out in such a way as to make heel-and-toeing easy. Creature comforts were not forgotten either, as demonstrated by the top-class stereo system (a dealer option in Japan), and the sensible heating and ventilation layout.

When asked what was the greatest difficulty the engineers had to overcome, Yoshida replied that it was "achieving high performance in both straight-line stability and cornering. Because the wheelbase is short and the front is light, straight-line stability at high speeds tended to suffer. European-specification cars must achieve speeds exceeding 125 miles per hour. To ensure safe handling at such speeds is absolutely essential, but this could not be achieved by the use of heavy steering. So we decided to use the high-caster, short-trail geometry to keep the centre of gravity as low as possible to emphasise the aerodynamic performance and particularly to reduce lift. We took the car to Europe, conducted repeated tests, and eventually we perfected the design.

"We wanted to ensure cornering at the very limit of the car's capability. In a mid-engined car, excellent cornering is almost inherent. But if the limit is high, the reaction tends to become proportionally more fierce when the

Japanese advertising from early 1984, showing the SV-3, FX-1 and TAC-3 recreational vehicle. With the latter, like the McLaren F1 road car, the driver sat in the centre, with the two passengers each side and behind in arrowhead formation.

An MR2 on a slalom test. In the dry, handling was superb, light and responsive, with excellent traction off the line and exiting corners. However, in the wet, as with all mid-engined vehicles, it paid to exercise a little restraint, although, it has to be said, with such modest power on tap, this problem was not nearly as acute as it was in the majority of cars with this layout.

Testing took place all over the world, and in all kinds of conditions. As Seiichi Yamauchi, MR2's Chief Designer, said in 1984: "In the past, Toyota produced the Sports 800 and 2000GT. We believed back then that there are always those that enjoy driving for driving's sake. Through the MR2, we hope that a wide range of people will discover the joys of driving."

27

Making final aerodynamic adjustments in the wind tunnel. The Cd was listed at 0.36 and the co-efficient of lift was 0.13 (or just 0.01 with the spoiler package) at the rear.

An interesting shot showing the MR2 being tested in strong crosswinds. This unusual test method prompted Toyota to change the rear spoiler found on the SV-3 prototype to a different type which, although it increased the car's aerodynamic drag a touch, allowed the car to react better in gusty weather. The front spoiler was also shaped to enhance the vehicle's high-speed stability.

Thankfully, the MR2 passed the statutory crash test with flying colours. Safety concerns were paramount, with the various bulkheads providing a strong, rigid passenger cell, augmented by other features such as a laminated windscreen and inertia reel seatbelts.

A couple of shots of the 1600G-Limited model at speed during endurance testing. The 1.6-litre vehicles gained an extra cooling fan in the engine bay to help reduce heat build-up after the powerplant was shut down after runs such as this, and all cars came with an oil cooler, complete with its own dedicated fan.

limit is exceeded. The rear wheels lose their grip and start to slide. To avoid this problem, the rear suspension setting was the key, and we believe we were very successful. But achieving this success required more testing than you can possibly imagine!"

Kazutoshi Arima, second in command on the project, stated that "the car has just the right amount of excitement and tension at the wheel, at the same time imparting confidence and relaxation in the handling ... two contradictory elements have been successfully combined."

Testing took place all over the world to acquire valuable data of the various extremes the car would encounter in service, from the searing heat of Death Valley in America to Arctic conditions; from pottering about town to flat-out runs on the German autobahn; and, of course, a number of race tracks for good measure. A European-specification prototype comfortably exceeded 125mph (200kph) on the test track, and this was almost exactly the same as the top speed recorded for production models: the first car leaving the line in May 1984.

It was noticeable that the nose profile and rear spoiler seen on the SV-3 were modified for cars destined for the showroom (the new rear spoiler helped the vehicle to react better against crosswinds), and the SV-3's digital

29

Cutaway drawing of the MR2 showing engine location and major components. A cutaway vehicle was actually produced; displayed at the press launch of the MR2, and later at the various motor shows across Europe and America. (Courtesy Yoshihiro Inomoto)

speedometer was replaced by pure analogue instruments for production. The co-efficient of drag on a bespoilered model was said to be Cd 0.36 (or 0.34 without door mirrors), which was more than reasonable, given the length of the car.

Although quite heavy for its size, with thick sound-deadening materials installed between the engine and driver (with the MR layout, mechanical noise was found to be some 5dB greater in the driving seat than with a typical FF car), and no fewer than five bulkheads (one up front behind the front-mounted radiator, at the front and rear of the cockpit, one behind the engine, and another in the rear panel), the steel-bodied MR2 felt solid under all conditions.

Much of the front boot space was occupied by the spare wheel, jack, tool kit, and washer bottle, although small items could be packed in there, along with the removable glass roof panel (optional in Japan, but standard in the UK), secured by two pads and a latch.

An interesting idea was to place the fuel tank under the transmission tunnel between the two seats, for while this reduced the size of the tank (and therefore the range of the vehicle), it meant that no matter what level of fuel was in it, handling wasn't affected. In addition, this clever piece of packaging enabled the seats to recline a little, or a small amount of luggage to be placed behind them (in reality, the space was almost certainly reserved for storing the forthcoming T-bar roof panels, as seen on the SV-3). Another advantage was cited: in this position, the nine-gallon (41-litre) tank was also less likely to rupture in the event of a rear impact.

Described in *Motor* as "the most exciting new car from the East since the Mazda RX-7, and arguably much more significant," for production models, the MR2 designation was adopted. This was said to represent Midship (which refers to the engine location) Runabout (a personal car), while the 2 tacked onto the back signified that it was a two-seater.

By happy coincidence, MR also describes the vehicle's layout (ie Mid-engine, Rear-wheel drive). Incidentally, the trademark MR2 bird is supposed to symbolise power and speed, and "aerodynamic beauty through evolution." Joining the Celica and Supra in the speciality car line-up, the MR2 further enhanced Toyota's new-found sporting image.

Toyota decided to manufacture the MR2 in a subsidiary plant – the Central Motor Co Ltd in Sagamihara, near Yokohama, interestingly, a far less automated factory than the majority of those found in Japan. With a capacity of 80,000 vehicles per year, MR2 production was scheduled to be 60,000 units in the first year before settling down to 5300 a month (the projections being 3000 for America, 2000 for Japan, and 300 for Europe).

Shoichiro Toyoda, Kiichiro Toyoda's son, was on hand to introduce the MR2 to the Japanese press in Tokyo.

	1.6MT	1.6ECT	1.5MT	1.5AT
1st	3.166	2.810	3.545	2.810
2nd	1.904	1.549	1.904	1.549
3rd	1.310	1.000	1.310	1.000
4th	0.969	0.706	0.969	0.706
5th	0.815	–	0.815	–
Rev	3.250	2.296	3.250	2.296
F/D	4.312	3.837	3.941	3.837

The home market

Toyota chose to introduce the car to the press at the Laforet Museum in Akasaka, Tokyo, more usually the venue for high-class fashion shows rather than car launches, but it gave a quality feel to the presentation, which was complete with large video screens and dry ice. Shoichiro Toyoda was there, proudly giving the spiel on Japan's first ever mid-engined production car.

Sales started from June 8th 1984 on the home market, with three grades available initially – the top-of-the-range 1600G-Limited, the 1600G, and the 1500S. The two 1.6-litre cars were powered by the Corolla GT's normally-aspirated, twin-cam 16v 4A-GELU engine, delivering 130bhp (at 6600rpm) and 110lbft of torque.

Featuring a cast iron block and an aluminium alloy head, equipped with T-VIS (the Toyota Variable Induction System, which acted rather like a two-stage throttle – a set of secondary butterflies opening above 4650rpm – enhancing response and fuel consumption) and EFI-D fuel-injection, transistorised ignition and an automatic choke, it provided very high power output for its size, combined with good economy.

The 1500S used the 1452cc 3A-LU (or 3A-II) sohc unit with a twin-choke carburettor, rated at 83bhp and with 87lbft of torque available. An automatic transmission could be specified on both engine options, with an electronically-controlled, two-way overdrive (ECT-S) on the 1.6-litre unit, although a five-speed manual gearbox came as the standard MR2 fitment, with fifth up and to the right of the standard 'H' pattern, and reverse below it. The gear ratios were as per the above table.

The basic 1500S had a fairly simple exterior and 5.5J steel wheels mounted with 185/60 HR14 tyres. The 1600G was basically the same car but with the 1.6-litre engine, whilst the top model featured special 5.5J x 14 cast aluminium alloy wheels shod with 185/60 rubber, side skirts, a clear plastic roof spoiler and a rear wing, although the 1600G was given the option of the rear spoiler package as a cost extra, and both of the cheaper grades could be bought with the alloy wheels.

Differences in interior trim levels were more marked, however. All cars came with high-back fabric sports seats with height adjustment, full instrumentation (including a tachometer), a tilt facility on the steering column, a heated rear window, door pockets, remote fuel door and boot releases, and a digital quartz clock.

A photograph taken in time for the MR2's announcement. The car carries French number plates, as this is where the picture was taken, although it is actually a Japanese-specification G-Limited model.

Overleaf: Pages from a preliminary Japanese catalogue printed in June 1984. They clearly show the power units employed for the home market models, the engine's location in the car and the suspension and braking systems.

Twin cam 16 Valve

ハートは16バルブ。ミッドシップ特性を最大限にいかすLASRE 4A-G搭載。

ミッドシップのために、ツインカム16バルブ。

正確なステアリングレスポンスと限界性能の高いコーナリングを特長とするミッドシップ、トヨタMR2。新しいファントゥドライブのためにMR2にはLASREα4Aツインカム16バルブを搭載。軽量・コンパクト、ポテンシャルの高さはトヨタのツインカムテクノロジーが証明する直列4気筒4A-GELU型、総排気量1,587cc、最高出力130ps/6,600r.p.m.、最大トルク15.2kg-m/5,200r.p.m.のスペックが示す高性能パワーユニット。

LASRE α 4A TWIN CAM 16VALVE

低中速でトルクフルにするT-VIS(TOYOTA-Variable Induction System)。燃料噴射量をエレクトロニクスがコントロールするEFI-D(Electronic Fuel Injection)。エンジンを総合コントロールするTCCS(TOYOTA Computer Controlled System)。優れたドライバビリティとパフォーマンスをもたらしている。10モード燃費12.8km/ℓ(運輸省審査値マニュアル車)という数字もファントゥドライブにふさわしい。

ツインカム16バルブにECT-Sを採用。

高性能を誰もがイージーに楽しめるようにとMR2は16バルブに先進のオートマチックECT-Sを採用している。

夢の世界へ、レーザーα4Aツインカム16。

Sには軽快なユニット、LASRE3A-Ⅱを搭載

1500には経済性の高いLASRE3A-Ⅱ。10モード燃費は15.0km/ℓ(運輸省審査値マニュアル車)だ

LASRE 3A-Ⅱ

New Concept Suspension

足はペガサス。新しいテクノロジーが快走シーンを演出する。

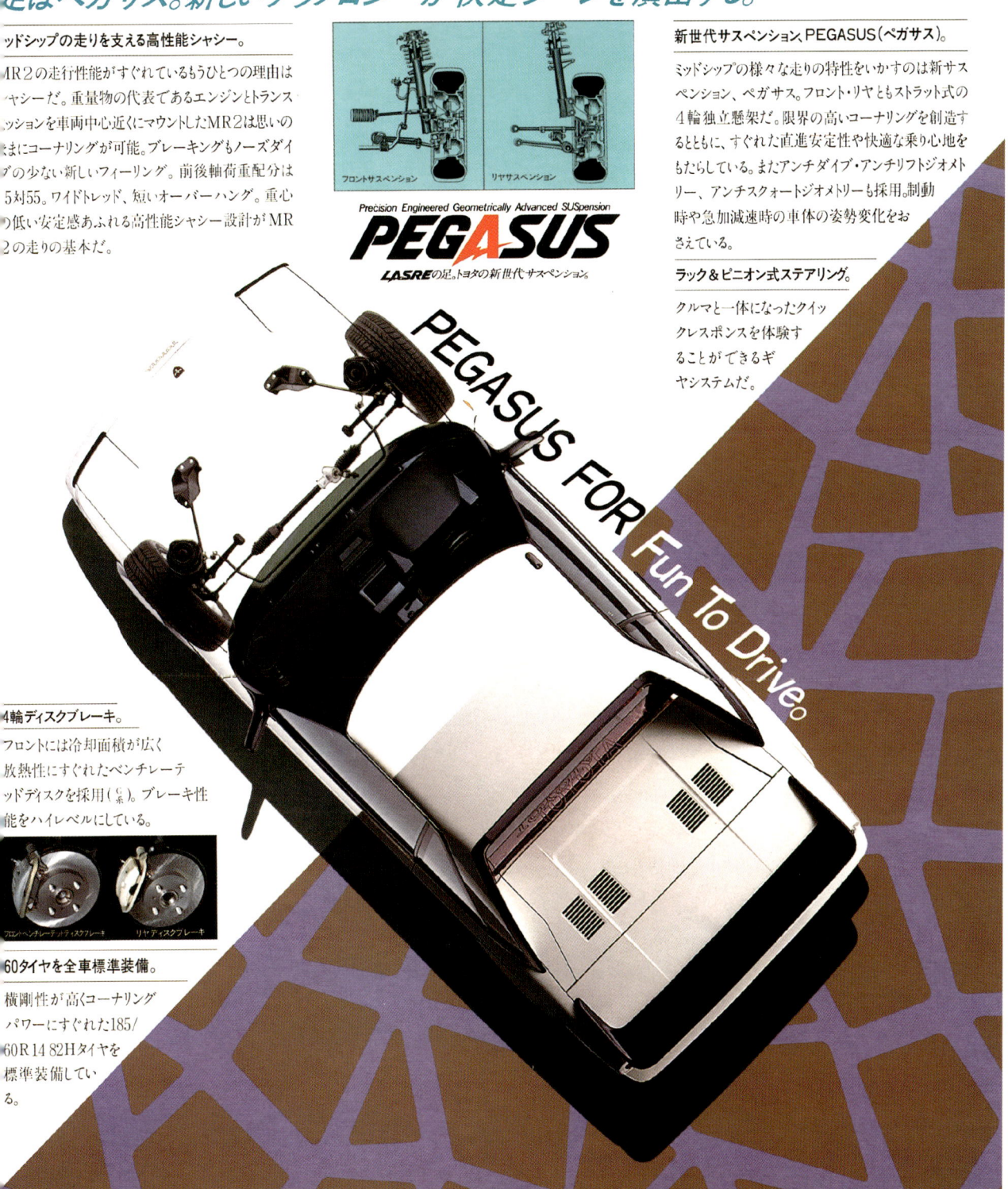

ミッドシップの走りを支える高性能シャシー。
MR2の走行性能がすぐれているもうひとつの理由はシャシーだ。重量物の代表であるエンジンとトランスミッションを車両中心近くにマウントしたMR2は思いのままにコーナリングが可能。ブレーキングもノーズダイブの少ない新しいフィーリング。前後軸荷重配分は45対55。ワイドトレッド、短いオーバーハング。重心の低い安定感あふれる高性能シャシー設計がMR2の走りの基本だ。

Precision Engineered Geometrically Advanced SUSpension
PEGASUS
LASREの足。トヨタの新世代サスペンション。

フロントサスペンション　リヤサスペンション

新世代サスペンション、PEGASUS（ペガサス）。
ミッドシップの様々な走りの特性をいかすのは新サスペンション、ペガサス。フロント・リヤともストラット式の4輪独立懸架だ。限界の高いコーナリングを創造するとともに、すぐれた直進安定性や快適な乗り心地をもたらしている。またアンチダイブ・アンチリフトジオメトリー、アンチスクォートジオメトリーも採用。制動時や急加減速時の車体の姿勢変化をおさえている。

ラック＆ピニオン式ステアリング。
クルマと一体になったクイックレスポンスを体験することができるギヤシステムだ。

PEGASUS FOR Fun To Drive。

4輪ディスクブレーキ。
フロントには冷却面積が広く放熱性にすぐれたベンチレーテッドディスクを採用（G-Limited）。ブレーキ性能をハイレベルにしている。

フロントベンチレーテッドディスクブレーキ　リヤディスクブレーキ

60タイヤを全車標準装備。
横剛性が高くコーナリングパワーにすぐれた185/60R14 82Hタイヤを標準装備している。

photo:G-Limited（ボディーカラーはスーパーホワイトⅡ）

The Japanese range at the time of the MR2's introduction.

The First Generation MR2 top of the range in Japan was the G-Limited. This picture dates from June 1984, and shows a car finished in a colour scheme known in Japan as Sherwood Toning. Testers from all corners of the world soon ran out of superlatives to describe it.

The door mirrors went from manual to electrical adjustment when one moved up to the G grade, the three-spoke steering wheel was trimmed in leather instead of urethane (as was the gearlever), higher-quality door trim was specified, an oil pressure gauge was added, and a voltmeter was fitted on five-speed models.

The G-Limited featured seven-way seat adjustment, individual headrests

Both photos below: A G-Limited model pictured at the press launch by the highly-respected Japanese journalist, Hideo Aoki. (Courtesy Hideo Aoki)

34

Interior of the G-Limited, seen here with an automatic gearbox.

One of a series of publicity shots taken in France, this particular shot showing the tail of the G-Limited. Note the rather apt number plate.

and larger side bolsters, while the moonroof, which could be stored in the front boot when removed, was classed as an option on all grades. Power windows and central locking were maker options on the G and G-Limited models. Dealer options included items such as air conditioning, various stereo systems, mudguards, foglights and a rear console box.

Prices ranged from an exceptionally low 1,395,000 yen for the 1500S in manual guise, rising to 1,642,000 yen for the cheapest 1.6-litre model; the flagship 1600G-Limited was listed at 1,795,000 yen with a manual gearbox, or 1,894,000 yen with an automatic transmission.

Four standard colours were listed – white, red, silver and blue – and interiors came in black and red (for red or white coachwork) or black and blue for the other two paint schemes. There was also the option of two-tone metallic dark green over beige (known as Sherwood Toning) on the G-Limited, and this came with black and yellow trim.

Kevin Radley was in Japan at the time of the launch, and, having driven the 1.6-litre car, wrote the following for *Motor* magazine: "A dab on the throttle and the tacho needle dances up the scale. The left foot finds the clutch, which goes home with remarkably little effort. The gearlever snicks effortlessly into first. Lower the parking brake, and move out. The steering is alive. Barely 20mph is showing on the speedometer, but one is already sensing the motion of the front wheels. And the response is instantaneous – like the proverbial go-kart. Into second, and then third.

"A truck ahead. Slow down, drop back, into second. Dare I pass? This is no time to equivocate. This road

The 1.6-litre engine used to power the 1600G and G-Limited. (Courtesy Hideo Aoki)

Fascia of the 1600G. The automatic transmission dictated that the voltmeter (usually in the top left-hand corner of the instrument binnacle) be deleted, as the space was needed for the gearbox mode indicators.

Front three-quarter shot of the 1600G at the time of the home market launch.

is straight and clear. Hard down on the throttle and the engine sings to 7500rpm. Shift up into third and continue the unburstable quest for the stars. There is 80mph showing on the dial and a notoriously deceptive 90-degree right-hander approaching at a ludicrous rate. How many times has my heart stopped on this corner as I have found it tighter than it at first appears? How will this new car take it? There is no time to ponder. The pedals are beautifully sited for heel-and-toeing, and the engine is once again rejoicing in second. And then the corner is gone. Can it be true? No car I have ever driven, from microcar to mighty 911, has made that bend so effortless. There is a total absence of all the usual tell-tales – tyre squeal, understeer, oversteer, body roll: it is uncanny.

"A Lamborghini? A Ferrari? A Lotus? For sheer driving pleasure it could have been: but it wasn't ... Judged as a sports car, the MR2 is a resounding success. It is pretty yet dramatic to look at. It is quiet, yet produces the right

Interior of the 1500S, featuring the highback seats used in the 1.5-litre model and the 1600G, although the trim was slightly different, as were the door panels. The G-Limited had higher quality seats altogether, with seven-way adjustment and individual headrests.

36

The MR2 viewed from above. This is the 1500S model with optional sunroof.

noises at the right time. It is quick in a straight line and, more importantly, it is ultra-quick in the turns. Toyota could have followed fashion and produced a muscle-bound supercar like the Nissan 300ZX. Instead, they've built a lithe, nimble athlete that can and will run rings round the opposition."

On the practical side, John Hartley noted: "Although the MR2 is low, you don't have to go through any contortions to get in and the driving position is not unlike that of the Corolla Levin.

"But the fairly high position is certainly practical; forward visibility is excellent, as you can just see the bonnet, which slopes away sharply. You can also see behind fairly well, although the mirror is a little smaller than is desirable, and I found the spoiler on top models does limit rear vision.

"As is common in mid-engined cars, there is little space for oddments inside the cockpit, although some rather inaccessible space is provided behind the seats. The interior is neat in a plasticky manner – instruments are grouped in a small nacelle – and seats offer reasonable support. Recognising that this one is earmarked as an enthusiast's car, Toyota have avoided using their awful digital instruments.

"The glovebox is small, and the door pockets, too. There is an optional console between the seats, which will just about hold a pocket handkerchief. Although the rear boot can hold some small suitcases, its use is limited because it gets fiendishly hot."

Nonetheless, during the first six months of sales, a total of 10,534 cars were sold on the home market, around 65% of which were G-Limited models – the 1600G accounted for approximately 30% of sales, while the 1500S made up the remaining 5%. Obviously, utilitarian matters were overshadowed by the fun element, and the difference in price between the top and lower grades had little bearing on the public's desire to own the more powerful and better-equipped machines.

At the end of 1984, the MR2 was named Japan's 'Car of the Year 1984-85,' voted ahead of competition such as the 16v Honda CRX and the latest Nissan Laurel. To celebrate this achievement, a limited edition was

An atmospheric shot of the G-Limited. Depending on the light, the 'Toyota' script on the roof spoiler was often reflected in the rear screen. It was a neat and unusual touch.

produced called 'White Lanner.' Based on the G-Limited model, each of the 100 examples built featured Super White II coachwork, with the same colour extending to the bumpers, spoilers, door mirrors and mudguards; a red or black interior could be specified.

Below: Early Japanese advertising for the new MR2.

Both photos: The limited edition 'White Lanner,' named after a European falcon. Note the G-Limited interior trim.

The new car in Britain

"Rarely if ever have we been so totally confident about a new Toyota model as we are about the MR2," said Mike Copeland, Toyota GB's National Sales Manager. "It is an exciting car which we feel will add lustre to our entire product range. It combines speed with

39

The MR2 was first seen in the UK at the 1984 Motor Show held in October. This is one of the original press photographs from the time. The first batch of UK press photographs were actually printed back-to-front, the left-hand drive car being fitted with a specially-made registration plate to make it appear correct (not a difficult exercise with modern perspex items, especially if the numbers and letters are chosen carefully). Surprisingly, no-one seemed to notice, despite the fact that the fuel door, air intake and exhaust pipes are on the wrong side in an attempt to show a rhd model.

A second shot from the first British press release. The pop-up headlights took little away from the car's appearance. When in the closed position, combined with the sharply-raked screen and bonnet, they helped to keep the drag coefficient down to just Cd 0.36 (or 0.34 without door mirrors).

The MR2 looked good from most angles. Only the rear three-quarter view was criticised by a few members of the contemporary press.

A final photograph from the original press release in which the vehicle was printed up as a reverse image in order to give the impression of a right-hand drive model. Note the windscreen wipers are correct, though, as Toyota went to the expense of having different wipers for lhd and rhd cars.

Early advertising for the British Isles. By now, proper UK-specification models were appearing in the media.

safety, performance with fuel economy. It also shows that Toyota engineering can match that of any other nation. We are convinced it will be a great success in the UK and worldwide."

Initially priced at £9295.16, the little Toyota was often referred to as the new MG Midget, and Copeland's confidence proved fully justified – the MR2 quickly found a large number of willing buyers in Britain after its official UK launch on 13th March 1985.

However, the public got a preview of the new model at the 1984 Motor Show, held at the NEC during the latter part of October. This was the car's first appearance outside of Japan, and the main display model was finished in striking metallic blue over light grey. It was joined on Stand 138 by the cutaway version, brought over from Japan, the FX-1 concept vehicle, and the Safari Rally-winning Celica Twin-Cam Turbo.

The press release stated: "Small, low, compact and devilishly fast, the MR2 endeavours to combine three conflicting strands of motoring aspiration. A car that is inexpensive to buy and to run; a car with out-and-out sporting pedigree, performance, ride and handling, and yet a car that will run quietly and docilely in the congested urban traffic of our times."

Only one MR2 model was sold in Britain, a well-equipped 1587cc machine with a five-speed gearbox, discs all round (ventilated up front), and front and rear anti-roll bars. It also featured 5.5J x 14 alloy wheels as standard (the same as those found on the Japanese G-Limited), shod with 185/60 HR-rated rubber. Gearbox ratios, as well as that specified for the final-drive, were carried over from the home market's 1.6-litre cars, incidentally.

The promise delivered

Other sports cars promise – the MR2 delivers. And how. 122bhp from a 16 valve twin-cam engine mounted forward of the rear axle in the classic mid-engined position for superb handling and exceptional manoeuvrability.

In every department, in every respect, the MR2 is an outstanding sports car. What gives it even more of a competitive edge is the name Toyota.

Begin the affair with the MR2 at one of our dealers listed on the next 2 pages, and discover what sports driving should be.

That's motoring

TOYOTA

Standard features included a full set of analogue gauges (including tachometer and voltmeter), a leather-covered, three-spoke steering wheel and gearlever, fabric G-Limited type seats and the higher-grade door trim, a glass sunroof, electric windows with tinted glass, remote door mirror adjustment, central locking via a switch on the driver's door armrest, and a stereo radio/cassette.

Journalists got their first drive in Portugal in January, three months after the MR2's NEC debut. *What Car?* noted: "In the same way as the exotic two-seater 2000GT stood proud in Toyota's range back in the mid-1960s, the MR2 looks set to become the jewel in the crown in the 1980s. Even before one is near the £9295 MR2 it's clear there simply isn't any competition to speak of; the nearest thing is the ageing and much

continued on page 45

Dating from March 1985, this picture was taken at the time of the British launch. Note the MR2 trademark on the rear bumper, and the badging on the nearside combination lamp (1.6-litre models in Japan had 'Twin-Cam 16 G' badges).

In this picture, one can just see the seven-way sports seats which were standard for the UK, as was a leather-wrapped, three-spoke steering wheel and gearlever. Internal releases for the boot and fuel flap were provided, and heating and ventilation was said to be very effective in most of the contemporary road tests. Note the front indicators: unique for Europe, with the clear sidelight lens.

A UK-specification model in profile. Alloy wheels and the aerodynamics kit came as standard.

Early reports were highly complementary. As Mike McCarthy said shortly after the UK launch: "The Toyota MR2 is more than just a new sports car: it is the trendsetter against which similar machines are going to be judged."

42

The MR2 wasn't the only sporting machine to be launched in Britain during the early part of 1985. This is the Corolla GT, which was powered by the same 16v 1.6-litre engine.

The Corolla GT Coupé was another model to employ the 4A-GE power unit, although it featured an FR layout, as opposed to an FF arrangement in the boxy GT, or MR in the MR2. It was a clever piece of engineering, getting the same engine to provide three completely different chassis characteristics.

43

The affair begins at first sight.

The MR2

THE MR2 COSTS £9295. PRICE CORRECT AT TIME OF GOING TO PRESS AND INCLUDES CAR TAX, VAT AND SEATBELTS BUT EXCLUDES ROAD TAX, NUMBER PLATES AND DELIVERY CHARGES. OFFICIAL FUEL CONSUMPTION FIGURES: URBAN CYCLE – 34.9 MPG (8.1 L/100KM); CONSTANT 56 MPH – 47.1 MPG (6.0 L/100KM), CONSTANT 75 MPH – 36.7 MPG (7.7 L/100KM).

16 v

red

hav

Please send
Redhill, Surrey RH

Name

British advertising from spring 1985.

may be attracted to our new baby by its revolutionary 1600cc, twin-overhead-cam, fuel injected engine.
erhaps it is the mid-engine layout which will appeal.
oyota engineering at its best (the engine will idle to less than a second).
it getting to 60 in 8.2 seconds that thrills you to bits?
atever makes you finally fall for our MR2, you only ke one look to be seduced.

TOYOTA *That's motoring*

chure: The Sales Dept., Toyota (GB) Ltd., The Quadrangle,
el: 0737 68585.

___Address and Postcode___

FL 5/M

less sophisticated Fiat X1/9 which would put up only a half-hearted battle against the Toyota."

Fortunately, the new car lived up to its promise. The magazine continued: "Within the MR2's short wheelbase is a screamer of an engine ... Traction is excellent – the rear wheels are most effective in putting power down during a standing start.

"Handling and ride are the ideal balance; much, much better than the uneasy Corolla GT. Not only does the MR2 handle beautifully, aided by precise rack-and-pinion steering – showing initial understeer turning to controllable oversteer – but the ride is comfortable, too. The same delicate poise, in fact, as you'd find in a mid-engined Lotus.

"Add to the sensible packaging the near immaculate Toyota standard of build, and you have one of the most sensible uncompromising sports cars to appear for many a year."

With equal enthusiasm, *Motor* said: "Not only is Toyota's significant mid-engined MR2 the company's first new sports car for 16 years, it's also the closest thing yet to an affordable exotic. Yes, it really is that good ...

"In broad terms, the MR2 is a quick car. Moreover, the sweetness of its power delivery is a revelation. Throttle response is ultra-crisp yet delightfully smooth; if there is a criticism of the engine it is that it doesn't sound very sporting unless you rev it hard, a treatment on which it thrives. The trade-off, though, is that engine noise seldom intrudes.

"We cannot think of any gearchange which better deserves the knife-through-butter metaphor: with short, positive, baulk-free movements through a narrow gate, the MR2's cable-operated gearshift is superbly easy and quick. It combines these qualities with a smooth throttle response, a perfectly-weighted, well-cushioned clutch and a completely snatch-free driveline: the MR2 flatters its driver."

The testers concluded: "It could be improved in detail but, as it stands, it is very, very good – probably the best sports car ever to come out of Japan. It stands comparison with Europe's best. Here, at last, is the mini-exoticar enthusiasts have been waiting for."

Following a full road test, *Autocar* was quick to point out in its summary that "none of the opposition can match the all-round competence of the Toyota ... If price is the limiting factor, then the Fiat [X1/9] seems a good bet; if not, it's worth having a long look at the MR2, which sets new standards in a number of areas and is great fun to drive."

Jeremy Coulter, writing for *Classic Cars* in June 1985, noted: "The main appeal of this car is in its handling, which is predictable and impressively grippy. The near ideal weight distribution of the mid-engined design gives snappy steering response with lightning turning ability. Altogether the car has a very delicate light feel to it."

The staff at *MotorSport* were equally smitten, pointing out: "Toyota has been clever with its use of its splendid 1600cc 16v 122bhp 4A-GE engine. It powers the Corolla GT coupé (front engine, rear wheel drive), the Corolla GT hatchback (tranversely mounted front engine, front wheel drive) while, in the MR2, in conjunction with the Corolla GT transaxle, it appears transversely mounted behind the driver.

"A mid-engined layout can lead to a nasty gearshift, but not in this case. One grips the leather-clad gearlever around the middle and if there's a better gearchange, then I've yet to encounter it. A weight bias of 44/56% helps the 14-inch 185/60 HR Continental Super tyres to transmit the power to the road without a hint of wheelspin, which is unusual given that the engine revs freely to 7600rpm.

"Toyota UK offers only one optional extra, metallic paint finish at £42.36 above the basic price of £9295, for the cars are brought in with a high level of equipment which includes electric windows, central locking, easily-adjustable headrests, a good quality radio/cassette player, detachable 'moonroof' (the aerodynamics of the car allow normal conversation at 90mph with the panel removed), tinted glass and electrically-adjusted door mirrors.

"Everything in the interior of the car feels natural, it's as though one wears it like a favourite pair of shoes ... There is also a sunshade which goes under the [moonroof] panel to complete the transition to a coupé, and this stores in the rear boot [when not in use]."

Thanks to 122bhp and 105lbft of torque in a body weighing only 977kg (2149lb), the manufacturer's claim of a 124mph (198kph) top speed with the five-speed car seemed spot-on. However, due to poor conditions, the best that *MotorSport* could muster was 120.4mph (193kph) in a one-way run. Toyota claimed a 0-60mph time of 8.2 seconds, but some independent tests recorded a best time of just 7.7 seconds; the 30-50mph increment was covered in 3.4 seconds in top gear, while 50-70mph was dismissed in 5.5 seconds. Average fuel consumption came out at roughly 30mpg.

Shortly after the launch, *Fast Lane* stated that the "overall impression of a highly 'chuckable' car dominates: stable at motorway speeds, although a little susceptible to crosswinds, and nimble through traffic. The brakes, discs all-round, ventilated at the front, fit in with the car's character. Strong and fade-free, even after numerous 100mph stops with little 'breathing space' in between, they provide a firm pedal and grab-free action."

However, *Fast Lane* did observe that the "two rear spoilers, one on the boot and one on the trailing edge of the roof, do limit the view out of the back, especially for parking." Actually, a number of testers in Europe made the same comment, and handling in the wet also required a certain amount of care. Another gripe was the full-sized spare wheel fitted to UK specification models, which further compromised the already limited front boot space.

The same magazine continued: "Cars are starting to filter through to eager markets in the UK, Germany, Switzerland, Belgium and Holland. France is the notable exception. MR2s will not be sold there because, according to Brian Townsend, Toyota's PR Manager, there is insufficient demand ... One theory is that 'MR2' pronounced the French way comes out something like 'merde.'"

Eventually, the MR2 did make it into France, where – it is interesting to note – it was simply called the MR! In Switzerland, however, where French is one of the official languages, the cars were still badged as the MR2. Specifications across Europe were basically very similar to those of the British cars, with the obvious exception of the steering wheel location.

The 1985 model year MR2 in American trim. Note the front indicator position compared with European and Japanese versions. US cars also had a mandatory reflector at the rear, mounted on the small piece of trim between the back bumper and wheelarch.

Meanwhile, praise continued to be heaped on the little mid-engined machine. *What Car?* did a comparison test involving the new Japanese model and the Fiat X1/9. It noted: "Rarely does a car receive such a rapturous reception as Toyota's MR2. Its unique combination of race-track handling, smooth injected performance from an engine that's willing to rev past 7000rpm, brilliant gearchange and sleek shape has made it a very impressive debutant. Everyone who drove it returned with eyes shining and appetite whetted for another shot in what is undoubtedly Japan's best sporting model to date.

"Not only is the MR2, with its feather-light controls, exceptionally satisfying to drive, it's also a highly civilised machine, being neither as noisy nor as impractical as some other mid-engine cars. Though some aspects of its styling border on the fussy – the engine body vents and dashboard layout, for example, it's a good looker, nevertheless and aerodynamic with it. Driven sensibly, it will return 34mpg, which is good for such a powerful car."

The 125mph (200kph) top speed and 7.6 second 0-60 time recorded by the magazine put the Toyota in a different league to the Fiat, and also intimated that it was quicker than cars like the Volkswagen Golf GTi, the Ford

Tail of the US-specification MR2. As with Japanese models, the number plate lights were closer together than those of British cars (due to the latter's longer registration plates). Note the lack of a badge on the left-hand combination lamp (the same arrangement as on home market 1500S models).

Escort XR3i, Peugeot's 205GTi – and even the BMW 323i. Having awarded the Japanese model five out of five, against three for the Italian machine, *What Car?* concluded: "The MR2 is such a refined all-rounder that, at the moment, it's difficult to see what can beat it."

The MR2 reaches America
The popularity of the mid-engined layout went into rapid decline during the early-1970s, with only the Fiat X1/9 remaining an affordable, mass-produced example of the breed by the start of the following decade.

Chrysler was thought to be working on a car, but then, in 1983, GM's Pontiac division introduced the mid-engined Fiero, thus stimulating the two-seater sports car market after a long lull in the States. The timing for

47

A picture from the first American catalogue. The text alongside it read: "Once before I saw this car, but only in my mind. It did not exist yet I could feel its power. And now that it's real, it races with my soul."

the launch of the mid-engined Toyota, "intended to offer Americans exotic car looks and excitement without the exotic price," wasn't perfect, but it wasn't far off either. Available only with the 1.6-litre 16v engine in the States, the latest Toyota was introduced to the American press at the Firebird International Raceway Park near Phoenix, Arizona, in the first week of November 1984.

Road & Track previewed the new MR2, and stated: "There is a smooth flow of power in any gear and we were less conscious of the relatively short gearing (almost the same as the Corolla's overall), with a lower level of engine noise being transmitted. On the other hand, there was a fairly high level of road surface vibration being picked up by the structure.

"Braking is truly impressive, with extremely short stopping distances under full control. With the same vented-in-front, four-wheel disc system as on the Corolla (which also did extremely well), and the same size tyres, the MR2's lower weight and better weight distribution simply shortened the stops.

"The MR2 exhibits neutral handling characteristics in most situations, responding accurately to the steering even if there is no real feel through the wheel. At all times the MR2 responds to the throttle, giving the driver the choice of working the chassis either by steering or throttle or a combination of both.

"The gearlever, with a nicely contoured grip, works quickly and logically through a smooth gate, and we never had to fumble for the right gear. A truly excellent ventilation and air conditioning system with a good blower and vents in the right places and Toyota gets the highest marks for ergonomics.

"If the price is anywhere near the expected $10,000 mark in the US, the MR2 simply cannot fail. It has everything going for it: instant appeal, convenient and functional operation, high performance and, best of all, Toyota's reputation for absolute reliability.

"When spy photos of the SV-3 started circulating, there was initial disappointment in the car's aesthetic conception. It seemed too conservative and too angular, especially for an all-new mid-engine sports car in an age of aero-conscious design. But when I first saw the MR2 production model, unchanged in most details, I was pleasantly surprised by its purposeful stance, good overall proportions and general harmony."

Compared to the majority of the competition, the 121mph (194kph) MR2 was a quick machine. According to *Road & Track*, 0-60mph was covered in 8.9 seconds (against 9.7 for a Mazda RX-7 or 11.6 for the Fiero), whilst the standing quarter was passed in 16.9 seconds with a terminal speed of 82mph (131kph). The RX-7 and the American machine were 0.2 seconds and 1.5mph (2.4kph) and 1.3 seconds and 9.5mph (15.2kph) slower respectively.

Advertising space was taken in

A couple of American 1985 models at speed. Tony Assenza observed: "By far the biggest problem with the MR2 is that there won't be enough to go around!"

a number of enthusiast publications during December and January, the gatefold adverts finishing with the line, "The Toyota MR2 – designed for high-performance, but you'll drive it just for fun." In March, the ads spread to consumer magazines, and a national TV advertising campaign was launched in the same month.

Having made its debut at the 1985 Chicago Show, which opened on February 9th, the MR2 went on sale in the United States later that month. As one observer stated, "people tended to either love it or hate it" but, judging by initial sales figures, the overall response was very favourable. Interestingly, the FX-1 and cutaway MR2 also made the long journey to the Windy City.

As mentioned earlier, only the 1.6-litre model was sold in the States. The 1587cc twin-cam engine developed 112bhp and 97lbft of torque in US trim, with the T-VIS system coming into operation at 4350rpm. It was linked to the five-speed manual transmission, with the gearing (including the final-drive ratio) the same as that found on the equivalent home market and European models. Not surprisingly, the chassis details were much the same, too: strut-type independent suspension all-round, with low-pressure gas dampers, anti-roll bars front and rear (as in Europe), disc brakes on all four corners (ventilated up front), and non-assisted rack-and-pinion steering. The familiar 5.5J alloys came as standard, shod with 185/60 HR14 tyres.

For a pure sports car, the MR2 was certainly well-equipped. Standard features included seven-way adjustable cloth seats, a full set of instruments (with tachometer and voltmeter), leather trim on the two-spoke steering wheel and gearshift, power door mirrors, tinted glass, intermittent wipers, a tilt facility on the steering column, AM/FM stereo radio, heated rear window, a rear console box, digital quartz clock, internal releases for the fuel door and boot, and full carpeting. However, the $10,999 price tag was slightly higher than expected due to the unfavourable exchange rate (about 220 yen to the dollar), and options such as air conditioning ($840), an AM/FM stereo radio cassette (including three speakers, at $365), the 'Power Package' (with electric windows, central door locking switch and cruise control, priced at $305), a sunroof ($300), rear spoiler ($150) and mudguards ($30) sent the price soaring. Incidentally, cruise control was available separately for $185.

Writing for *Car & Driver*, Michael Jordan noted, rather tongue-in-cheek: "The only things that stand between the MR2 and true sports car status are a coat of BRG paint and a pool of oil underneath the engine. Get behind the wheel and you feel the tradition at work, as if Toyota had been mucking around in the graveyard of the sports car and brought the beast back to life with the aid of special effects cribbed from old Godzilla movies. This is the car we stopped hoping for ten years ago when it became clear that the Triumph

49

American advertising proudly stating the fact that the MR2 was awarded the 1985 'Import Car of the Year' title by Motor Trend magazine.

TR7 and Fiat X1/9 just weren't going to make the cut."

After a truly rapturous reception from journalists in the States, the MR2 was awarded the title of '1985 Import Car of the Year' by *Motor Trend*, which described it as "the ultimate training car for would-be road racers." Equally significant was the first year's US sales figures – around 32,000 units.

Standard colour schemes for 1985 included Super Red II (with black/red interior trim), Light Beige Metallic (black/beige inside), Light Blue Metallic (with black/blue trim), and Super White and Super Silver Metallic, both coming with two-tone black/grey interiors.

Minor changes

In June 1985, a number of minor changes were announced in Japan. The bumpers were now in body colour on all models, as were the side skirts/mudguards on the G-Limited, and the rear spoiler (still available on the 1600G model as an option). Bronze laminated glass became a feature on the G-Limited, and white over silver metallic was listed as an option for all cars. In addition, there was a coloured side protection moulding, new side stripes, and a front boot mat.

Two months later, the 1600G Sports Package was announced. High-quality Bridgestone Potenza RE71M tyres were standard, along with a rear anti-roll bar, and uprated springs and shock absorbers. Available only with the five-speed manual gearbox, Toyota was aiming to sell 200 a month.

The Japanese range now included the 1600G-Limited (priced at 1,884,000 yen in manual guise, with the ECT-S automatic transmission adding 99,000 yen), the 1600G Sports Package (at 1,773,000 yen), the standard 1600G (1,659,000 yen in five-speed guise, or 1,758,000 with the four-speed automatic), and the 1500S, the manual car being listed at 1,412,000 yen, with the four-speed automatic transmission adding 79,000 yen to the price.

Meanwhile, across the Pacific, the press in the United States were still enthusing over the MR2. The mid-engined Toyota duly became a member of *Automobile* magazine's 'All-Star' listing, and made it into the *Car & Driver* '10 Best' ranking. *Sports & GT Cars* noted that: "the big news [for 1986] is the availability of an automatic transmission. Similar to the Camry and Supra option and priced at $600, it's Toyota's four-speed electronically-controlled type, with lock-up torque converter, manually selectable overdrive, and shift points that can be switched from 'Normal' to 'Power' to suit driving conditions.

"Added to the paint chart are monochrome black metallic and a dark

Another US-specification MR2 showing its very flat handling characteristics on a tight bend. In the dry, the MR2 was a class act, but care was needed in the wet.

jade/light beige two-tone, and there's a new black leather interior package for seats, door panels and centre armrest.

The extra cost 'aero' exterior dress-up returns with rear-deck spoiler, rocker-panel extensions and rear mudguards, all now done in body colour as are the bumpers.

"Ask the MR2 to dance and you have to decide whether to lead or follow. Though it doesn't have much low-end torque, the engine pulls smoothly from as low as 1000rpm in fifth gear because of the short overall gearing (18.5mph/1000rpm). The short gearing also contributes to strong through-the-gears performance. Ride is quite good for a 'middy,' the MR2 exhibiting much less pitching over undulations and freeway expansion joints than is customary with this layout.

"Exhaust boom is prominent most of the time and tends to drown out what wind noise exists. Tyre rumble is

The 1600G Sports Package of August 1985 vintage.

51

Interior of the Japanese G-Limited model, seen here in manual guise.

noticeable on coarse pavement but not excessive. But the MR2's noise should disturb no-one who is attracted to it in the first place; its size and looks alone mean that nobody will approach it looking for luxury."

In addition to the changes outlined in the article, the rear anti-roll bar was deleted on 1986 model year American-specification models, although a high-mount rear brake light was fitted to comply with the latest regulations. Prices started at $12,548, incidentally, with the automatic transmission adding $670. The new options, including the Leather Package, Spoiler Package and two-tone paintwork, were priced at $730, $475 and $220 respectively. Other major options included the Power Package ($350), air conditioning ($765), cruise control ($210), moonroof with sunshade ($340), rear spoiler (complete with black mudguards at $200), an AM/FM radio/cassette ($175, or $405 with ETR), and mudguards ($30); all-weather tyres could be specified at no extra charge.

While comparing various sports cars in the $8000 to $13,500 price range with different drivetrain layouts, *Road & Track* declared that the MR2 was the car it would most like to take down a favourite piece of road. It stated: "Toyota engineers have taken what should be a very good layout and made it especially so. The MR2's steering and suspension communicate well and respond crisply and predictably to input. The car rewards a skilled driver, but it doesn't absolutely snap back when mistreated. In this price range, it's the layout to beat."

In England, *Motor* had one of the mid-engined Toyotas as part of its long-term test fleet. Richard Bremner reported: "The fact is that we're as

Press photograph of the American 1986 model year MR2. The caption noted: "The critically-acclaimed Toyota MR2 receives an optional spoiler package in 1986, enhancing its sporty, aerodynamic design. Also new in 1986 is the availability of a four-speed automatic transmission model."

ecstatic now about our MR2 as we were on the day it was collected. With the running-in period complete it was taken for a week's driving in Scotland, where it proved fabulous. When you consider that the MR2 was engineered thousands of miles away in Japan, it seems all the more remarkable that it should behave as though it were built for the roads of Scotland.

"Our chief discovery was the car's phenomenal dry-road grip – the Toyota corners at speeds on an altogether higher plane, and with such finesse that it tempts you into manoeuvres that would be reckless in most other cars. Eventually you have to temper the pace with a dash of sanity.

"You need a little more sanity if it's raining. A well-driven Renault 4 can probably outflank the Toyota on a greasy roundabout, because the sportster often can't make up its mind whether to let go at the front or the

Tail of the 1986 MR2 in Stateside trim, seen here with the $475 Spoiler Package.

Another view of the American car at speed. Note the colour-keyed bumpers and body kit.

rear, and because it doesn't appear to have grip anyway.

"And this is our sole serious complaint with this car, and it's one that we suspect may be overcome with a change of tyres – the so-called Continental Super Contacts may well have been named by an optimist."

Prices in the UK had gone up to £9499 within three months of the launch, and were set to increase by a further £440 in October. The colour-coded bumpers and aerodynamic aids announced in Japan in mid-1985 were adopted worldwide for the 1986 model year, which for most markets (including Britain) meant from October 1985 onwards. Proper, key-operated central locking and chrome wheelnuts were introduced at the same time.

In the meantime, cars on the European mainland were available in White, Super Red or Dark Green over Beige Metallic. In America, standard colours included Super White, Super Red, Super Silver Metallic, Light Beige Metallic, Metallic Black, and Light Blue

53

When Toyota went to Long Beach... Tokico went along for the ride.

When the new MR2 pace car hit the streets at the Toyota Grand Prix of Long Beach this year it was equipped with TOKICO twin tube gas shocks... not specially designed trick parts, but the same top quality shocks that you can buy from your local performance retailer. The reason that Toyota chose TOKICO is simple... a clearly superior product that will outperform any gas shock on the market.

TOKICO, the world's largest manufacturer of shock absorbers has been on the forefront of gas shock technology for years... developing innovative designs that provide the ultimate in performance handling. So when you're looking for a performance shock... do what Toyota did at the Grand Prix... choose TOKICO.

TOKICO performance suspension products, including our new line of springs and anti-sway bars, are available at better performance retailers everywhere or by mail with prices starting at $42.00.

TOKICO Shocks

3555 West Lomita Blvd., Suite E, Dept. RT, Torrance, CA 90505-5016 (213) 534-3300

JULY 1985 181

The MR2 had some excellent reviews in the States, and soon found its way onto the race tracks. A number were seen competing in the IMSA Showroom Stock Endurance Series, but this is the Pace Car for the 1985 Toyota Grand Prix of Long Beach.

Advertising from America during the early part of the 1986 model year. Note the colour-coded bumpers on the production car in the lower part of the advert.

Right: An MR2 won the Touring Class in the IMSA Firehawk Showroom Stock Endurance series in 1985, and again in 1986. Here are a few of the cars that competed during the 1986 season.

MR2 DOMINATES!

*Touring Class
© 1985 Toyota Motor Sales, U.S.A., Inc.

WHO COULD ASK TOYOTA FOR ANYTHING MORE!

TOYOTA MOTORSPORTS

RIGHT OFF THE SHOWROOM FLOOR, MR2 DOMINATES ITS CLASS.

How many production cars can you take fresh out of the showroom and start winning races? Not many. Unless your car is the Toyota MR2.

Maybe that's why MR2 was the most popular car in its class* during the IMSA-sanctioned Firehawk Endurance Series, the most grueling showroom stock series in the U.S. Eight races, between March and October, that ground up showroom stock cars for 3 to 24 hours at a stretch. MR2 not only went the distance. It won the series.*

This kind of performance isn't beginner's luck. The MR2 comes from a heritage of quality and technology that demands better balance in a sports car. Like the balance from mid-engine design. A heritage that demands Electronic Fuel-Injection, twin cams and sixteen valves for better performance. A heritage that demands 4-wheel independent suspension, 4-wheel disc brakes and a 7-way adjustable driver's seat for better command of the road.

And most important, a heritage that demands all this performance as part of a car you can count on. Trip after trip. Or race after race.

Toyota MR2. A winner. Because that's all Toyota builds.

GET MORE OUT OF LIFE—BUCKLE UP!

54

Metallic, while Dark Jade over Light Beige was listed as an option.

As a matter of interest, it was thought that Nissan would join the mid-engine brigade with the replacement for the Z31-type 300ZX. Prototypes given the MID-4 appellation had been displayed on the 1985 and 1987 Show circuit, but rumours that the cars were due to enter production were unfounded on both occasions.

Another project worthy of mention was the so-called Michelotti Clas, which made its debut at the 1986 Turin Show. This represented a renewal of the famous Italian styling house's links with Japanese cars, as the design was based on the MR2. Featuring 2+2 seating, exposed headlights and far more glass area than the production model, it also had softer lines and a partially-covered rear wheel, a styling accent found on many of the show cars from the period. Although the lines were far from the best to come from Italy, the Clas was nonetheless an interesting prototype, and the vehicle deserved more exposure than it received. Sadly, the Michelotti concern closed down not long after.

Competition news

The MR2 had a one-make series in both the United States and Britain, and also did well in IMSA and SCCA racing Stateside. During 1984, a four-wheel drive rally version of the MR2 was under development by Toyota Team Europe (TTE), designed to compete in the proposed new Group S, due to be inaugurated in 1988.

The birth of Toyota Team Europe came about in 1972, when the accomplished Swedish rally driver, Ove Andersson (he won the Monte Carlo, San Remo, Austrian Alpine and Acropolis Rallies in 1971), asked if Toyota in Japan would prepare a car for him to use in international rallying. A deal was struck, and Andersson drove a Celica to ninth overall and a Class win in the 1972 RAC Rally.

This immediate success so impressed Japanese personnel that Toyota helped Andersson establish a team, comprising just four mechanics, Andersson, and his co-driver, Arne Hertz. At that time, it was run from Andersson's house in Uppsala, as there seemed little point in having big premises. However, the team moved to Brussels in February 1975 and was soon attracting top drivers – a string of fine results was assured with talented hands in charge of tough and dependable steeds, and the name 'Toyota Team Europe' was officially adopted. Based in Cologne since 1979, TTE now employs over 200 people, and has done a sterling job in bringing the Toyota marque to the attention of so many.

The MR2-based rally car came about when TTE was looking at different engine layouts for a Group S contender. With safety concerns running high on the agenda, sadly, the demise of the rally supercars meant a premature end for the Group S category, and the MR2 project Toyota Team Europe was in the middle of developing.

A new Celica, a new Supra

"With 16 candles on its birthday cake,

The MR2 developed by Toyota Team Europe to run in the stillborn Group S of the World Rally Championship. Unfortunately, the project came to an end before the car had a chance to run after the Group B supercars were banned.

the 1986 Toyota Celica has left its Mustang-inspired heritage behind, taken on front-wheel drive and been given a refreshingly smooth and cliché-free body design. It is a new car in every respect and, most importantly for Toyota's marketing strategy, will no longer share its structure nor its components with the Supra." – *Road & Track*, October 1985.

Announced in August 1985, the new Celica – with its smooth, aerodynamic styling – quickly gained a reputation for fine handling and balance, and moved Toyota into the upper echelons of sports car manufacturers. The latest Celica also brought the company an immense amount of publicity through its success in the field of motorsport, particularly in the World Rally Championship.

The old Celica Supra was listed until mid-1986, when it was replaced by a distinctive new model, not linked to the Celica in any way. The impressive all-new, three-litre Supra was a refined GT with excellent performance, bettered only by the turbocharged model that followed a couple of years later. Toyota was now the only manufacturer to offer three sports cars alongside a full range of saloons.

The MR2 was voted 'Best Coupé' by *What Car?* in its 1986 'Car of the Year' competition, but many changes were on the cards for this popular model.

The T-bar roof

In a 1985 article, the British journalist, Jeremy Coulter, mentioned: "I can't help noticing that the MR2 would make a lovely convertible, so how about it Toyota ...?" Sadly, there was too much strength in the roof, so a T-bar was the best the engineers could do without compromising the rigidity of the vehicle.

On 26th August 1986, Toyota officially announced the T-bar roof option, even though it had first been seen three years earlier on the SV-3 prototype. According to the press release: "The T-bar roof has detachable glass panels (with sunshade panels) on both sides, and when these are removed the bar-shaped section remains along the middle. This roof has been introduced for the 1.6-litre 16v twin-cam engine models."

A rear view of TTE's Group S MR2, designed to give cars like the Peugeot 205 T16, Audi Quattro and Lancia 037 a run for their money.

As one magazine put it: "There's no need to worry about scuttle shake or leaking roof panels. In topless mode, the Toyota shell still feels as taut as that of the current, glass sunroof MR2 (which continues alongside the T-bar car) and with the roof panels in place, there's no disturbing wind roar to spoil refinement. Fit and finish is excellent." When not in use, the glass panels could be stored behind the seats.

A new front bumper and spoiler was a key distinguishing feature on the latest cars, along with a restyled engine air intake and tail-lights. The deeper spoiler helped reduce lift, and was also a useful ally against crosswind. Different, higher-grade material was used to trim the interior, a smaller diameter steering wheel and new instrument graphics were adopted, and the heater controls were modified to the push-button type at the same time. A number of chassis modifications were also introduced, but more on this particular subject later.

A supercharged model

In August 1985, *Motor* ran the story: "Toyota is expected to become the first Japanese car maker to offer a production car fitted with a supercharger. While the first application is likely to be the big Crown, a later step will be of particular significance – for it will be a supercharged MR2.

"This would answer the widely-voiced call for more power and particularly mid-range punch for the little two-seater – a plea which apparently cannot be answered by the new Celica's two-litre engine due to lack of space."

Sure enough, one year later, at the same time as the T-bar roof appeared, Toyota introduced the supercharged MR2. It featured the same chassis and suspension modifications as the T-bar models; namely, uprated shock absorbers and springs, repositioned rear suspension arms, and a tower bar between the front suspension turrets. Larger brake discs and servos were adopted, with the supercharged car featuring tandem brake boosters and stiffer anti-roll bars and springs up front.

The main feature of the supercharged model, however, was, of course, the power unit, which was basically the existing MR2 1.6-litre

British advertising showing the T-bar roof in all its glory. Note also the reprofiled nose and deeper spoiler – another change announced in Japan in August 1986. The body modifications and new roof option were introduced to all markets for the 1987 model year.

top: a 4.29:1 final-drive was specified. The driveshafts were also heavier duty, incidentally.

The supercharged model came with a T-bar roof, full aerodynamics kit and colour-coded mirrors, as well as a new louvred glassfibre engine cover to help disperse heat from the power unit and intercooler.

Regarding the supercharged model, writing for *Motor*, Kevin Radley stated that "Toyota told us they had chosen a supercharger because it gave better responsiveness than a turbo. A turbo might have been preferred for Europe, where high-speed operation is the rule rather than the exception, but for Japan bottom-end torque and response were deemed essential.

"The green light on the tachometer is on, indicating that the supercharger is pumping its contribution. [There is] certainly no lag. The speed builds up in a linear fashion as the tach swings round the dial. Toyota claim a healthy car can run the standing-quarter mile in just 15.2 seconds.

"Toyota say they have tried to make the car easier to control, and have worked hand-in-hand with their tyre makers (Bridgestone and Yokohama) to raise the limits of grip and improve controllability. This translates into a loss of the knife-edge nervousness of the original car, though at the low speeds enforced by the nature of the road, understeer looms large as it is not possible to get the back end to break away. The result is rather clumsy.

"It is not, as hoped, the exciting sports car to end all sports cars, but supercharging does help to keep the MR2 on its pedestal as arguably Japan's best sports car."

Sadly, the supercharged car never made it to Europe, as poor availability

engine with the addition of a belt-driven, Toyota SC12 Roots-type blower. Interestingly, in order to reduce tiresome supercharger whine and enhance the 4A-GZE unit's economy, it went into action only on demand, using an electromagnetic clutch and bypass valve, and the rotors were resin-coated to prolong life.

With new bi-directional injectors, forged aluminium pistons (giving an 8.0:1 compression ratio), reprofiled camshafts, an electronic knock-sensor and an air-to-air intercooler, maximum power rose to 145bhp at 6400rpm, while torque output increased to 137lbft at 4400rpm.

The gearbox and clutch were suitably uprated to handle the extra power, with the ratios changed to 3.23:1 on first, 1.91 on second, 1.26 on third, 0.92 on fourth and 0.73 on

A superb shot of the Japanese 1600G model, proudly displaying its new nose. Note the steel wheels.

of unleaded fuel made selling it there somewhat impractical. At least the T-bar roof would be marketed worldwide. As a matter of interest, the supercharger installation added around 50kg (110lb) to the overall weight of the MR2, while the T-bar roof added a further 30kg (66lb).

UK news

Despite a post-budget price increase in April 1986 which took the MR2 to £10,600, the mid-engined machine continued to be extremely popular in the UK, with sales far exceeding expectations. In 1986, *MotorSport* stated that the "British appetite for sports cars remains undiminished despite the decline of the home-based volume producers, and the UK is one of Toyota's most important markets for its sports cars. We took 20% of all MR2 production last year." While Japan and the USA accounted for the majority of sales, it is interesting to note that West Germany took only 8% of the 51,000 built.

The respected British weekly, the *Autocar*, covered the new T-bar model in October 1986, when it made its UK debut. Recording a top speed of 119mph (190kph) with a one-way best of 122mph (195kph), 0-60mph was covered in just 7.7 seconds. The standing quarter-mile came up in 16.5 seconds (at a terminal speed of 85mph, or 136kph), all whilst returning an average of 28.6mpg. The magazine noted: "Not a company to sit back on its laurels, Toyota has now responded to the main criticism of the MR2, its fixed top. With much of the car's structural strength provided by the roof, Toyota has not been able to offer a true convertible, so has therefore produced the next best thing, a T-top in the style of a number of American sports cars.

"What the new generation MR2 offers, apart from a removable roof, is the suspension pack and the bodywork and interior alterations of the supercharged version now available in Japan. Even without the supercharger, the alterations have a beneficial effect on an already accomplished car.

"Externally, the front bumper and nose of the car are smoother and longer, and there's a deeper front spoiler,

Fascia of the 1500S for 1987. Note the new instrument graphics, heater controls and steering wheel (now three-spoke for all markets). The voltmeter and oil pressure gauge were still missing on the 1.5-litre model, although both were there on 1.6-litre cars. 1987 also saw a new ashtray arrangement, adopted worldwide (left-hand drive vehicles now had the handbrake on the same side as right-hand drive ones).

At first glance there was little to distinguish the new supercharged model from the standard 1.6-litre car. Those with keen eyes will spot the very understated 'Supercharger' badge on the left-hand side, the latest combination lamps and new location for the 'Twin-Cam 16 G' insignia.

Two Japanese-specification supercharged models, with the new T-bar roof, restyled frontal area and the latest 6J x 14 alloy wheels.

while the air intake on the rear offside has been restyled. Inside, the T-bar acquires restyled fascia switches and instruments and the heater/ventilation controls are now of the push-button variety. The [three-spoke] steering wheel has been reduced in diameter by 60mm (2.4in) and the standard stereo radio/cassette player has been uprated [with an electronic tuner and five speakers] ...

"Suspension and braking have also been uprated. A strut brace has been fitted across the front suspension turrets ... Restyled alloy wheels are increased in width to 6J from 5.5J but retain the same type and size of tyre. Ventilated front discs are increased in diameter by 15mm (0.6in) and the rears by 23mm (0.9in).

"Removing one or both of the [roof] panels is simplicity itself. The original MR2 has a sunshield which fits under the sunroof and the T-bar goes one better: it has two sunshields which are stored in the front boot-space when not in use.

"The MR2 is a classic in its own lifetime and by bringing out the T-bar, Toyota has ensured that this will not change. Performance, handling, good driver ergonomics, good fuel economy and the ability to get the wind in the hair all combine to make the MR2 T-bar a car in a class of its own."

It would be fair to say that *Motor*'s Roger Bell was not so comprehensively impressed. He pointed out: "There are no dramatic changes to the car's handling. It's as brilliant as ever, if not quite the paragon of perfection it's sometimes cracked up to be. To my mind, the steering is not alert enough for that.

The supercharged model photographed by Hideo Aoki at its launch. (Courtesy Hideo Aoki)

Interior of the supercharged model, based on the G-Limited.

The 4A-GZE power unit. (Courtesy Hideo Aoki)

"It's easy to see how the MR2's seductive charms have coloured previous assessments. The car is such enormous fun, so forgiving, such an agreeable partner. But I'm not wearing my rose-tinted glasses this time. For all its great qualities, it seems to me this fine evening that the car needs bringing down a peg or two. Pious reverence is over the top. Huge respect is nearer the mark."

In its February 1987 issue, *Performance Car* looked at the T-bar roof model, and observed: "There is little in the way of wind noise, road noise is limited, and the general standard of ride is better than in most Japanese cars of whatever type, which is saying a great deal about why the MR2 has made sports cars acceptable again." Priced at £11,559 on introduction, options included leather trim at £441, metallic paint at £93, and duotone paint at £299; the standard car was £11,099 at this time.

This stunning overhead publicity shot shows the louvred engine cover employed on the supercharged models (the normally-aspirated cars continued to use the original panel).

61

Another view of the supercharged MR2 at speed. Note the 'Supercharger' badge on the door, the T-bar roof and the slightly-modified front end of these latest cars.

Tasteful Japanese advertising for the 1987 model year. Sadly, Toyota felt that a full convertible was not possible without compromising the rigidity of the vehicle, but the MR2 T-bar managed to introduce the mid-engined Toyota to a wider audience. In Germany, however, the Schwan concern of Wurzburg-Heidingsfeld was converting the Celica and MR2. (The MR2 conversion, called the MR2 Cabriolet, featured a single removable panel that could then be stored on the rear deck in a special holder.) In California, too, the MR2 was getting the drophead treatment, this time by a company called Motor Style.

Rear three-quarter shot of the supercharged MR2. Available in Japan only initially, it was shipped to the States for the 1988 season. Britain, the mid-engined Toyota's next biggest market, was destined not to import it, as the distinct unavailability of unleaded fuel would have played havoc with its catalytic converter.

To the end of 1987, UK MR2 sales totalled 7413. Of this total, 1304 were T-bar roof models, but, naturally, with its late-1986 introduction, the majority of those sales (actually 1197 of them) came in 1987. As regards the coupé, 2116 were sold in 1985, and 2322 in 1986. The remainder, 1671 of them, were sold in 1987.

By this time, MR2 prices had increased another two times in Britain – once in June and again in October – taking the list price of the coupé to £11,990, with the T-bar at £12,992. Prices for both went up by a further £250 the following January!

The US 1987 model year

There were big changes outlined for the 1987 season in America. As elsewhere, the T-bar roof model joined the line-up for 1987 and, of course, the body, chassis and interior upgrades were carried over to Stateside models, but there was much more to it than that. In effect, the basic specification was lower than before, with a number of new options allowing the buyer to create a custom vehicle.

Steel wheels were now standard fare across the range, shod with 185/60 HR14 rubber, while alloys became a $425 option; all-weather tyres were available at no extra cost. The seats were cheaper, cloth-trimmed, high-back items; the steering wheel and gearlever were finished in urethane rather than leather, and mirrors came with manual adjustment, unless the $465 Power Package was specified, which also included power windows and door locks. However, the Power Package

The 1987 model year MR2 for the UK, pictured at the time of the 1986 Motor Show, held that year at the NEC.

1987 model year MR2 T-bar roof for the US market. This is a 'fully-loaded' vehicle, fitted with optional aerodynamic aids and alloy wheels.

American advertising from the 1987 model year.

The basic coupé was priced at $12,548, or $13,238 with automatic transmission, while the T-bar roof car was introduced at $13,738 ($14,428 in automatic guise). The model ranges with transmission options for the 1985 to 1987 model years are listed in the table opposite, complete with the serial and prefix numbers.

The MR2 was listed in *Car & Driver*'s '10 Best' ranking, with standard colours for 1987 being Super White, Super Red, Dark Blue Pearl, Silver Metallic, Beige Metallic and Metallic Black; two-tone Jade over Beige was classed as a $230 option. Interior trim could be specified in either Black, Blue or Beige, depending on the coachwork.

Minor changes

In August 1987 it was announced that the normally-aspirated, 1.6-litre engines had been upgraded to LASRE Alpha spec (4A-II), with modified camshaft and valve timing, plus larger exhaust manifold ports. Although there was a drop of 10bhp, the new unit complied with all of the latest regulations.

On the supercharged model, a new AD Package was announced in which the springs and shock absorber rates were modified, and a rear anti-roll was added, along with Potenza 185/60 R14 tyres. White alloy wheels became an option on the G-Limited, and two-tone grey found its way onto the colour scheme listing.

Although a Californian concern known as Motor Style had carried out an attractive conversion to make the MR2 into a full convertible, Toyota still had no plans to follow suit. Few were sold in any case, as the rag-top cost around $19,000 in 1987 and, for that money,

could only be bought in conjunction with the Performance Interior Package.

The Performance Interior Package brought back the seven-way adjustable sports seats, leather-trimmed steering wheel and gearshift, and better quality carpets. Priced at $340, it came as standard on the T-bar roof model. If the owner wanted something really special, he could opt for the $760 Leather Package.

A three-speaker AM/FM radio with electronic tuning came as standard, but could be upgraded to a five-speaker system with cassette for $250, or to a radio/cassette with amplifier and graphic equaliser ($455 on the base model or $400 on the T-bar version).

Other options included a $475 Aerodynamic Spoiler Package (featuring colour-coded front and rear spoilers, side skirts and mudguards, and the additional spoiler on the trailing edge of the roof), a rear spoiler only ($210), air conditioning ($795), cruise control ($220), a moonroof ($355) and mudguards ($30).

Year	Code	Model
1985	JT2AW15C	Coupé (5-sp. manual)
1986	JT2AW15C	Coupé (5-sp. manual or 4-sp. auto.)
1987	JT2AW15C	Coupé (5-sp. manual or 4-sp. auto.)
	JT2AW15J	T-bar (5-sp. manual or 4-sp. auto.)

it was possible to buy a Porsche 924S or a top Mazda RX-7.

1988 model year in America

For 1988 power rose to 115bhp and torque to 100lbft on the basic 1.6-litre engine. In addition, the supercharged engine joined the line-up, delivering 145bhp at 6400rpm and 140lbft of torque at 4000rpm in American trim. The MR2 Supercharged could be bought with a manual or optional automatic transmission.

Based on the T-bar roof model, the 'Supercharged' logos soon identified the car. In addition, the MR2 Supercharged came with the 6J alloy rims found on home and European market MR2s, whilst the optional 5.5J alloy wheels for normally-aspirated cars featured a different design. (Both were shod with 185/60 HR14 tyres, as were the steel rims.) The Spoiler Package was standard equipment on the faster machine.

Although the team at *Car & Driver* had mixed reactions, the main gripes being concerned with the chassis, after recording a 0-60 time of just 7.0 seconds, *Road & Track* said: "You don't wait for acceleration and you never seem to run out of it." (*Car & Driver* clocked just 6.5 seconds for the same yardstick.) *Road & Track* went on to class the supercharged model as one of the 'Ten Best Cars in the World,' on the grounds of both passion and value. It noted: "The supercharger makes this neat little runabout a giant-killing marvel, smooth and strong all the way up. If it doesn't start a trend, we'll eat our hats and all other affordable GTs will continue to eat dust."

The success of the MR2 was undoubtedly one of the main reasons for the early demise of the mid-engined Pontiac Fiero (production ended in the latter half of 1988 after around 370,000 units had been built), and Fiat's X1/9 (sold later as the Bertone X1/9 in America) was shortly to follow.

Ironically, the proposed mid-engined Honda was cancelled in early 1987, presumably because it was thought that returns would be reduced with such a large number of competitors in this niche market, although it has to be said that the nippy little CRX probably did the job of providing enjoyment for the driver just as well. Indeed, in a comparison test involving the V6-powered Fiero, the normally-aspirated MR2 and the front-wheel drive Honda, *Car & Driver* declared the CRX the winner on 16 points, against 15 for the Toyota and 11 for the Pontiac – it was a very accomplished performer!

On the downside for all manufacturers in the Land of the Rising Sun, 1985 had seen the yen move strongly against the dollar, making Japanese exports harder to sell. With the exchange rate in 1988 at around 120 yen to the dollar, prices were pushed up to unprecedented

The MR2 seen racing in America in the 1987 IMSA Showroom Stock Endurance Series.

The Japanese range for 1988

Model	Body	Engine	Code	Price
1600G-Limited	Coupé	4A-GELU	E-AW11-WC*QF	1,908,000 yen
1600G-Limited	T-bar	4A-GELU	E-AW11-WJ*QF	2,058,000 yen
1600G-Limited	Coupé	4A-GZE	E-AW11-WC*QR	2,100,000 yen
1600G-Limited	T-bar	4A-GZE	E-AW11-WJ*QR	2,250,000 yen
1600G-Ltd AD	Coupé	4A-GZE	E-AW11-WC*QR	2,120,000 yen
1600G-Ltd AD	T-bar	4A-GZE	E-AW11-WJ*QR	2,270,000 yen
1600G	Coupé	4A-GELU	E-AW11-WC*QF	1,691,000 yen
1600G	T-bar	4A-GELU	E-AW11-WJ*QF	1,841,000 yen
1600G	Coupé	4A-GZE	E-AW11-WC*QR	1,883,000 yen
1600G	T-bar	4A-GZE	E-AW11-WJ*QR	2,033,000 yen
1500S	Coupé	3A-LU	E-AW10-WC*SS	1,447,000 yen

* replace with M for manual or P for automatic.

Another piece of US advertising from early 1987. It features Craig Horning's MR2, which took the Firehawk Showroom Stock Endurance Series crown. The model was still winning in 1989, with Michael Galati claiming the SCCA Showroom Stock C title.

Functional dashboard of the American MR2. Note the relocated handbrake, which had been standardised with the right-hand drive cars in time for the 1987 season.

The MR2 Supercharged joined the American line-up for 1988.

levels. The basic coupé cost $13,458, the T-bar version was $14,808, and the MR2 Supercharged started at $17,068: opting for automatic transmission added a further $730 to these prices. Options, although a fraction more expensive, were much the same as they were in 1987, although a Value Package was added. Priced at $1075, it included air conditioning, the Performance Interior Package, Power Package and Spoiler Package.

Standard colours included Super White, Super Red, Dark Blue Pearl, Orange Pearl, Metallic Grey, and Metallic Black, with two-tone Metallic Grey over Super Silver coachwork being

TOYOTA TECHNOLOGY

REV REVIEWS!

ENTHUSIAST PUBLICATIONS ENTHUSIASTIC ABOUT TOYOTA TECHNOLOGY.
Those in a position to know have always applauded Toyota reliability, quality, styling and solid engineering. They still do. Now, they're paying tribute to Toyota's extraordinary technological advances, as well. Here's why they're so revved up:

MR2 SUPERCHARGED
"Simply a blast. The supercharger makes this neat little runabout a giant-killing marvel... all other affordable GT's will continue to eat its dust." **Road & Track**
"...it's easy to realize that the MR2 can be driven as a race car." **Sports Car Illustrated**

COROLLA GT-S
"This high-line coupe has everything going for it... motor that makes your mouth water... bucket seats that hug you... and a chassis that knows how to fondle the curves... this is one Toyota that loves to play Ferrari." **Car and Driver**

CELICA ALL-TRAC TURBO
"...the Celica All-Trac Turbo is the next best thing to wings... rather like a Learjet for the road." **Car and Driver**
"Among Import Sports Coupes... the most potent, quickest-handling vehicle... for either foul-or-fair weather fun..." **Consumers Digest**

SUPRA TURBO
"...one of the best GT cars ever offered for sale in this country." **Automobile**
"...(Supra) brings an impressively high level of genuine performance credentials to the game." **Motor Trend**

TOYOTA QUALITY
WHO COULD ASK FOR ANYTHING MORE!

Get More From Life...Buckle Up!
© 1988 Toyota Motor Sales, U.S.A., Inc.

By the end of the 1980s, Toyota had an enviable sports car line-up. The Fourth Generation Celica had changed to a front-wheel drive machine (seen here in All-Trac Turbo guise, the US version of the GT-Four), whilst the new Supra became a distinct model, losing its links with the Celica, thus giving the three sports cars in the Toyota range completely different layouts – MR2 (MR), Supra (FR) and Celica (FF). To make up for the lack of a convertible on the MR2, Toyota went on to produce a rag-top version of the new Celica.

Honda CRX and the Nissan EXA (aka Pulsar NX). The MR2 took the fancy of two of the testers, with the third tester favouring the Nissan. It was a surprisingly close test, showing that Toyota couldn't rest on its laurels for too long. Interestingly, the same journal continued to admire the MR2, stating later in the year that it was a "mid-engined jewel" and choosing it as its favourite sports car of 1988, winning on value-for-money.

On the other side of the world in England, *What Car?* compared the T-bar roof model with the slightly cheaper Nissan Sunny ZX Coupé, and observed: "We asked at the beginning of this test whether the Nissan Sunny ZX Coupé stood as a creditable alternative to Toyota sportster MR2. We now know that it

listed as an option. Trim came in either black, blue or beige depending on the shade of the exterior paintwork.

News from the Antipodes
In its March 1988 issue, *Wheels* magazine tested the MR2 against a

doesn't. Maybe one day something will come along and *really* challenge it. Maybe ..."

67

Although it still looked fairly modern in its high-spec UK trim (this car dates from the 1988 model year), there was no doubt that the lower grades in Japan were starting to look dated. The little mid-engined model was still getting some rave reviews in the media, however.

American advertising for the 1989 model year MR2. A tuned version of the engine from the normally-aspirated MR2 was used in the single-seaters entered in the Toyota Atlantic Championship Series.

Perhaps the new breed of 'hot hatch' could offer some competition? Not according to *Autocar*, which voted for the MR2 in a comparison test between the mid-engined Toyota and the 16v Volkswagen Golf GTi.

More minor changes!

In August 1988 the T-bar roof glass became half-mirrored in order to maximise the efficiency of the air conditioning unit. At the same time, the rear spoiler gained an auxiliary LED brake light like that found on the 1989 US-specification models, and colour-coding was extended to the mirrors and door handles on all models. The optional leather trim was upgraded across the range, and bronze tinted glass was fitted.

In January 1989 the Toyota MR2 Super Edition was launched. Based on the supercharged version of the G-Limited with AD Package and T-bar roof, it featured a dark blue mica metallic finish, Recaro seats, a MOMO steering wheel and gearknob, cut-pile carpeting and special door trim. Just 270 were built with a price tag of 2,492,000 yen.

Although there were reports that the supercharged engine used in the MR2 could produce up to 40bhp more through a simple pulley change on the blower, this was not introduced for production models, presumably because Toyota wanted the engine to be reliable rather than highly-strung. The fact that warranty claims on the model's power unit were virtually non-existent would justify this decision, but probably also meant that the engine could happily handle more power. However, time was running out for

A normally-aspirated 1989 model year MR2. Note the optional alloy wheels used on American-specification models, unique to the non-supercharged cars for that market, and the adoption of colour-coded mirrors.

A US advert for the 1989 MR2 Supercharged.

0-60 IN 6.8 SECONDS.* IT'S ENOUGH TO MAKE A GROWN MAN FLY.

Give the exhilarator pedal a little love tap and you're off on a whirlwind affair. The 1989 Toyota MR2 Supercharged is mid-engined for more neutral handling in the corners. And with a twin-cam, 16-Valve, 145-hp supercharged engine, it makes short work of straightaways too. The Toyota MR2 Supercharged. Schedule a flight today.

A **36-month/36,000 mile** basic new vehicle limited warranty with no deductible and no transfer fee applies to all components other than normal wear and maintenance items.

Call 1-800-GO-TOYOTA for more information and the location of your nearest dealer. Get More From Life...Buckle Up!

TOYOTA QUALITY
WHO COULD ASK FOR ANYTHING MORE!

United States Auto Club certified performance figures for 1988 MR2 Supercharged.
© 1988 Toyota Motor Sales, U.S.A., Inc.

the First Generation MR2, and it was therefore left in the same state of tune as before.

Bowing out from the States

For the 1989 season, a rear anti-roll bar was added on the MR2 Supercharged, but otherwise specifications remained pretty much unchanged. Detail revisions included colour-keyed door mirrors and door handles across the range, and the Value Package option was deleted.

However, the 11mm diameter rear anti-sway bar was the most important change. *Motor Trend* felt it was worthwhile, stating: "Very neutral and forgiving during low to medium effort flogging, at the limit it can become a bit of a handful when subjected to radical throttle chops or overly enthusiastic braking. However, the new rear anti-roll bar does a yeoman job under most circumstances. And once this tantalizing Toyota takes a firm set, it will happily whiz through high-speed sweepers like it was on rails. When things do tighten up, a well-timed and modulated stab at the throttle or brake will bring the rear around just enough to power out smoothly and go in search of the next twist in the road." Mike Banks concluded: "This is four-star entertainment!"

The basic coupé had a $13,798 sticker price, the T-bar roof model started at $15,268, and the MR2 Supercharged was $17,628; the four-speed electronically-controlled

Distinctive. Charismatic. Powerful. And fun.

The MR2. The classic two-seater sports car. Sheer pleasure on four wheels.

No power steering. No cruise control. No room for more than you, a passenger and an overnight bag. No compromise. This car is for driving.

Turn the stereo up high. Move on to the open road with a mighty 123 bhp at 6600 rpm in your hands. The power to accelerate from 0–60 mph in a mere 8.2 seconds. And a top speed capability of 125 mph.

All controlled from a cockpit skilfully designed to combine the essential two-seater feel of a bygone age with the equally essential comfort demanded by today's motoring enthusiast.

As *"Autocar"* said, 'a car in a class of its own'.

MR2

A four-cylinder, 16-valve, 1587cc engine. Electronic fuel injection. Pent-roof combustion chambers. And the same exclusive T-VIS Variable Induction System as the Celica.

A formidable combination that gives the MR2 push-in-the-back acceleration, but with quite remarkable fuel economy.

And perfect close-ratio gearing delivers the 125 mph maximum speed just below the power peak of 123 bhp.

The mid-engine mounting (behind the cockpit, but just ahead of the rear axle) gives outstanding road holding and stability, with 55% of the kerb weight distributed to the rear wheels.

This balance and traction combine with the enormous rigidity of the monocoque chassis and the modified MacPherson-strut independent suspension to produce exhilarating agility and excellent cornering, smoothly and safely.

Behind the alloy wheels there is enough stopping power from the large diameter disc brakes to bring you just as smoothly and safely to a halt.

But it's not only the advanced technology of its mechanical components that make the MR2 a truly contemporary classic.

The interior environment offers everything you look for in a sports car. The right look and feel, but with a few discreet improvements made so you can revel in all the power and glory of this superb performance package from a position of perfect comfort. For example, there is a 6-way adjustable sports seat, a compact and competent cockpit layout, crisp good looks and a high-quality finish, together with electric windows and door mirrors, central locking, four-speaker electronic stereo radio/cassette. And in original hardtop form, a removable/refit glass sunroof.

But for those who like a little more wind-in-the-hair with their two-seater sports car, we have created the MR2 T-bar – with a distinctive central roof-brace and removable glass panels. And the two seats and steering wheel in sumptuous black leather.

Real open-top motoring as it used to be. With one or two rather impressive improvements, that moved *"MOTOR"* magazine to call it, quite simply, 'an all-time great'.

MR2

A page from the last UK catalogue to feature the First Generation MR2.

Another page from the same brochure, this one showing the interior and fascia for the British market (the leather trim came as standard on the T-bar roof model).

A final shot from the winter 1989/90 catalogue. It features the MR2 T-bar roof, the fourth version of the Celica (also about to be replaced), and the Supra Grand Tourer. The Toyota marque had long since ceased to be dependent on selling economy cars, and its sporting machinery made a definite upmarket move over the coming years.

automatic transmission (available for all cars) added $750. Prices rose by around $250 before the year was out, however.

Options included the Leather/Power/Performance Interior Package at $1730 (or $1200 on T-bar models), although the Power Package and Performance Interior Package continued to be available separately, priced at $920 ($390 on T-bar models) and $530 respectively. The Aerodynamic Spoiler Package was listed at $560. Individual options were alloy wheels for the normally-aspirated MR2s at $435, all-weather tyres, air conditioning ($795), cruise control ($225), the uprated stereo systems, a rear spoiler ($285), sunroof ($380) and mudguards.

Standard colours included White, Super Red, Black, Medium Red Pearl, Ice Blue Pearl, Dark Blue Pearl, and Metallic Grey, with two-tone Grey over Silver being listed as a $245 option. Trim came in either black, blue or red depending on the coachwork shade.

News from Europe

In October 1988, the MR2 coupé was listed at £12,551 in Britain and the T-bar roof model commanded £14,174. Prices went up by around £400 the following January, but, as some consolation, leather upholstery was made standard on T-bar cars in the UK for the 1989 model year.

Announced in September 1989, the Fifth Generation Celica made its public debut the following month at the Tokyo Show. The press release noted: "The new Celica was developed on the basic concept of creating a car to satisfy the desires of fashion-conscious individuals, providing futuristic features in style and ride." It would later go on to give Toyota its first World Rally Championship title.

The Second Generation MR2 also made its debut in Japan in October 1989, but was not introduced in Europe until six months later. Prices in the UK at this time started at £13,320 for the MR2 coupé, while the T-bar was quoted at £15,041, and there they stayed until the new model made it into the showroom. To put this into perspective, the standard Celica GT was priced at £16,720, while its four-wheel drive stablemate was listed at £21,447; the normally-aspirated Supra was a fraction over £20,000. An interesting alternative was the Corolla 1.6 GTi 16v at just £11,381; at that price, no doubt it took a good many sales from the mid-engined car.

As for options, metallic paint was £187 extra on the MR2, but two-tone coachwork was not available, nor was automatic transmission. Standard colours included Super White III, Super Red II, Blue Mica and Light Blue Mica.

What Car? compared the MR2 T-bar roof with the TVR S, declaring it a split decision. "These two cars appeal to two very different sorts of driver," it was noted. "But what can't be denied is the sheer competence of the little Japanese sports car. Well-equipped, ultra-reliable and cheap to run, the Toyota will no doubt reward your pocket just as it does your driving enjoyment."

The original MR2 was a great success, with around 163,000 being sold (over half of them going to America), but the sharp-edged styling was now starting to look dated. There was also some new, strong competition, such as the similarly-priced Mazda MX-5, to be considered. However, with such a well-loved concept, the Second Generation was eagerly awaited in Europe.

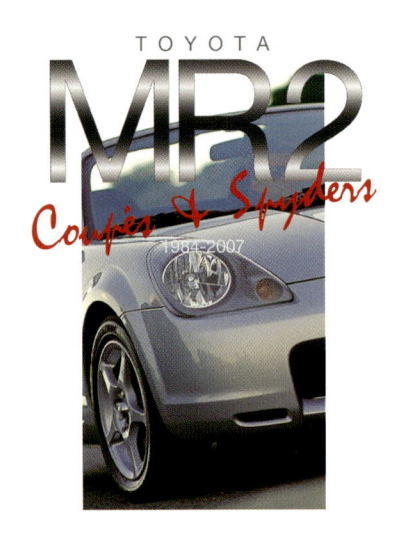

TOYOTA MR2
Coupés & Spyders
1984-2007

3
THE CONCEPT MATURES

The British catalogue from 1994 noted: "Like many champions on the track, the MR2 has its powerful engine sited amidships. This configuration allows a low centre of gravity, a short, sharply raked bonnet and a high rear deck, delivering the ultimate in aerodynamic efficiency and the optimum weight distribution. The result is an exhilarating performance and responsive handling to meet the toughest driving challenges in style."

The leading feature that sets the MR2 apart from the majority of other mass-produced sporting machinery has always been its mid-engine layout. Naturally, this was retained for the Second Generation car to provide it with ideal weight distribution and balance, but the aerodynamic body was now larger, smoother and undoubtedly more attractive.

The priority of the design team, led by the project's Chief Engineer, Kazutoshi Arima, was again to make the car "fun to drive." Arima, second in command on the original MR2 since 1982, was educated at Kyushu University. The Corona Mk II was the first vehicle he was involved with at Toyota.

However, at the start of the project numerous other goals were set. The car should have distinctive, exciting and refined styling, with increased comfort and quality for the interior; ergonomics, good seating and overall design were quite rightfully deemed important factors in making the driver feel part of the machine. It is interesting to note that Arima quotes "style" at the top of his list for desirable sports car attributes.

The key people entrusted with giving the new SW20 model "style" were the Styling Room No 2 chief, Kunihiro Uchida (born in 1942, he joined Toyota in 1966), who led the body design team, and Hideichi Misono (a Toyota man since 1969, with experience both in Japan and at Calty in the States), who looked after the upgraded interior. Uchida was certainly a versatile character, as he

continued on page 81

Kazutoshi Arima, Chief Engineer on the Second Generation MR2.

Kunihiro Uchida, Chief Designer of the new model.

72

An early styling sketch submitted by the Tokyo Design Office. In common with a lot of Japanese Second Generation models, the brief dictated that the new car was to be bigger, faster and more expensive than its predecessor.

Above, left and overleaf: Various styling proposals from the start of the project. Some of the sketches displayed lines that gave the car considerable bulk, others a low, wide appearance, while some designers opted for a lither profile. Certain MR2 features were already starting to show through in a number of the drawings.

73

(For caption see previous page)

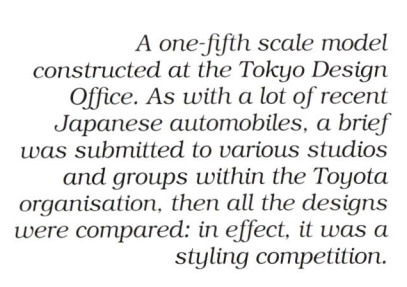

A one-fifth scale model constructed at the Tokyo Design Office. As with a lot of recent Japanese automobiles, a brief was submitted to various studios and groups within the Toyota organisation, then all the designs were compared: in effect, it was a styling competition.

74

The one-fifth scale model put forward by the Planning & Development Team at the Toyota Head Office. This particular proposal was very similar to the Panther Solo.

Another model from Head Office, but this time submitted by the Mass-Production Development Team.

75

A final one-fifth scale model; this rather unconventional shape was put forward by the Design Office at the Central Motor Co Ltd. This concern had built the First Generation (AW10) MR2s, and would once again be entrusted with production of its ultimate replacement. Meanwhile, decisions had first to be made on the new car's lines.

Front and rear views of a full-size clay from the Tokyo Design Office. The tail and roofline still had to be refined, but already one can see the origins of the SW20 model.

76

A full-size clay from the Planning & Development Team. This attractive design was much more conservative than the original proposal but, sadly, did not make it through to the next round of the competition.

The Mass-Production Development Team's full-size clay. This, too, was destined for rejection by Toyota management. Note the 'Twin-Turbo' badge on the front wing.

In addition to the Tokyo Design Office proposal, this one, from the Central Motor Company, was chosen for further development. The front was very stylish but, at this stage, the tail seems to be lacking that certain something that makes the difference between a good and an indifferent design.

In the second stage of the proceedings, the Tokyo Design Office further refined its proposal to ultimately develop 'Model A.'

Model A as it was presented to Toyota management. Note the use of clear windows on this full-size clay.

78

When the designers at the Central Motor Company went back to the drawing board, this is one of the sketches they came up with for 'Model B.'

Model B – ultimately, not all that different to the original Central Motor Company proposal. The Model A clay was the one finally chosen for further development. Although it was surprisingly conservative compared to its immediate predecessors, it was certainly attractive, and definitely more viable as a production model.

After the Model A clay was selected, the design was further refined. A Toyota press release noted: "When designing the exterior, we did countless tests to provide a sports car with aerodynamic form and beauty. Overall, we spent five times the average in wind tunnel and actual driving tests."

This page & bottom left: Three views of the final prototype. The front three-quarter shot shows the car without a rear wing, but it is fitted in the other two. Note the rear roof 'spoiler' (like that fitted on some of the First Generation models), a feature that was integrated into the flying buttresses on production vehicles, and the rear screen shape, which went on to ape that of the classic Ferrari Dino.

has also been credited with the lines of the contemporary Celsior (or Lexus LS400) – a completely different kind of automobile.

Another key point for the development team to consider was the adoption of larger engines, endowing the car with a higher level of performance and substantially more low-end torque, thus making it easier to drive in everyday situations. The team also wanted precise, top-level handling from a communicative chassis, and improved practicality.

As with almost all sports cars, America was cited as the primary market, but while the original MR2 had been deliberately aimed at a very wide-ranging group of people, the new model was given a more sporting flavour – at the end of the day, surely the main point of adopting a mid-engined layout in the first place – and definitely taking a more upmarket position than that of its predecessor. At the same time, research had shown that potential buyers required more luggage space and a roomier cockpit, so, as a consequence, the body had to become bigger.

Whilst remaining a pure two-seater coupé, compared with the AW10 model of 1984, dimensions had certainly changed somewhat. The length was now quoted at 4170mm (164.2in) against the 3925mm (154.5in) of the original,

continued on page 88

81

Both pages: A small selection of the interior styling sketches put forward by the various design studios. A key theme was the feeling of individual cockpits, partly dictated by the unusual fuel tank location, carried over from the First Generation cars.

83

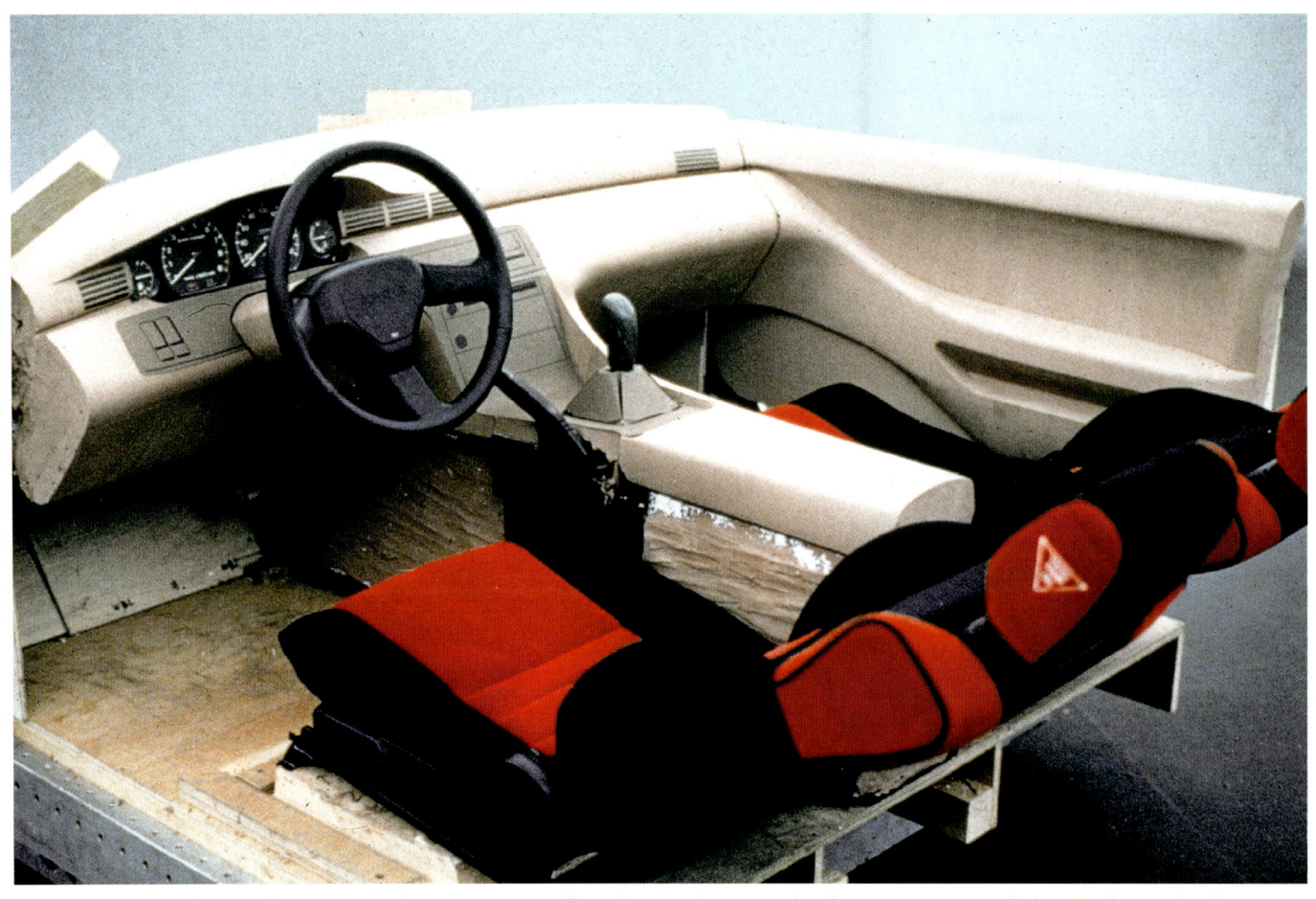

To suit the advanced exterior styling, some equally advanced interior bucks were prepared during the early design stages.

Interior of the Model A clay.

Interior of the Model B clay.

85

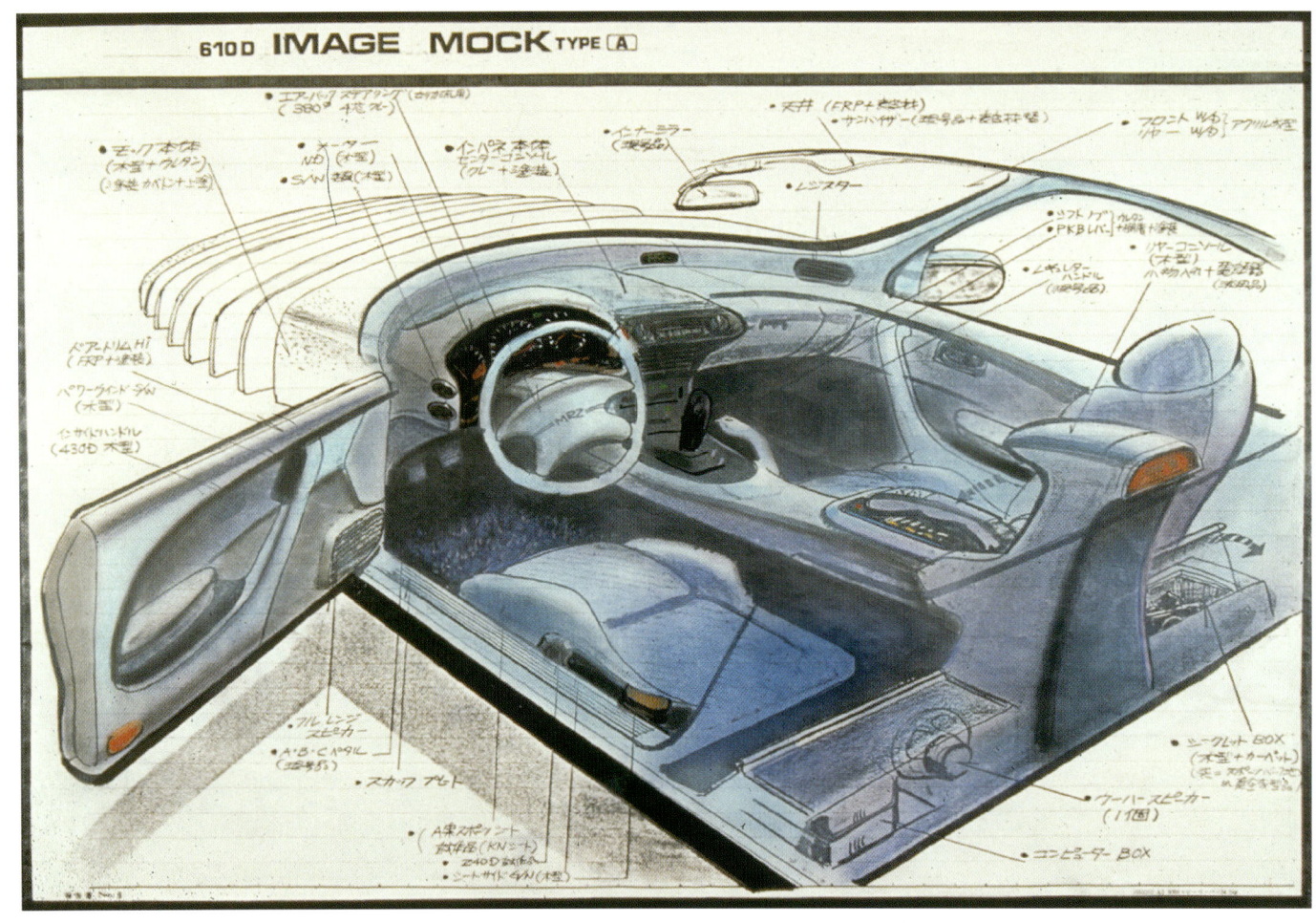

Together with the exterior, the original Model A interior was further modified.

Opposite page: Final mock-up of the interior. A Toyota spokesman said: "The MR2's interior is intimate without being claustrophobic. In true sports car tradition, all controls are close at hand, yet the rounded instrument panel gives excellent visibility and a feeling of spaciousness."

This particular steering wheel design was adopted for the American market (as a driver's-side airbag was specified for the US), but Japanese and European models ultimately had three-spoke items, minus the SRS system, when the car was launched.

The second Model A fascia.

87

Midship Express
NEW MR2 接近

while the width had also increased – at 1695mm (66.7in), it was 30mm (1.2in) wider than the first MR2. Height was now listed at 1240mm (48.8in), which was 10mm (or 0.4in) lower but, at 2400mm (94.5in), the wheelbase was some 80mm (3.2in) longer. The front and rear track dimensions on the SW20 were specified at 1470mm (57.9in) and 1450mm (57.1in) respectively: compared to the original, considerably wider at the front, but not so different at the back.

Uchida and his team certainly succeeded in giving the car style, with many observers comparing the lines of the new MR2 with the best of Italy's sporting machinery. A T-bar roof was offered again and, with the help of flush-fitting glass, underbody fairings and the continued use of pop-up headlights, the rigid body displayed a slippery Cd figure of just 0.31 (with the rear spoiler in place); lift was also reduced compared to the First Generation model.

All of the steel employed in the monocoque was treated against rust, with a fair percentage of it being high-tensile steel, in order to give the body greater strength and to enhance the car's level of safety. On the subject of safety, the MR2 came equipped with impact absorbing bumpers, and crumple zones to help direct forces away from the reinforced passenger cabin in the event of a collision.

Inside, the interior was dominated by the high 'transmission' tunnel, necessary because of the central positioning of the fuel tank. The tank itself was enlarged to 54 litres (11.9 Imperial gallons) on the SW20, giving the car greater range, or at least making up for the use of larger power units. In line with the move upmarket, the new MR2 would come fully-equipped, and extra attention was given to reducing noise in the cockpit, with the engine being supported by fluid-filled mounts and connected to the body by lateral rods. On the practical side, luggage capacity was also increased by around 50% in total, with lockable storage boxes being installed behind the seats, a bigger rear console and larger boots fore and aft.

Mechanically, there was a new series of advanced, powerful LASRE-Alpha engines to provide increased performance, with various four-cylinder units being listed depending on the market. On top models, some

The 'Midship Express Japan Tour' certainly brought the new MR2 to the public's attention! A car was loaded onto a special trailer and taken all over Japan. Almost five-and-a-half years separated the First and Second Generation models – a much longer than usual gap for Toyota at that time.

countries were given the chance to buy a 225bhp turbocharged powerplant, which basically replaced the supercharged version found in the original MR2.

After the rumoured four-wheel drive failed to materialise, again, either a five-speed manual or four-speed automatic transmission would transmit drive to the rear wheels, the latter gearbox option still being extremely popular in the States and on the home market. Interestingly, whichever transmission was used, the gearbox was moved slightly closer to the driver in order to improve the car's weight distribution.

As before, suspension was via MacPherson struts with low-pressure, gas-filled shock absorbers on all four corners (with a dual-link set-up at the back), but every component was modified to suit the new car, and the geometry revised with the intention of providing the automobile with improved "handling and high-speed straight-ahead stability."

For all markets, ball-joint type anti-roll bars were fitted at both ends to enhance the vehicle's cornering capabilities (tests showed the latest MR2 would pull 0.89g on a skidpan), along with a front tower bar; an additional rear brace was employed on Japanese-specification models and turbocharged cars destined for export.

Computer-controlled, speed-sensing, electro-hydraulic, power-assisted steering (EHPS) was adopted on most models. The advantage of EHPS was the use of an electric motor to provide hydraulic assistance, instead of a belt-driven pump off the engine, meaning that the entire system could be housed at the front of the car. Therefore, there was no need to have lengthy hoses running from the power unit, and there was absolutely no drain on engine power. The steering was via rack-and-pinion in all cases, incidentally.

Larger tyres were specified, fitted to aluminium alloy or pressed steel 6J x 14 rims at the front and 7J items at the rear. In keeping with the extra weight and power, the servo-assisted brakes were also uprated, featuring ventilated discs all-round (258mm, or 10.1in up front, and 263mm, 10.3in at the back) and larger calipers, with ABS being available on some grades. Production took place at the Central Motor Co Limited factory again, close to Yokohama.

The range in Japan

On the home market, the new MR2 went on sale on 17th October 1989. It was presented to the press at the then-popular Rail City site in Shiodome, Tokyo, before setting off on the 'Midship Express Japan Tour.' This involved a car being loaded on a special trailer and then displayed at various cities, including Sapporo, Sendai, Tokyo, Yokohama, Shizuoka, Nagoya, Kyoto, Osaka, Kobe and Fukuoka.

A few days afterwards, at the 1989 Tokyo Show (the first to be held at Makuhari Messe, incidentally), the Toyota stand was graced with a red T-bar model, although, it has to be said, the 4500GT concept car, the gullwing Sera coupé and the new Celsior (Lexus LS400) stole a lot of the limelight.

Advanced two-litre, fuel-injected engines included the 16v dohc

A home market GT model from the time of the car's launch. The front foglights fitted to the turbocharged GT and the normally-aspirated G-Limited were steering-actuated, allowing them to follow the road.

3S-GE and its turbocharged brother, the 3S-GTE. The 3S-GE, with its knock sensor and variable length induction tracts ensuring greater output over the entire rev-range, was rated at 165bhp with 141lbft of torque. If automatic transmission was specified with this unit (which also found service in the new Celica, though in FF format rather than MR), Toyota's highly-efficient Super Flow Torque Converter was fitted to extract the maximum performance from the powerplant; in addition, the manual transmission was improved for both MR2 models.

The 1998cc 3S-GTE featured a reinforced iron block, a forged crankshaft (instead of a cast one), forged connecting-rods, a twin-entry ceramic turbocharger for reduced lag, an air-to-air intercooler (mounted on the right-hand side of the engine bay), and a catalytic converter. Developing no less than 225bhp and 224lbft of torque, a similar unit was used in the Celica GT-Four.

On both powerplants, an aluminium alloy head and stainless steel manifold was employed, the latter resisting higher exhaust gas temperatures, thus allowing the engine to run at high speeds with a lower fuel-to-air ratio, enhancing fuel economy as a consequence.

A manual transmission was mandatory on the turbocharged cars, although it had slightly different ratios to the normally-aspirated (NA) models. On both five-speed gearboxes, however, fifth was up and to the right of the traditional 'H' pattern, with reverse

An interesting shot of the GT taken by Hideo Aoki at the car's press launch. (Courtesy Hideo Aoki)

below it. The ratios were as per the table on page 91.

As for the other chassis details, power steering was standard on the GT and G-Limited, and optional on the entry-level G model, although all vehicles came with an adjustable steering column, featuring tilt and telescopic movement. Cars powered by the turbocharged engine had ABS braking as standard, and it was optional on the others. Alloy wheels (6J x 14 at the front, 7J x 14 at the rear) were included as part of the package on the GT and G-Limited grades, while the G had steel rims of the same size, finished with a plastic trim – the cast five-spoke alloys were an extra on

90

Tail of the GT. Note the raised areas on the engine cover, just visible through the gap between the body and the spoiler – a distinguishing feature on the turbocharged model. The rear spoiler was standard on the more expensive grades.

Another view of the GT, a T-bar roof model, with the panels locked in place. As well as the different engine cover (to more quickly dissipate heat from the engine bay), the turbocharged models also had markings on the side protection mouldings.

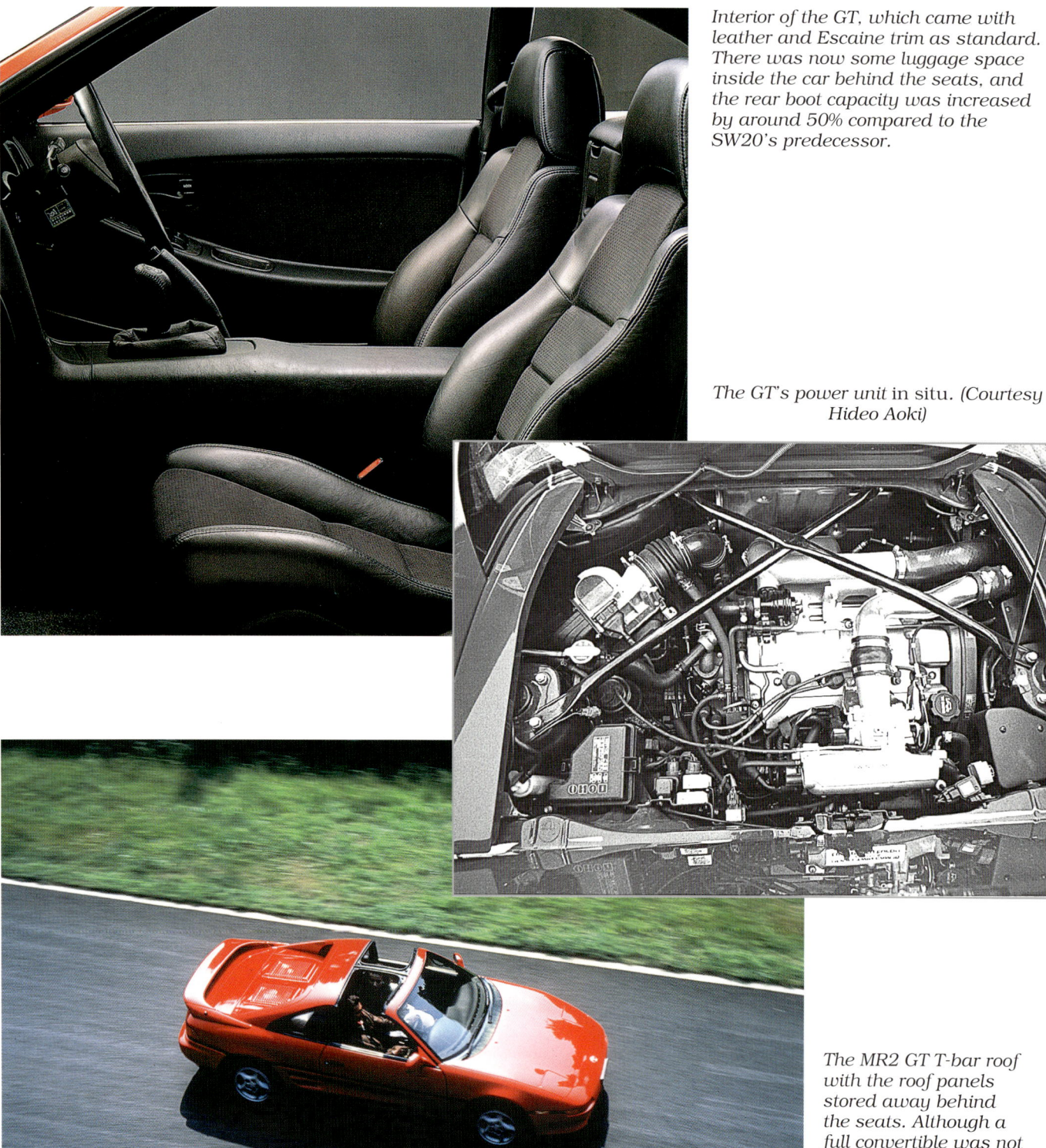

Interior of the GT, which came with leather and Escaine trim as standard. There was now some luggage space inside the car behind the seats, and the rear boot capacity was increased by around 50% compared to the SW20's predecessor.

The GT's power unit in situ. (Courtesy Hideo Aoki)

The MR2 GT T-bar roof with the roof panels stored away behind the seats. Although a full convertible was not available – at least not at this time – the targa arrangement, carried over from the previous model, proved very popular.

	Turbo (MT)	NA (MT)	NA (ECT)
1st	3.230	3.285	3.643
2nd	1.913	1.960	2.008
3rd	1.258	1.322	1.296
4th	0.918	1.028	0.892
5th	0.731	0.820	–
Rev	3.545	3.153	2.977
F/D	4.285	4.176	2.892

the basic model. In all cases, 195/60 HR-rated rubber was specified for the 6J wheel, with 205/60s coming on the 7J rim. Front and rear anti-roll bars were standard across the range, incidentally.

Automatic air conditioning came with all home market cars – an absolute necessity in Japan – as did leather trim on the steering wheel, gearknob (manual gearbox only) and handbrake lever. Tinted glass was also standard, along with remote boot, bonnet and fuel flap releases, a digital quartz clock, door pockets, halogen headlights, front foglights (those on the GT and G-Limited were linked to the steering and actually followed the road, while those fitted on the cheaper G grade were fixed), and an LED high-mounted auxiliary brake light.

The MR2 G was priced at 1,820,000 yen on introduction, with a T-bar roof adding 140,000 yen, or automatic gearbox 93,000 yen. Both of these options added 30kg (66lb) each to the basic 1160kg (2552lb) package.

Moving up to the GT and G-Limited grades brought a two-position rear spoiler (optional on the G, although a front spoiler was standard on all cars), electrically-operated door mirrors instead of manually-adjusted items, a buzzer to remind the driver that the lights were left on, and better, seven-way sports seats with individual headrests and map pockets (trimmed in leather and Escaine on the GT, rather than fabric).

The GT and G-Limited also came with electric windows, central locking and door courtesy lights, all of which could be bought as part of a package on the G, while the option of wireless central locking and cruise control remained unique to the more expensive models. Whilst even the basic G grade came equipped with a six-speaker AM/FM radio and an electric aerial, the top cars had a 'Super Live' 160W seven-speaker system. Radio/cassette units and CD players were classed as dealer options for all vehicles, as were front and rear mudguards.

Again, a closed coupé or T-bar roof body could be ordered. The G-Limited, weighing in at 1180kg (2596lb), was priced at 2,155,000 yen, with the automatic version costing 2,248,000 yen. Adding the T-bar roof added another 140,000 yen. The turbocharged

Interior of the G-Limited, similar to the GT but with fabric trim (leather was optional). In Japan, a black interior meant bronze glass was used for the windows, whilst a blue one meant the glass had a blue tint. Note the rear console box between the seats.

Dashboard of the G-Limited. One of the most important differences in this area between the normally-aspirated car and its turbocharged brother was in the centre of the instrument cluster. This car has a voltmeter lurking behind the steering wheel, whereas the GT had a boost gauge.

Rear view of the G-Limited. Note the different badge on the tail, and the '4.ABS' sticker in the back window, showing that this particular car was equipped with the optional braking system (standard on the GT).

Fascia of the basic G grade, seen here trimmed in blue, a shade that was available only on the normally-aspirated models with cloth trim. The automatic gear selector was quite a sporty design, but could have benefited from a better-defined gate.

PHOTO : G-Limited. ボデーカラーはダークターコイズマイカ(742). 4輪ABSはオプション.

G-Limited

Interior of the same car. The G had four-way adjustment only on the driver's seat rather than the seven of the GT and G-Limited.

95

Front three-quarter view of the G grade, which sported plastic wheel trims instead of alloy wheels. The foglights were fixed on this model, and the rear spoiler was classed as an option.

GT, meanwhile, started at 2,638,000 yen, with the 1270kg (2794lb) MR2 GT T-bar roof model coming in at 2,778,000 yen.

Standard coachwork colours included Super White III, Black, Super Red III and Dark Turquoise Mica. A bright yellow shade was also revived, a hue that hadn't been seen on a Toyota for a long time, but particularly suitable for a sports car; Crystal Pearl Mica II was optional. Early interiors in Japan were finished in either Black or Dark Blue (the latter being optional on the G and G-Limited) only, while export models had these two shades, and red as well. It was hoped that a tan colour could join the line-up in due course.

Despite Toyota's best efforts, as with the original MR2, public opinion regarding the new model was very strongly one way or the other. *Motor Magazine* liked the exterior styling very much, but felt disappointed with the interior, especially the rather bland instrument panel, which lacked the glamour of the car's lines. Interestingly, it was generally full of praise for the 225bhp GT model, stating that this exciting machine would reward highly-experienced drivers, but felt it was perhaps a little too much for those with only average driving skills.

On the other hand, the Japanese monthly, *Car*, thought the dashboard was "trendy." In another article, Kiyondo Sato (now the author's colleague on *Jaguar World* magazine), declared that the styling wasn't distinctive enough. However, he was in agreement with *Motor Magazine* that wet weather handling would take many by surprise.

The new MR2 In Britain

Great Britain had continually provided the MR2 with the second biggest export market outside the USA. Indeed, such was the importance of the British Isles in relation to the mid-engined model that Toyota engineers had descended on the UK with two prototypes in 1989 to fine-tune the suspension and steering to better suit British taste.

It was ultimately decided not to offer the EHPS, give the manual rack a 20.5:1 ratio (3.7 turns lock-to-lock), and specify a 17mm (0.67in) diameter anti-roll bar for the front, with an 18mm (0.71in) one at the back. Also, in view of the higher speeds of European roads, the twin-pot front brake calipers from the Japanese turbocharged model were adopted, minus the ABS system.

Having sold no less than 13,580 of the original 1.6-litre MR2s in the UK (2116 in 1985, 2429 in 1986, 2868 in 1987, 3159 in 1988 and 3008 in 1989), the new car was duly launched in Yorkshire, going on sale from April 11th 1990.

UK buyers were initially given the choice of four two-litre models – the basic MR2 (with manual or automatic transmission), the GT and the GT T-bar. In the June 1990 issue of *MotorSport* it was stated: "Priced at £14,000.68, the base model is unique to Britain and identified by its lack of a rear spoiler and the use of the ex-Carina 3S-FE 16v dohc four-cylinder engine. There is a standard catalytic converter demanding lead-free fuel only."

With more torque available from the unit's larger cubic capacity, there was greater mid-range punch than that found in the original 1.6-litre model, but a similar top speed; with the S54 manual gearbox (featuring the same internal ratios as the normally-aspirated cars in Japan, but a 3.944:1 final-drive), Toyota claimed 124mph

The British market had a unique 3S-FE powered MR2 listed as a base model. Note the lack of front foglights and a rear spoiler, useful identifying features on the basic MR2. Even this cheapest version came with alloy wheels and a glass sunroof.

Right, below: A UK-specification MR2 GT; this closed version cost around £1110 less than the T-bar. Both GT models had manual transmission only, although the basic MR2 was given the option of an automatic gearbox.

(198kph) and a 0-60 time of 9.3 seconds.

An electronically-controlled, four-speed automatic transmission was also available on the 3S-FE powered machine. Designated type A241L, it came with a 3.034:1 final-drive, adding £735 to the invoice and knocking 3mph (5kph) off the car's top speed.

This cheapest model lacked the rear spoiler and auxiliary driving lights of the GT, but alloy wheels (6J at the front, shod with 195/60 VR14 rubber, and 7J at the back, fitted with 205/60s), central locking, power door mirrors, electric windows with tinted glass, a glass sunroof, seven-speaker radio/cassette with electric aerial, an alarm and a digital clock were all standard items, as was a three-year warranty.

In its test of the 119bhp version, *Autocar & Motor* noted: "[The] MR2 is nimble and finely balanced, providing thrills aplenty on twisty roads. Ride is very firm yet absorbent. The two-litre engine from the Camry lacks the GT's sparkle but is still torquey and willing. Engine noise, [however], is sometimes irritating ... The cabin is snug and user-friendly with adequate headroom and an excellent driving position."

Right, above: Tail of the same car, proudly showing off its rear spoiler. Note the different side repeater lights on European models. The rear bumper differed, too, to take the larger registration plates used in Britain and on the Continent.

Right: British version of the MR2 T-bar. From this angle, in particular, it's quite easy to see why some journalists called the Second Generation car "a scaled-down Ferrari."

97

A different view of the top model in the UK line-up – the MR2 GT T-bar. This picture dates from April 1990, the time of the British launch. Note the tiny air deflectors on the leading edge of the roof aperture.

The UK range as it stood in 1990, with the T-bar in the foreground, the GT to its left (the glass sunroof could be tilted, as seen here, or removed completely, incidentally), and the base model in the background, minus the rear spoiler.

Far from basic, *Autocar & Motor* felt it was this car that was the closest in concept to the original MR2, offering "fine grip, handling and poise" as well as "great value for money." However, the steering was thought to be a little heavy (at first, power-assisted steering was not offered on any MR2 in the UK), and the performance was said to be "disappointing" compared to that of the GT.

The two-litre GT was listed at £15,440.86, while the T-bar cost £16,650.50. The GT had the 158bhp 3S-GE engine, seven-way adjustment on the seats, and the rear spoiler. The T-bar model was basically a GT with black leather trim (extending to the steering wheel), and with the glass sunroof replaced by a targa roof.

With such a comprehensive specification, the car had dramatically gained in size and weight, now being a 1285kg (2827lb) vehicle in T-bar roof guise. Fortunately, power was increased substantially to compensate for this. With the GT, power went up from 123 to 158bhp (both at 6600rpm), while torque increased from 107lbft at 5000rpm to 140lbft at 4800. This meant that the two-litre engine was delivering an impressive 79.4bhp per litre, on leaded or unleaded fuel, as the three-way catalytic converter was not fitted to the 3S-GE engine. Using the same gearing and hydraulically-operated 224mm (8.8in) diameter clutch as the basic model, official figures quoted a 137mph (219kph) top speed, and a 0-60 time of just 7.6 seconds.

"The old MR2 was a gem in many ways," said *Autocar & Motor* in its report on the GT. "Nippy, almost incredibly wieldy and usually very forgiving, it acquired the sort of bullet-proof reputation and cult following that was always going to be hard to follow.

"It would be easy to assume that its bigger, faster successor had forsaken the original's intimacy and finesse for an altogether bolder assault on the senses. It's true, the new MR2 GT is a thrilling car, but don't get the impression that it's in any way its predecessor's inferior when it comes to dynamic deftness. This is still a friendly and entertaining car that offers a driving experience of the highest calibre. The difference is, it's also a pleasingly fast one."

Test results confirmed the GT's top speed, although the 0-60 time proved very conservative, with the magazine recording 6.7 seconds! Equally interesting, the standing-quarter was dismissed in 15.2 seconds, yet average fuel consumption was a remarkable 27.2mpg. The only real complaint concerned the "harsh low-speed ride."

A number of journalists in Japan, and also at *Car* magazine in the UK, had encountered sudden, breakaway oversteer. However, *MotorSport* dismissed the handling worries voiced elsewhere, deciding that most of the stories from Japan concerned the 225bhp turbo model, not available in Europe. It concluded: "I enjoyed

The American-specification MR2 Turbo, classed as a 1991 model, despite arriving in the States during the spring of 1990. This particular model is sporting the T-bar roof, an option on both the turbocharged and normally-aspirated cars.

Interior of the Turbo, complete with optional leather trim. All American cars came with a driver's-side airbag as standard.

Tail of the MR2 Turbo, with its standard rear spoiler and five-spoke alloys. Although the front side marker was the same as that used in Japan, the rear combination lamp design was different, the wraparound part being red to meet Federal regulations.

American advertising dating from spring 1990.

THE PASSION IS B

It's the all-new MR2 Turbo. And its soul is passion. The passion of a Toyota design team who view performance as the difference between cars that are made for transportation and cars that are made for driving.

If passion is the MR2 Turbo's soul, its heart is a two-liter, twin-cam, 16-valve turbocharged engine with air-to-air intercooler that pumps out 200 horse-

power. Zero to sixty is a 5.96-s

Controlling this power and gett an extremely rigid mid-engine to chassis rigidity, the mid-eng contributes to better overall ba center of gravity. This, combin independent MacPherson strut

*1991 MR2 Turbo United States Auto Club certified performance figures.
Call 1-800-GO-TOYOTA for more information and the location of your nearest dealer. Get More From Life...Buckle Up! © 1990

---

the blend between absorbent ride, outstanding traction and accurately 'weighted' brakes.

"The Targa Top MR2 shows that a mid-engine car can be practical fun, offering most of the thrills of the open [Lotus] Elan with a better finish and the easy to live with thoughtfulness of so many Japanese products."

Another Japanese vehicle making an impression at this time was the Mazda MX-5. In June 1990, the British magazine, *What Car?*, looked at the two newcomers (the MX-5 made its debut in the UK at the 1989 Motor Show). Although the Toyota was awarded higher points in three of the six categories (the others drew with the Mazda), the final verdict was to award both machines top marks! However, forced into a decision, the writers came down in favour of the Toyota as "it achieves what it sets out to do fractionally better than the MX-5."

Specifications across Europe were virtually the same as those found on UK-specification cars, but only the 3S-GE engine was listed. In France, for instance, power was listed at 118kw CEE, with torque at 19.1kgm. Converting these figures into more familiar British measurements gives a similar story on both sides of the Channel, while 0-100kph (62mph) was quoted as being 7.8 seconds. One of the few differences, apart from the obvious left- and right-hand steering, was that owners in the United Kingdom still had to endure a full-sized spare on a 6J steel rim, as opposed to a spacesaver.

Reaching American shores

In the March 1990 edition of *Toyota Today*, a magazine for the marque's dealerships, the new MR2 was

porating offset coil springs and gas shock absorbers, gives the MR2 high-performance handling. And a new anti-dive/anti-squat suspension geometry enhances acceleration and braking stability.

Ventilated disc brakes at all four wheels and optional Anti-lock Brake System (ABS) help put a stop to all of this performance.

Even the MR2's looks perform. With a .31 coefficient of drag, the MR2's styling is as slippery as it is beautiful.

On the inside, the feel of a true cockpit envelops the driver. A thickly padded, tilt-adjustable steering wheel (with standard air bag Supplemental Restraint System) and short-throw gearshift fall immediately to hand. A seven-way adjustable seat holds the driver firmly yet comfortably in place. An optional seven-speaker state-of-the-art compact disc stereo system is available for those occasions when the road isn't entertainment enough. And a full complement of instruments measures the MR2's pulse and completes a package that will quicken yours.

The Toyota MR2 Turbo. Put the passion back into your driving.

MR2

"I love what you do for me."

TOYOTA

The 2.2-litre coupé in virtually basic trim. A sunroof has been fitted, but the wheels remain standard, and the rear spoiler option rejected. Note the flat engine cover on the normally-aspirated cars.

Another view of the 2.2-litre machine. The lack of front foglights and black door mirrors (they were colour-keyed on the Turbo) serve as useful identifying features, as do the seven-spoke plastic wheel trims.

introduced as follows: "In the late-1980s, sports car enthusiasts were asking 'where's the beef?' So Toyota took its original, award-winning MR2 and put it on a body-building programme. The result is the 1991 model year MR2 – a high-performance sports car with the muscle and grace of a lean, mean professional athlete.

"This spring, Toyota's mid-engined sports car for the driving enthusiast debuts with a fresh design and benchmark performance."

The new MR2, offered with both coupé and T-bar bodies, was announced in America as a 1991 model year car, although 1990.5 would have been more accurate, as vehicles started to appear in dealerships in the spring. As such, there were no 1990 MR2s in the States.

Two twin-cam engines were offered – a 130bhp 2164cc four-cylinder unit (the 5S-FE), and the 3S-GTE turbocharged two-litre powerplant. Rated at a healthy 200bhp, the latter replaced the supercharged engine in the line-up, while the 2.2-litre four provided a 40% improvement in torque over the previous normally-aspirated unit, thus giving better low- to mid-range response, and more relaxed driving around town.

While the 3S-GTE came with a five-speed manual gearbox only, it was possible to buy the 2.2-litre car with a manual or four-speed automatic transmission. In all cases, gearing was exactly the same as that used on Japan's two-litre models, except for a 3.034:1 final-drive ratio on the automatic model.

Manual steering racks (3.7 turns lock-to-lock), and front and rear anti-roll bars were standard on both turbocharged and normally-aspirated versions, but there were differences in the braking, and in the wheel and tyre specifications. As in Japan, the Turbo came with larger twin-pot calipers up front, but the ABS system was optional instead of standard. Although of the same sizes (6J x 14 and 7J x 14 wheels shod with 195/60 and 205/60 tyres respectively), the turbocharged car had aluminium alloys and VR-rated rubber, while the 2.2-litre model came with steel rims (finished with seven-spoke plastic trims) and HR tyres.

In America a number of articles noted tricky handling close to the limit. As *Motor Trend* put it in the June 1990 issue: "The transition from neutrality to slight push to definite oversteer happens at a far quicker pace than in the Miata [the American name for the MX-5], and recovery demands considerably more skill than it does in the extremely forgiving Mazda." Unfortunately, many people took this, and similar statements, the wrong way. The very high cornering speeds attainable under most circumstances were far greater than the majority of sane people would encounter on public roads anyway – it should, perhaps, be remembered that ex-Formula One driver, Dan Gurney, was involved with the fine tuning of the chassis.

Despite double-page adverts for the new car in leading American journals, buyers stayed away, reading the headlines only and not bothering to compare the handling characteristics of other mid- or rear-engined machines. However, it wasn't all doom and gloom. *Road & Track* carried out a test on the MR2 Turbo in April 1990 and observed: "With its own front airdam with integrated foglights, aerodynamic rear spoiler, louvred engine cover and distinctive alloy wheels, the Turbo resembles a scaled-down Ferrari or Nissan 300ZX. And performs like one too, thanks to a free-revving 200bhp powerplant that is the only major component the MR2 shares with other Toyota models.

"What the Turbo loses in throttle response to its supercharged predecessor, its 55 additional bhp more than compensates for. Only near red-line is the turbo engine's whistle louder than the smaller supercharged engine's whine."

As well as gaining a foothold in the US luxury car market through the Lexus brand, Toyota was extremely active, and successful, in the field of motorsport. Thanks to Dan Gurney, the marque was a force to be reckoned with on America's race tracks, while TTE would deliver the WRC crown to its Japanese masters. The Celica shown is one of the new Fifth Generation models, incidentally.

TOYOTA *Technology On A Fast Track*

While most people design cars on computers, we prefer to do it somewhere more exciting.

There is still one thing a computer can't be programmed to comprehend:
 The basic human thrill of driving.
 So we take the bugs out of our ideas by taking our ideas out to the racetrack. Where there's no other way to learn but to learn fast.
 Racing is our acid test. A technological graduation day at a blurred speed. An anxiety-ridden moment of truth.
 And a rush like you wouldn't believe.
 So we race. And we learn. Recognizing that there's no substitute for designing Toyotas in the real world.
 Because that's where people drive them.

© 1989 Toyota Motor Sales, U.S.A., Inc.

The 1990 Celica All-Trac Turbo.

TOYOTA
"I love what you do for me."

Get More From Life... Buckle Up!

 Perhaps ironically, the magazine continued: "The MR2's rear weight bias needs to be respected only in the most severe cornering situations. At a lesser pace, it's a useful asset in adjusting the Toyota's course, while supplying extra grip exiting corners.
 "To reap the fruits of Toyota's (and Gurney's) labours, one need only tackle the ubiquitous twisty two-lane where the well-behaved MR2 Turbo – it pulls 0.86g on the skidpad and averages 64.5mph in the slalom – is a touch more tenacious and a lot more mannerly than the First Generation car."
 Car & Driver described the MR2 Turbo as "an exotic for the rest of us." But it was also quick to point out that a certain amount of care was necessary with the 200bhp machine for those less experienced behind the wheel: "The new MR2 is always ready to remind you of its mid-engine design. Push it hard and the front end slides first, but in a brisk corner a hasty move off the power or onto the brakes will set the mass-filled rear end swinging wide. The oversteer is undramatic and easy to control with opposite lock or a move back on the power – which makes it useful for holding a neutral cornering attitude. But inattentive drivers could get themselves into trouble. (Few inattentive drivers will ever push the MR2 hard enough to set the rear end loose, of course.) Like an exotic, the MR2 Turbo rewards skilled moves but can become a handful if driven mindlessly.
 "Directing the MR2 Turbo is a joy, because the cockpit is a splendid place in which to work. The driving position is nearly perfect: the seat is form-fitting and feels good to your backside, and the fine four-spoke steering wheel lies in easy reach of your palms. The wheel feels good to the touch. The stubby shifter rests nearby, atop a smooth console; the lever is nicely shaped but is notchy through its pattern (a sad regression, for the old MR2's five-speed was one of the world's best). Ahead of the instrument panel, the nose drops away dramatically – providing an incomparable view for the pilot and giving the car an exciting feel of a glass-enclosed single-seater.
 "Simple gauges and handsome materials adorn the agreeably uncluttered cabin. The switches and buttons respond with a velvety, expensive feel – one of the intangibles so important in making a first-class automobile. Toyota is one of a handful of automakers capable of producing a cockpit as good as this one."
 Regarding the instruments, the Turbo came with a 160mph speedometer and 9000rpm tachometer, whilst the normally-aspirated car

103

was equipped with 140mph and 8000rpm items. Another difference was the voltmeter, replaced by a boost gauge on the turbocharged model, although both featured the usual coolant temperature and fuel level monitors. All US-specification cars were fitted with a four-spoke steering wheel incorporating an SRS airbag as standard, wrapped in leather, incidentally, on the Turbo.

At the time of the car's introduction, Bob McCurry, Toyota's Executive Vice-President in the States, went on record saying: "While the prices for exotic sports cars escalate to unreachable heights, Toyota's 1991 MR2 brings world-class performance, mid-engined handling, and exotic car styling within the reach of car buyers with more enthusiasm than money." Prices in America started at $14,898 for the basic 2.2-litre car. Options included a Leather Trim Package, a Power Package, automatic transmission, cruise control, air conditioning, alloy wheels, a rear spoiler, sunroof, the Turbo's seven-way sports seats (as part of the Leather Trim Package), floor mats, an alarm and better stereos (a four-speaker AM/FM radio with ETR came as standard, although it was possible to upgrade to the Turbo's six-speaker system with a radio/cassette, or go crazy with the seven-speaker set-up with a radio/cassette and CD player). The T-bar roof boosted the cost by roughly $1000, but, strangely, was not available with an automatic gearbox.

In a group test bringing together some of the finest sports cars on the market at that time, *Road & Track* noted that the "ride is the most supple and bump-absorbing of any car in the group, but the MR2 corners with no untoward body sway, quick and flat as a road-going manta ray." Performance-wise, 0-60mph was covered in around 8.5 seconds in the 2.2-litre machine.

The exchange rate (actually, from an export point of view, better than it had been in the late-1980s, at approximately 160 yen to the dollar) dictated that the Turbo was priced at $18,628 in basic trim. Options included the T-bar roof, a traditional glass sunroof, power-assisted steering (EHPS), ABS braking, cruise control, the uprated stereo with or without a CD player, suitably modified versions of the Leather Trim and Power Packages, an alarm and air conditioning.

On a par with the Porsche 944 S2 and Ferrari 328GTS through the standing-quarter; 0-60mph was covered in just 6.2 seconds, and one magazine later clocked it at 144mph (230kph).

Motor Trend voted the turbocharged MR2 as the car with the best 'Bang for the Buck' for 1991, which, in reality, only confirmed what a lot of enthusiasts already knew. The Penske MR2 Performance Club had been formed to bring together fans of the mid-engined model (as well as a successful racing team, Penske owned a Toyota dealership, and was one of the first to sign up for Lexus), which came second in the *Motor Trend* survey of the following year, just pipped by the Plymouth Laser RS Turbo.

For the 1991 model year, seven colours were available in the States: Super White, Signal Yellow, Aquamarine Pearl, Nautical Blue Metallic, Crimson Red, Black and, for the MR2 Turbo only, Steel Grey Mist. Black fabric trim was the norm, although the white and blue shades could be specified with a blue interior; black leather was an option.

News from Australia
In the first month of 1990, *Wheels* covered the new MR2 and was impressed: "Quieter, better finished and more practical, too. At a stroke the new MR2 answers many of the niggling drawbacks of its acclaimed predecessor.

"We're talking here of details; of the tiny [fuel] tank and boot, of high noise levels, ultimately tricky handling, lack of torque and overtaxed front brakes. Granted, none of these ever seriously dampened the rampant enthusiasm for Toyota's inspiring little car, but you always hoped they would be put to rights. And they have."

The same magazine confirmed the excellent chassis set-up of the MR2, stating that it "made our trackwork look easy and impressed the silicon chips out of our test equipment." At the end of the day, though, despite their admiration for the car, like the Americans they were concerned with the oversteer at the limit: "Once it breaks, the average enthusiast is not going to be quick enough or measured enough in his inputs to bring it back." Australia, incidentally, only ever received the normally-aspirated model.

The 1991 model year proper
In the States, the normally-aspirated MR2 entered the 1991 model year priced at $15,448; the T-bar roof added $950 and the automatic gearbox $750; oddly, a combination of these options was still not possible. As for the Turbo, prices started at $18,778, rising to $19,678 for the T-bar roof version.

The Leather Trim Package was $1710 on the base model, consisting of seven-way sports seats with leather trim and map pockets, leather-trimmed door panels, leather on the steering wheel, gearknob and

The entry-level 3S-FE powered MR2 continued in the UK for 1991. Although at £14,505 it offered good value, it was far from cheap. The BMW 3-series started at £11,839, for instance, or, for those looking for something more sporting, £14,899 would have secured a Mazda MX-5.

handbrake, an additional centre console, electric windows, central locking, the Turbo's colour-keyed power mirrors (manually-adjusted mirrors in black were standard on the normally-aspirated car), and door courtesy lights. The same set was $1235 on the Turbo, as the leather-wrapped steering wheel, gearshift and handbrake were already original equipment, as were the sports seats (albeit trimmed in fabric), courtesy lighting, centre console and the electrically-adjustable door mirrors finished in body colour. Likewise, the Power Package was also cheaper on the turbocharged car ($425 against $535), as power mirrors and courtesy door lighting were already standard features, but both cars received electric windows and central locking.

Other options included air conditioning ($825), ABS brakes ($1130), cruise control ($245), a sunroof ($380), rear spoiler ($225), power steering ($600), an alarm ($165), and alloy wheels (standard on the Turbo) priced at $360.

As for stereo equipment, to upgrade the basic model's radio to Turbo standards cost $250, while the Premium System, with seven speakers, a radio/cassette deck and an electric aerial (the latter was standard on the T-bar and Turbo) was $340 on the turbocharged car, and $655 on the normally-aspirated model; a CD player added a further $700. Alternatively, a separate radio/cassette or CD player could be purchased as a dealer option.

The MR2 Turbo came a gallant fourth place in *Motor Trend*'s 'Import Car of the Year' awards, one writer noting: "This is the quintessential driver's car. It has all the power and presence you'd expect from a sports car, with an attendant need to pay attention in order to make the car work. On the street, it's as docile as a lamb, and the seats are so form-fitting, they might have been tailor-made." The winner of the title, incidentally, was the Mitsubishi 3000GT VR-4.

Prices in the UK during September 1990 ranged from £14,505.24 for the basic MR2 to £17,251.04 for the T-bar; between them, the MR2 GT was listed at £15,995.25. Automatic transmission (available only on the basic MR2) was extra at £760, whilst metallic paint could be specified for £199. Colours included Super White III, Super Red III, Blue Metallic and Black.

In February 1991, a press release from Toyota GB noted that Bridgestone tyres were now supplied as standard equipment on all MR2 models. Although still 195/60 VR14 at the front and 205/60 VR14 at the rear, they had previously used Continental rubber. In addition, the original 185/60 spare tyre was replaced by a narrower T135/70 spacesaver to increase luggage capacity under the front bonnet.

MotorSport tested the T-bar model in its August 1991 issue, noting:

"Despite criticism from some quarters of inherent handling flaws ... we found no such defect in the Toyota during road, track or grass track use, the latter allowing us to balance the car in long power slides with one hand.

"There is a massive compensation from the coil spring rates; the rears are over 65% harder than the fronts, but neither are guilty of allowing an unduly harsh ride ...

"Despite sombre shades in heavy plastics, the MR2 cabin always feels a light and airy place, courtesy of the standard sunroof or the twin T-bar panels. Instrumentation is fairly simple, stretching to three supplementary dials, a 160mph speedometer and a 9000rpm tachometer that is red-lined at 7200rpm. Convenient interior releases are provided for the lid over a slim, but properly arranged and trimmed, rear boot, the fuel filler flap, engine cover and a bonnet that hides the spacesaver spare.

"The only major surprise was that Toyota have been trapped by that old TVR foible of having the handbrake and gearlever virtually interlock at certain points in their arcs. The gearchange itself veers toward clonky with its partial cable activation, but unlike a VW Passat/Corrado, it would be unfair to level any real criticisms at the change quality, for that seems fast and fluid in all circumstances, road or track.

"The view over the front bonnet is typical mid-engined 'front row of the stalls' in character, but is marred by some scattered reflections, worst in the mirror when gazing at the Porsche 959-style hoop rear spoiler. Three-quarter vision is certainly adequate to join motorways and the overall feeling is of the most practical mid-engine motor

The US-specification MR2 Turbo for 1992, complete with optional T-bar roof.

car we have driven since the £50,000 plus Honda NSX.

"We enjoyed the MR2 for its calculated combination of speed, reasonable 26.6mpg economy on cheaper unleaded fuels, and an assembly quality that was emphasised by the leather seating in the test example."

It was thought that the car, now priced at a hefty £18,413, needed ABS in wet weather conditions due to the light front end, and the T-bar arrangement was a bit fiddly compared with modern convertible tops.

However, 0-60 was covered in 7.2 seconds, with the 50-70mph increment being dismissed in 4.8; the standing quarter-mile came up in 15.5 seconds (at 90.8mph, or 145.3kph), and maximum speeds through the gears were 38, 69, 95, 123 and 137mph respectively, which equates to 61, 110, 152, 197 and 219kph.

As a matter of interest, at *Classic Cars*, Mark Dixon thought that noise suppression was very good, but he wasn't as happy with the sound of the GT, a view which echoed that expressed in an earlier *MotorSport* article.

Limited editions

While Toyota announced that cumulative car production had just reached the 70,000,000 mark, the Japanese economy, which had been riding on an amazing high since 1987, took a definite downturn in the early part of 1991.

Nonetheless, in April that year, Toyota announced a limited edition model known as the G-Limited Super Edition. Based on the G-Limited with T-bar roof, only 850 were produced for the Japanese market, with special features including Blueish-Grey Mica coachwork, a CD player, unique badging and GT-style seats. It was priced at 2,444,000 yen with the manual gearbox, an automatic transmission adding 93,000 yen.

By this time, Crystal Pearl Mica had been dropped from the home market's paint charts, but this was of little consequence to the tuning business. While the Japanese aftermarket industry was quick to react to the launch of the SW20, it took European concerns a little longer. Notwithstanding, a German company called HKS Fritzinger Motorsport GmbH offered the new MR2 with 240 and 280bhp engine conversions! Complete cars with body modifications and wider alloy wheels cost from DM 108,000 – not surprisingly, performance was said to be stunning.

1992 Stateside

In America, the MR2 was put through its paces with nine other of the best-handling cars on sale in the States at that time. *Road & Track* carried out the test in the early part of 1992, declaring that the "MR2 surprises us with its balance. The tail can, and will, come out, but just as with the Miata [Mazda MX-5] – which feels similarly under-tyred – it is predictable and easy to catch."

The normally-aspirated car started at $16,048 for 1992, with the Turbo coming in at $20,278. Options were the same as they had been in the previous year, with prices not all that different, despite the fact that substantial price increases had been applied to the basic cars. Colour schemes continued unchanged from the time of the SW20's introduction.

Minor changes

A Japanese press release dating from December 1991 noted that a limited-slip differential and Bilstein shock absorbers had become standard equipment on the GT grade, with a traction control system listed as an option on the same model. At the same time, the transmission was improved via multi-cone synchros.

The suspension, steering and clutch were improved across the range, and new 15-inch five-spoke alloy wheels replaced the old 14-inch type, fitted with larger, lower profile tyres specially developed for the MR2 by Yokohama. At the front, 195/55 VR15s were employed, while 225/50 VR15s were used at the rear; naturally, the spacesaver spare was changed to suit. Regarding the new tyres, it was stated: "By achieving a well-balanced contact area through the adoption of a multi-tread radius at the rear, the latest MR2 achieves even higher cornering forces along with better wet road performance, improved grip and control at all speeds, better steering feel and greater wear resistance. All this has been achieved with negligible effect on ride comfort, rolling resistance, and noise."

Able to take advantage of the bigger wheels, and therefore the greater

A picture taken from the American 1992 model year catalogue depicting a Turbo at speed. This dramatic photograph clearly illustrates the superb line of vision afforded by the large front screen.

clearance around the brake calipers, the engineers uprated the braking system at the same time. For the quicker models, the front discs increased in size from 258mm (10.1in) to 275mm (10.8in), while the rears went up from 263mm (10.3in) to 281mm (11.1in); both sets were also correspondingly thicker.

The Japanese market's GT model from December 1991. Apart from various improvements under the skin, there were new wheels, and a different front mask with a larger spoiler.

107

Interior of the latest GT model. Note the new gearknob.

Left: The GT T-bar roof at speed. The mechanical changes brought about at the end of 1991 certainly made a big difference to the car's handling and stopping power.

The Japanese seem fascinated by aftermarket tuning and custom parts – a fact not lost on the manufacturers. This is the optional MOMO steering wheel from the time.

A fantastic shot of the G-Limited with a T-bar roof. The elegant lines of the MR2 looked even better with the new 15-inch alloy wheels.

The turbocharged GT-S was a new grade that joined the home market line-up at the end of 1991. It was basically a cheaper version of the GT for those who wanted the performance but not the luxury.

The Japanese range:				
GT	Coupé	3S-GTE	5-sp Manual	2,842,000 yen
	T-bar		5-sp Manual	2,982,000 yen
GT-S	Coupé	3S-GTE	5-sp Manual	2,505,000 yen
	T-bar		5-sp Manual	2,645,000 yen
G-Limited	Coupé	3S-GE	5-sp Manual	2,279,000 yen
	T-bar		5-sp Manual	2,419,000 yen
G-Limited	Coupé	3S-GE	4-sp Automatic	2,372,000 yen
	T-bar		4-sp Automatic	2,512,000 yen
G	Coupé	3S-GE	5-sp Manual	1,964,000 yen
	T-bar		5-sp Manual	2,104,000 yen
G	Coupé	3S-GE	4-sp Automatic	2,057,000 yen
	T-bar		4-sp Automatic	2,197,000 yen

The car's appearance was improved by a larger, integrated bumper/front spoiler, the bigger wheels also helping to enhance the sporty image of the vehicle. Inside, the steering wheel rim and spoke positions were changed across the board to make room for the optional driver's airbag. On the G-Limited grade and above, a package – consisting of Recaro seats and a MOMO steering wheel and gearknob – was listed as an option.

Finally, the GT-S model was introduced, a slightly cheaper version of the GT, and given the option of traction control and four-wheel ABS braking as part of a package. Perhaps the sub-heading should have been 'Major Changes'!

Changes for the UK

In March 1992, the automatic option was deleted from the basic MR2 specification and, according to the Toyota GB press release, a number of changes were made to "enhance the areas of performance, safety, comfort and cleaner exhaust emissions."

Although the 3S-FE's power was unchanged at 119bhp at 5600rpm, the 3S-GE engine now delivered 154bhp at 6600rpm due to the addition of a three-way catalytic converter (the 3S-FE had always been fitted with one). Maximum torque output was also down a fraction, now listed at 137lbft at 4800rpm, while the FE unit remained at 130lbft.

As in Japan, the new front bumper and its integrated airdam was adopted, giving the car a smoother and cleaner look, while the front fog lamps (GT and T-bar models only) had

This Toyota GB picture of the GT from the start of the 1992 model year provides a useful comparison for the later cars, introduced to the UK market in spring.

A press shot of the latest basic MR2 for Britain, soon to become an endangered species. Note the new wheels and the changes at the front end.

A rear view of the UK-specification MR2 GT. The J prefix on the number plate indicates that this car dates from between August 1991 and July 1992. The bigger, 15-inch wheels narrow it down to being registered after March 1992.

The GT T-bar continued as top of the line in the British Isles, although the basic MR2 was dropped from the range by the time the autumn 1992 catalogue was released. The open roof shows off the standard leather interior nicely.

Another view of the UK-specification GT T-bar from March 1992.

clear lenses rather than the previous yellow tint.

Naturally, the latest five-spoke alloy wheels and Yokohama tyres were also a feature. Like the home market, 195/55 VR15s were employed upfront, mounted on 6J rims, while 225/50 VR15s on 7J alloys were used at the back.

In addition, the GT and T-bar models gained the electro-hydraulic power-assisted steering (EHPS) as standard. With a quicker 17.6:1 ratio, it reduced the number of turns necessary from lock-to-lock from 3.7 to 3.1. A slightly smaller diameter three-spoke steering wheel was adopted across the range.

The steering geometry was also modified, and there were stiffer anti-roll bars for both front and rear (up to 18mm and 19mm, or 0.71in and 0.75in respectively). Spring rates remained the same but the double-acting, gas-filled front shock absorbers were retuned to make them harder. At the same time, ride height was reduced by 10mm (0.39in), and the rearmost lower suspension arm was lengthened by 98mm (3.9in) to improve control at very high cornering speeds.

The larger brakes were also carried over from Japan, and quicker gear changes were aided by a shorter clutch movement. Strangely, however, ABS was still not an option for British buyers. However, most contemporary reports had few complaints about the more traditional set-up.

Meanwhile, passenger safety was enhanced by the inclusion of side-impact beams in the door assemblies. Inside, the handbrake lever was now leather-trimmed on all models, and the seven original speakers for the audio system were augmented by

111

American advertising for the 'new' 1993 MR2, dated May 1992.

Prices now ranged from £15,125.68 for the 3S-FE powered machine, with the GT commanding £17,058.31 and the MR2 GT T-bar £18,394.87. As noted earlier, an automatic transmission was no longer available, and metallic paint was £196 extra. Thankfully, a change in Special Car Tax (SCT) in the April budget actually saw sticker prices drop even further following a relentless series of increases.

America's 'New Car'

Although many of the modifications for the latest version of the US-specification MR2 simply mirrored those of Japan and Europe, Toyota Motor Sales so wanted to emphasise the major improvements that it called the vehicle a "new car" in its advertising.

An American press photograph announcing the 1993 model year MR2. This is the Turbo model with optional T-bar roof, although for the 1993 MY proper (ie from October 1992), it became a standard feature on the turbocharged car.

an additional bass speaker mounted behind the driver's seat. Noise insulation was also improved.

Autocar & Motor tried one of the latest T-bar models, and declared: "The MR2 has had the finer points of its dynamic cutting edge sharpened to a level that anyone with an ounce of enthusiasm for cars would have to stand up and applaud. Not only does it perform as a proper sports car should (this much was never in any doubt), but it also handles and steers like one, too. What's more, Toyota hasn't made these benefits even remotely hard on the pocket, the new car costing £18 less than the old."

A stunning picture of the Turbo (again with T-bar roof) from the US catalogue dated January 1992. Yes, that's how early the 1993 model year car was announced!

For 1993, it was possible to buy either full black or black/ivory leather trim (as shown here) in the States.

A US-specification MR2 Turbo shown in Steel Grey Mist. Colour schemes were revised for the 1993 model year line-up.

The appearance of the 2.2-litre car, now with an extra 5bhp outside California, was improved no end by the adoption of colour-keyed door mirrors and the new 15-inch alloy wheels.

For this reason, it was released as a 1993 model, even though 1992.5 would have been more accurate, as the American 1993 model year MR2 was actually launched in spring 1992.

The press release read as follows: "The superb all-round handling of the Toyota MR2 is raised to a new level of sophistication with the introduction of extensive suspension refinements on all 1993 models.

"Prioritizing improved road feel, high-speed control and cornering capability, chassis engineers began by stiffening suspension bushings and increasing spring and shock rates at all four wheels. The front suspension's caster trail was increased for improved tracking and on-centre feel. Key front strut mounting points were changed to reduce dive and lower ride height.

"In the rear, the lower control arm was lengthened nearly four inches to prevent toe-out when the suspension is compressed under hard braking and cornering, thus minimizing oversteer at the cornering limit. Additionally, the attachment height of the strut rods at the body were raised to decrease lift during braking and squat during acceleration.

"Improved cornering, road grip and tyre life – as well as enhanced appearance – are provided by larger 15-inch VR-rated tyres mounted to a new-design alloy wheel [for all cars]. Front tyres increased to 195/55-15 from 195/60-14, while rear tyres increased to 225/50-15 from 205/60-14.

"The MR2 has always been one of the best-braking vehicles in its category. For 1993, Turbo models feature improved braking thermal capacity with larger (in diameter and thickness) front and rear brake discs.

"Turbo models also offer an optional viscous-coupling limited-slip rear differential for enhanced traction.

"Improved shifting effort, and feel, on manual transmission Turbo models is realised with the use of multi-cone synchros for second and third gears, a synchro mechanism for reverse, a shortened and redesigned shift lever, and a reduction in clutch pedal travel of approximately one inch in Turbo models, and a half inch in normally-aspirated models. (Multi-cone synchros on non-turbocharged models will be available this Fall.)

"Exterior improvements to the 1993 MR2 include a redesigned front valance/spoiler, larger front air opening, dual colour-keyed power sideview mirrors, and four new exterior colours. Interior changes include a new Black and Ivory Leather Trim Package, and an additional rear sub-woofer for the Premium cassette and CD sound systems.

"The new 1993 MR2 offers the 80W maximum power, Deluxe ETR stereo radio/cassette, with six-speakers and manual antenna as standard equipment, with power antenna standard on Turbo models. The Deluxe unit offers Dolby B noise reduction, auto-reverse function, and the ability to expand the sound system by adding a dealer-installed CD player.

"For ultimate listening pleasure, the Premium ETR stereo radio/cassette and Premium three-in-one ETR stereo radio/cassette with CD are available. Both Premium systems feature: 200W maximum power output through eight speakers; a radio monitor function during rewind and fast forward of cassette tape, and Dolby C noise reduction for increased compatibility with home cassette systems.

"New this year is the addition of a second woofer located behind the passenger seat. The system features four 30W amplifiers for tweeters, and full-range speakers and separate 40W amplifiers for each woofer.

"Both the dealer-installed and factory CD units provide one-touch loading and ejection of CDs, fast forward and reverse at the touch of a button, endless play and repeat functions, as well as the ability to play three-inch CD singles without any adaptors."

A good ICE system is all very nice, of course, but, at the end of the day, the purpose of a sports car is to provide driving pleasure. Following the press launch in Arizona, testers from virtually every magazine noted a vast difference, especially when the 1993 model year car was driven back-to-back with an earlier example. Most felt that there was more understeer, but the handling was now "confidence-inspiring" and infinitely less tricky on the limit. The larger brakes – strong and virtually fade-free – were also appreciated.

Incidentally, most normally-aspirated cars gained an additional 5bhp at this time (California-spec models were unchanged at 130bhp), but all saw an increase in torque output, up 5lbft to 145 at 4400rpm; the turbocharged engine remained the same.

Only Brock Yates at *Car & Driver* seemed less than enthusiastic. Whilst acknowledging the improvements, he said: "On paper, the MR2 Turbo appears to be a fast driver's dream:

With the optional rear spoiler fitted, it was hard to tell whether or not the car was turbocharged or normally-aspirated. From this angle, though, the flat engine cover gives the game away – it's a 2.2-litre machine.

a close-coupled two-seater with a high-revving, mid-mounted twin-cam, turbocharged and intercooled four-banger linked to a five-speed transaxle, four-wheel independent suspension, disc brakes all-round, and a host of subtle mechanical nuances that would send the average Porschephile into paroxysms of joy if this little beauty had been created in Zuffenhausen. At about 25 grand, the MR2 Turbo would seem to be a miracle of bargain-basement exotica.

"Even so, the MR2 Turbo somehow seems more a pint-sized GT machine than an outright sports car. It will transport two passengers over long distances in relative silence and comfort. It can be zapped through all manner of switchbacks and jagged mountain corners with impunity, while displaying near-perfect manners. It will knock on 140mph without apparent effort and leap to 60 in under seven seconds. And like all Toyotas, it seems to have been carved out of a solid ingot of metal, implying that it will run forever without the faintest suggestion of flimsiness.

Another attractive shot from the first American 1993 model year catalogue.

"But somehow a critical ingredient has been lost in the recipe. Call it brio, call it zaniness, call it *cojones*. Call it soul. For all its mechanical sophistication, the MR2 remains mysteriously tepid. It reminds one of a straight-A student who never cracks a smile.

"Try as we might, our enthusiasm lags. Is it the rather bland, derivative styling? Is it the honour-student primness? Is it the strange, almost subliminal impression that the MR2 Turbo, for all its technical excellence, is less than the sum of its parts? This car demands to be liked. We want to love it, but outright lust escapes us."

As noted earlier, colour schemes were also revised for 1993. Exterior choices included Steel Mist Grey, Super White, Signal Yellow, Turquoise Pearl, Blue Metallic, Super Red and Black. Fabric interior trim again included shades of blue or black, but the optional leather was now available in all-black, or a combination of black and ivory.

For the 1993 model year proper, although the specifications for the

115

The British market's GT grade for the 1993 model year – now the entry level MR2 following the departure of the basic car in the autumn of 1992.

normally-aspirated car remained unchanged, the Turbo acquired a number of convenience items that were previously options as part of the standard package. Air conditioning, cruise control, the Power Package and Premium eight-speaker sound system were all included in the price, but the glass sunroof was no longer available on the turbocharged model after the T-bar roof was made mandatory.

Sadly, unstable exchange rates continued to push prices up. In 1993, the rate was roughly 100 yen to the dollar (it actually fell even more before settling back to this level), giving the basic 2.2-litre machine a sticker price of $18,948, with automatic transmission adding $800, or the T-bar roof a hefty $1890; as before, the two could not be bought together. The solitary turbocharged model came in at $24,728, which was very reasonable considering its extra performance and far higher level of equipment.

Options included the Leather Trim Package ($1705 on the 2.2-litre car, $810 on the Turbo), the Power Package ($530), an lsd for the Turbo at $400, ABS brakes ($1030), power-assisted steering ($600), air conditioning ($915), cruise control ($265), a sunroof ($380), rear spoiler ($300), various stereo upgrades and an alarm ($165). Of course, a lot of this equipment now came as standard on the turbocharged model.

Barry Winfield penned an article for *Car & Driver* in May 1993, and wrote: "Spending time behind the wheel and its integral airbag is no chore. Even with an engine mounted where other cars have rear seats, the MR2's cabin is surprisingly roomy, with comfortable and supportive seating and a tidy dashboard. Despite the short wheelbase and generous track, the ride is not the choppy affair you might have expected. The MR2 is clearly more user-friendly than it is knife-edged.

"Some people, seeing the mid-engined good looks, may find this easy-going personality something of a contradiction. In fact, the MR2 is one of the most delicately poised compromises, offering distinctive looks and accommodations in a durable package at a fairly reasonable price."

The magazine duly named the MR2 one of the '10 Best Performers' available in the States for the 1993 season.

UK update
The British catalogue from autumn 1992 noted that only two models were now available – the £16,375 MR2 GT and the £17,659 MR2 GT T-bar. Fitted with a catalytic converter and five-speed manual gearbox as standard, both cars could cover 0-60 in 7.7 seconds, and had a 137mph (219kph) top speed. However, they were still capable of returning up to 47.1mpg at a constant 56mph (90kph).

An advertising line stated: "The mid-engined magic of the MR2 prompted the *Financial Times* into quoting 'it looks and goes like a baby Ferrari.' Never was real muscle more exquisitely packaged."

The standard specification was as high as ever, but the inevitable price increases at the start of 1993 put the GT at £16,998 and the T-bar at £18,399. Metallic paint was the only extra, however, listed at just under £200.

The MR2 In competition
The Swiss Touring Car Championship again provided Toyota with an excellent string of results. The MR2 won its Class at Hockenheim (with J Strasser at the wheel), Dijon (J Durig), and the Osterreichring (Strasser again) in 1990.

L Calamia won the 1991 Swiss TCC Group N two-litre Class with the new MR2, and a number of worthy results were recorded around the world, notably in Thailand. In fact, Kasikam Suphot won the 1992 South-East Asian Supercars Championship in Thailand after winning four rounds outright. Suphot also gained overall victory in a round of the Thailand GP Championship with the SW20 MR2, and the Shah Alam round of the Malaysian series.

1993 and 1994 had further runs of Class wins in the Swiss Touring Car Championship, K Philipp and A Luthi being regular visitors to the winner's podium. The Swiss Mountain Races also provided Luthi with an arena in which to display his driving skills, this leading Toyota exponent taking no less than four Class wins in 1994.

Other Toyota sports cars
The latest Supra (the Fourth Generation of the breed) was, in the words of *MotorSport*, "Wild and alternative. This is the brashest Supra yet ..." Launched in the UK in August 1993 with a £37,500 list price, production had started midway through the year. Performance from this three-litre turbocharged machine was truly stunning, even marginally better than that of the Celica GT-Four.

YOU & US

When choosing a new car what exactly do different people look for? Some want reliability. Some economy. Others are attracted by comfort or individual flair.

There's one thing, however, that we all insist upon. The highest possible standards. Our reputation for building cars that combine practical economy and superior quality is one that we are justifiably proud of. But there's more to Toyota, far more. We don't just make cars to satisfy the many, we design cars that excite the few.

There's the exclusive mid-engine MR2 sports car with its agile, responsive handling. The innovative, aero-style Previa, a family car that adapts to your needs. And the rugged LandCruiser off-roader, which lets individualists get wherever they want to go.

We make a wide range of cars like these because we want everyone to be satisfied with Toyota: You and Us.

Specifications may vary from those illustrated.

TOYOTA

Advertising from the June 1993 issue of National Geographic.

The other model in the 1993 UK line-up was the GT T-bar. Many magazines likened its purposeful styling to that of a Ferrari. The rear spoiler was not just a gimmick, however, as it reduced drag, lift and a tendency for the car to react badly to sidewinds. The underbody tray was also developed in the wind tunnel.

117

An MR2 competing in the SCCA's Showroom Stock category. In America, SCCA racing has been well-liked for many years, and shows little sign of losing its appeal.

In Japan and America, the three-litre turbocharged version was available, along with a normally-aspirated three-litre. Wide Body and Sport Roof models were also listed on the home market, but Europe had to be content with the 326bhp straight-six coupé.

In October 1993, Toyota introduced the Sixth Generation Celica alongside the Carina ED and Corona EXiV four-door hardtops. The GT-Four followed at the beginning of February 1994, the year in which Toyota won the World Rally Championship for the second time, and Didier Auriol secured

The stunning Fourth Generation Supra made its UK debut in August 1993, and graced the cover of the Earls Court Show catalogue. Seven months later, the new Celica put in an appearance. Chief Engineer was Tadashi Nakagawa, who became involved with the MR2 shortly after it was launched. His name will crop up again in the next chapter as we profile the MR2's replacement.

The modified 3S-GTE engine, which developed another 20bhp. Sadly, only Japan would receive it, as the American market continued with the original turbocharged unit.

the Driver's Championship for his Japanese masters.

The 1994 model year

The 3S-GTE engine received a modified turbocharger, new valves and manifolds for better breathing, and an improved exhaust system. As a result, power was increased by 20bhp and there was also a far wider spread of torque. The 3S-GE also received a hike in power – 15bhp on cars with the manual gearbox, but just 5bhp on automatic versions due to a different camshaft profile.

In both cases, the majority of this extra horsepower came courtesy of ACIS (Acoustic Control Induction System), which varied the flow of air into the engine, helping to boost low-end torque and provide more vivid acceleration. With all the additional minor changes, effectively, this was a completely new generation of 3S powerplants.

At the same time, the suspension mountings were made stronger, new shock absorbers were adopted, and the geometry was changed slightly. Toyota's so-called 'Sports ABS' was listed as an option on the turbocharged cars, while the standard braking system was enhanced via the adoption of the GT and GT-S's larger discs and uprated servos.

Sills and side protection mouldings became body colour across the range, and the rear combination lamps were restyled to include rounded lights and a new garnishing piece; the rear spoiler was also of a new design. The seats were made more comfortable and given better trim, and on cars with a driver's airbag, a different 365mm (14.4in) diameter steering wheel was employed.

Japan had no less than 12 models listed for 1994. Prices ranged from 2,029,000 yen for the basic manual G grade coupé up to 2,969,000 yen for the GT with a T-bar roof.

After trying the latest model, the Australian *Wheels* magazine stated: "Out on the open road, pushing hard, the MR2 at last comes into its own. Now with unprecedented grunt and reformed suspension, the MR2 is pure unbridled joy, a car that hits the adrenalin button like none of its forebears."

The various suspension modifications of the last couple of seasons certainly made a vast difference in the handling department. *Wheels* continued: "The MR2 changes direction with go-kart speed, agility and deftness, and on Hakone's snaking hill passes, that's just the kind of thing you need.

スピードはひかえめに。シートベルトは忘れずに。

Would y

midship

きっと、このリニアな走りにあつくなる。

テクノロジーの進化がある意味でスポーツカーの存在を稀薄に
容易に堪能できるようになった。しかし所詮、「意のままに走るた
このMIDSHIP SPORTSにはかなわない。エンジン、サスペンシ
チューニング、セッティング、幾度となく行われた走行テスト……
現段階においてパーフェクトと呼べる領域へ限りなく近づいたこ

NEW MR2

● 3S-GTE(GT,GT-S) MAXIMUM POWER:NET245PS/6,000r.p.m., MAXIMUM TORQUE:31.0kg-m
● 3S-GE(G-Limited,G) MAXIMUM POWER:NET180PS/7,000r.p.m.(M/T), MAXIMUM TORQUE:1
● MIDSHIP ENGINE LAYOUT ● TIRES:195/55R15 84V(FRONT), 225/50R15 91V(REAR)
● BRAKES:VENTILATED DISCS(FRONT/REAR) ● SEATING CAPACITY:2 PASSENGERS

Photo:GT Tバールーフ仕様車(オプション装着車)　お求めはトヨタオート店・トヨタ

"After a few kilometres of pretty slopes, S-bends, dips and blind corners, the MR2 Turbo is still on the road and the grin factor is rising rapidly. Over this same route (admittedly in drizzle), its '89 forebear was such a handful it was a relief to give it back.

"Four-and-a-bit years later, all that MR2 nervousness has gone. The car stays flat and grips like the proverbial leech. Cornering poise is phenomenal. Back then, the Turbo's right pedal needed a lot of respect. The rear wheels kept wanting to overtake the fronts. Today, different story. The MR2 has transformed into a neutral car that goes exactly where you point it ..."

More changes for Europe
The UK catalogue from 1994 noted: "The MR2 is powered by the two-litre dohc 3S-GE engine, which generates a maximum 173bhp at 7000rpm, or 137lbft at

Japanese advertising from the 1994 model year. The new rear lights, the modified trim piece between them and new rear spoiler can clearly be seen in this atmospheric shot of the GT. Colour-keyed sills and side protection mouldings were introduced for all models at this time.

Fascia and interior of the 1994 model year GT.

4800rpm. In only 7.7 seconds, this car can reach 60mph from a standing start, and carry on to a possible top speed of 137mph where the law allows. As for the competition – *what* competition?

"In the MR2, 55% of the weight is borne by the rear wheels when the car is standing still, and this load increases

121

A superb publicity shot of the home market GT model for 1994. On careful inspection, the turbocharged car's markings on the side protection moulding can just be seen.

Above & left: Fascia and interior of the GT-S. Comparison with the GT model from the same year gives a clear indication of why the GT-S was cheaper.

during acceleration. As a result, power is transferred to the rear wheels more efficiently because of the greater downward force on the tyres and road surface. Steering effort is reduced by the smaller load on the front wheels, while the cornering performance is further improved by the siting of the engine and other heavy components near the centre of the car."

Rear view of the Japanese 1994 model year MR2 G-Limited T-bar roof.

A full model line-up in Japan, this picture also from October 1993. The car nearest the camera is the GT, then the GT-S, the G-Limited, with the basic G grade in the background.

The UK-specification MR2 GT T-bar (left) and GT of 1994. Autocar & Motor tested the very GT model pictured here, praising its "fine steering, great brakes, good looks and secure handling." They were less impressed with the "reduced performance, coarse engine note and firm ride," however. The lack of zip was a real anomaly.

The more powerful version of the 1998cc 3S-GE power unit had a 10.3:1 compression ratio and incorporated ACIS. It was introduced to the European market in March 1994, along with the various suspension, bodywork and interior changes outlined for Japan, and an advanced four-wheel ABS braking system, now fitted as standard.

The list price for 1994 was set at £17,689 for the MR2 GT in Britain, while the T-bar model commanded £19,145. This compared to £19,230 for a Celica GT, or a massive £38,989 for the Supra (with either manual or automatic transmission for the same price).

The latest Celica GT-Four duly joined the UK line-up in the spring, introduced at £29,235. However, by this time, the cost of an MR2 had risen again, with the GT at £19,275 and the T-bar at £20,760 following the March changes.

After testing the closed GT model, *Autocar & Motor* said: "Through it all, the MR2 remains something special, something palpably out of the ordinary. From the low-slung driving position and the pleasure of hearing the engine start behind you to its new and truly

An American 2.2-litre coupé for the 1994 model year. A rear spoiler now came as standard on the normally-aspirated car, as well as its turbocharged brethren.

124

In March 1994, Eiji Toyoda was inducted into the Automotive Hall of Fame in Detroit – only the second Japanese person to be successfully nominated. To date, there are still only four Japanese in the AHF; the first was Soichiro Honda in 1989, then Toyoda, Professor Genichi Taguchi and, in 1998, the author's friend and mentor, Yutaka Katayama.

The 2.2-litre model for the US 1995 model year. For America, this was the end of the line.

excellent handling, it sets itself apart from the crowd. Fearsomely flawed though it is, the MR2 will earn its place in the hearts of those who drive it – and, for a car like this, that's the most important job of all."

Although black was the only interior option, the choice of coachwork colours included Pure White, Astral Black, Sunburst Red, Goodwood Metallic and Caribbean Blue Metallic. Options on both models included air conditioning and a CD player.

Britain continued to be a massive market for the MR2. A total of 13,580 First Generation models had been sold, but, by the end of 1994, that figure had already been surpassed by the Second Generation car: 3457 examples found new homes in 1990, 4053 in 1991, 3022 in 1992, 2170 in 1993 and 1357 in 1994.

In France, the MR was listed at 204,450 FF in July 1994 (11,500 more than the two-litre Celica GT). Power output was quoted as 175bhp at 7000rpm, with 137lbft of torque at 4800rpm. Top speed was said to be 141mph (226kph), no doubt thanks, in part, to the low Cd figure of just 0.31.

Meanwhile, Toyota Switzerland, which sold 1808 First Generation MR2s, was also finding the new car a better seller, with sales of 932 in 1990, 1173 in 1991, 407 in 1992, 159 in 1993 and 95 in 1994.

News from America

Some magazines had been predicting the end of the MR2 since 1992, which was perhaps a fair assumption given Toyota's traditional four-year gap between models. However, a lot of the speculation was centred not so much on what to expect from the Third Generation car, but whether or not there would even be one. In May 1993, *Car & Driver* stated: "Despite luggage space better suited to golfers than travellers, the MR2 easily handles the daily transportation challenges of its strongest constituency – those young upscale singles. Unfortunately, so do other cars that do not have the complex mid-engined layout. So this will be the last generation of small, mid-engined Toyotas, and we'll miss them."

In the meantime, the 1994 model year saw a few more changes in a bid to give the buyer better value for money, and dual airbags became a feature. As well as the styling and suspension refinements introduced in Japan (although, for some reason, the US-specification, non-turbocharged model retained its black body side mouldings), a rear spoiler was now standard across the board, as was air conditioning, which now used CFC-free gas; both of these had previously been standard on the Turbo only, and options on the normally-aspirated car.

While the other options remained unchanged, prices ranged from $22,538 for the basic 2.2-litre coupé, up to $27,588 for the Turbo. This represented a $3500 increase on the entry-level MR2, for which the buyer did at least get more than $1200 worth of air conditioning and rear spoiler thrown in, but the Turbo driver, who was being asked to pay almost $3000 extra compared with 1993, gained nothing on the previous year's specification.

Steel Mist Grey, Black, Super Red and Super White continued, but Tropical Blue Metallic, Solar Yellow and Dark Emerald Pearl were new coachwork colour options introduced to freshen the image of the car. Monotone black fabric or leather, or a black and ivory leather trim, could be specified for the interior.

In the annual 'Bang for the Buck' contest, *Motor Trend* stated: "What a hoot! The MR2's limits are a little lower than those of the monster cars, but this is pure fun ... Think of it as a baby Ferrari for 20% of the price." Ultimately, after beating some strong competition, the MR2 Turbo came second behind the Chevrolet Corvette Z28.

The MRJ concept car, introduced at the 1995 Tokyo Show. Apparently the 'J' stood for joyful!

News from Japan

In January 1995, a Tenth Anniversary model was launched, based on the G-Limited coupé. Featuring silver and black paintwork, grey alloy wheels and badging, a MOMO steering wheel and gearknob, Bilstein shock absorbers and stainless steel treadplates, it sold for 2,337,000 yen (automatic transmission adding 93,000 yen).

The standard range of MR2 colours in Japan at that time included Super White II, Black, Super Red II, Super Bright Yellow, Dark Green Mica and Strong Blue Metallic. A shade known as Blueish-Grey Argentum Mica was available as an option on all models.

In February 1995, Japan's *Car* magazine observed: "The early Second Generation's handling incurred some criticism but, following a series of minor changes, the MR2 has been endowed with many improvements, transforming it into a sports car which people can really enjoy."

Bowing out from America

Most people thought that the 1994 model was going to be the last year of the Second Generation cars, but it appeared again the following season. Apart from the fact that the Turbo could no longer be bought with California emissions equipment, specifications and options were unchanged, but the prices were a far cry from those of 1985. The basic 2.2-litre coupé was $24,038, with a T-bar roof adding $1790, or automatic transmission an additional $800; the MR2 Turbo was a massive $29,238.

In the July 1995 issue, *Motor Trend* carried out a fascinating test to establish the top speed capability of a number of powerful cars. Having remarked that the MR2 Turbo was now a touch expensive, it noted: "The MR2 Turbo is a potent mid-engine sports car in the tradition of Lotus, Lamborghini, and, dare we say, Ferrari. It offers hard-wired-to-your-brain handling, impressive all-round performance, superb-for-sports car comfort, plus Toyota reliability."

However, by this time, production of US-specification cars had ended (the last one left the line in June), and, by the end of the year, the MR2 had been dropped from the Stateside line-up "due to changing market demands."

In the August 1995 issue of *Toyota Today*, it was noted: "Today, the high-performance segment overall appears to be declining. Recent studies show a dynamic market and new trends have contributed to consumers' dwindling appetite for sports cars ... Another reason the MR2 is leaving US dealerships is stringent emissions laws."

Confirming this observation, Robert Maling of Toyota Motor Sales Inc. mused: "Function and comfort these days are high on buyers' priority lists. Sport utilities are the new trend because they offer a sporty image with a lot more practicality.

"If we're going to continue selling the same volume of MR2s as we have in recent years, the cost to recertify the car for the Environmental Protection Agency [EPA] doesn't justify reimporting and distributing the product."

Maling continued: "The MR2 will be discontinued this year, but there are a lot of new things in store for the future." With the Tokyo Show just around the corner, that was an interesting statement to make ...

However, with regard to the Second Generation MR2, generally speaking, the consensus in America was that the designers' brief to make the car "fun to drive" had been well and truly met. In a 1997 *Car & Driver* owner's survey, a number of people compared the cross-country capability of the mid-engined machine with that of their motorbike. Those questioned had reported a 91.8% satisfaction rate with the product.

The 31st Tokyo Show

At the 1995 Tokyo Show, which opened on 25th October, the author witnessed the debut of a mid-engined concept car known as the MRJ. There were many indications that this was going to be the Third Generation MR2, but no date set. With fewer people buying sports cars in the Land of the Rising Sun, Toyota cannot be blamed for not rushing into another mid-engined project. The trend in recent years has been towards RVs (Recreational Vehicles) and people movers, despite

The top-of-the-range GT T-bar roof model following its mid-1996 face-lift.

The G-Limited of June 1996 vintage, seen here finished in two-tone black and silver. Note the latest polished finish on the five-spoke alloys, and the clear front indicator lenses that were adopted at the same time.

Dashboard and interior of the GT T-bar roof model. Note the passenger-side airbag mounted on the top of the fascia.

The GT-S coupé from June 1996. Although the T-bar roof has its fans, from a pure styling viewpoint, the author actually prefers the closed body.

128

		The Japanese range:		
GT	Coupé	3S-GTE	5-sp Manual	2,958,000 yen
	T-bar		5-sp Manual	3,098,000 yen
GT-S	Coupé	3S-GTE	5-sp Manual	2,716,000 yen
	T-bar		5-sp Manual	2,856,000 yen
G-Limited	Coupé	3S-GE	5-sp Manual	2,363,000 yen
	T-bar		5-sp Manual	2,503,000 yen
G-Limited	Coupé	3S-GE	4-sp Auto	2,456,000 yen
	T-bar		4-sp Auto	2,596,000 yen
G	Coupé	3S-GE	5-sp Manual	2,138,000 yen
	T-bar		5-sp Manual	2,278,000 yen
G	Coupé	3S-GE	4-sp Auto	2,231,000 yen
	T-bar		4-sp Auto	2,371,000 yen

the fact that they are completely unsuitable for tight Japanese roads and parking areas.

However, in fashion-conscious Japan, common sense doesn't come into it; manufacturers simply have to follow trends very closely or get left behind in the race for buyers: it's harsh, economic reality. If nothing else, the Second Generation MR2 was allowed to continue at least.

A brilliant piece of UK advertising for the 1996 model year. Toyota's sports car line-up really was impressive at this time, dispelling once and for all the Japanese marque's conservative image. The vehicles featured here are the Sixth Generation Celica (in GT and Cabriolet form), the MR2 GT T-bar and the Fourth Generation Supra.

Front and rear views of the 1996 model year GT for the UK market.

The 10th Anniversary MR2 GT T-bar. This particular example is finished in Lucerne Silver, but it was also available in Caribbean Blue. Note the darker grey finish on the alloys of the limited edition model.

Two views of the British-specification 1996 model year GT T-bar in standard trim.

131

A rather cute piece of advertising that appeared in Australian Vogue during December 1995. It was one of many suggestions the magazine put forward for Christmas presents that year. Despite a number of subtle hints that the MR2 was a good idea, the author had to be content with a pair of socks!

Wrap it up, I'll take it
That's how you'll feel when you see the stylish, sexy MR2 from Toyota. As well as looking a treat, the MR2 sports car is an absolute joy to drive; it's powerful yet safe, handling both city streets and highways like a dream. So if you're in the running for a new car this Christmas, the MR2 has to be the year's most exciting stocking filler. If you're not, well... dreams are free.
For more information on the Toyota MR2, telephone: 1 800-032 255.

TOYOTA MR2

The Toyota sports car range for 1996 included no less than 14 models on the home market: the Soarer, Supra, Cavalier Coupé, Celica, Celica Convertible, Corona EXiV, Carina ED, Curren, MR2, Corolla Ceres, Corolla Levin, Sprinter Marino, Sprinter Trueno and the Cynos. These were sold through five completely different sales networks – the MR2 being available alongside the Sprinters in one outlet, the Supra batched with the Celicas and Corollas, and the Curren and Cynos in another.

Despite ailing sales, MR2 development continued. In June 1996, ABS braking became standard across the range, as did dual airbags, and a limited-slip differential was now optional on the manual G and G-Limited grades. In addition, new colours were added to the range, including an attractive Black over Silver two-tone paint scheme, and the alloy wheels were given a polished finish.

By the end of 1996, no fewer than 105,750 MR2s had been sold on the home market. However, despite sales officially finishing in America in 1995, the States still accounted for the largest share of MR2 sales with a total of 122,720 units – equivalent to just over 40% of production.

UK news round-up

By spring 1995, the GT model was just £45 shy of the £20,000 mark, whilst the T-bar commanded £21,493. However, the MR2 was still popular amongst enthusiasts – the massive MR2 Drivers' Club in the UK (founded in 1991 and affiliated to Club Toyota) being proof if ever it were needed.

In fact, 27,639 MR2s had been sold in Britain from March 1985 to the end of 1994 (the two generations splitting this figure roughly down the middle), representing almost 10% of Toyota's mid-engined production. During 1995, a further 997 MR2s found new homes in Britain, 611 of them the more expensive T-bar versions.

News of a limited edition model broke in *Auto Express* in March 1996: "Toyota is celebrating ten years of MR2 production with a special anniversary edition of its 173bhp GT T-bar sports car. Only 250 of these cars will be made – in blue or silver with black leather upholstery. The £23,149 roadster features stainless steel sill plates bearing the MR2 logo, five-spoke alloy wheels, and a leather and wood steering wheel with an anniversary badge."

The 10th Anniversary MR2 GT T-bar, available in either Caribbean Blue or Lucerne Silver, was launched just ahead of St Valentine's day, in "perfect timing for the car lover who has an eye for a classic sports car design." As well as the special MOMO steering wheel, other features included a grey finish on the alloys, commemorative badges (with the car's serial number) and treadplates, and the addition of a single-disc CD player to augment the standard eight-speaker stereo radio/

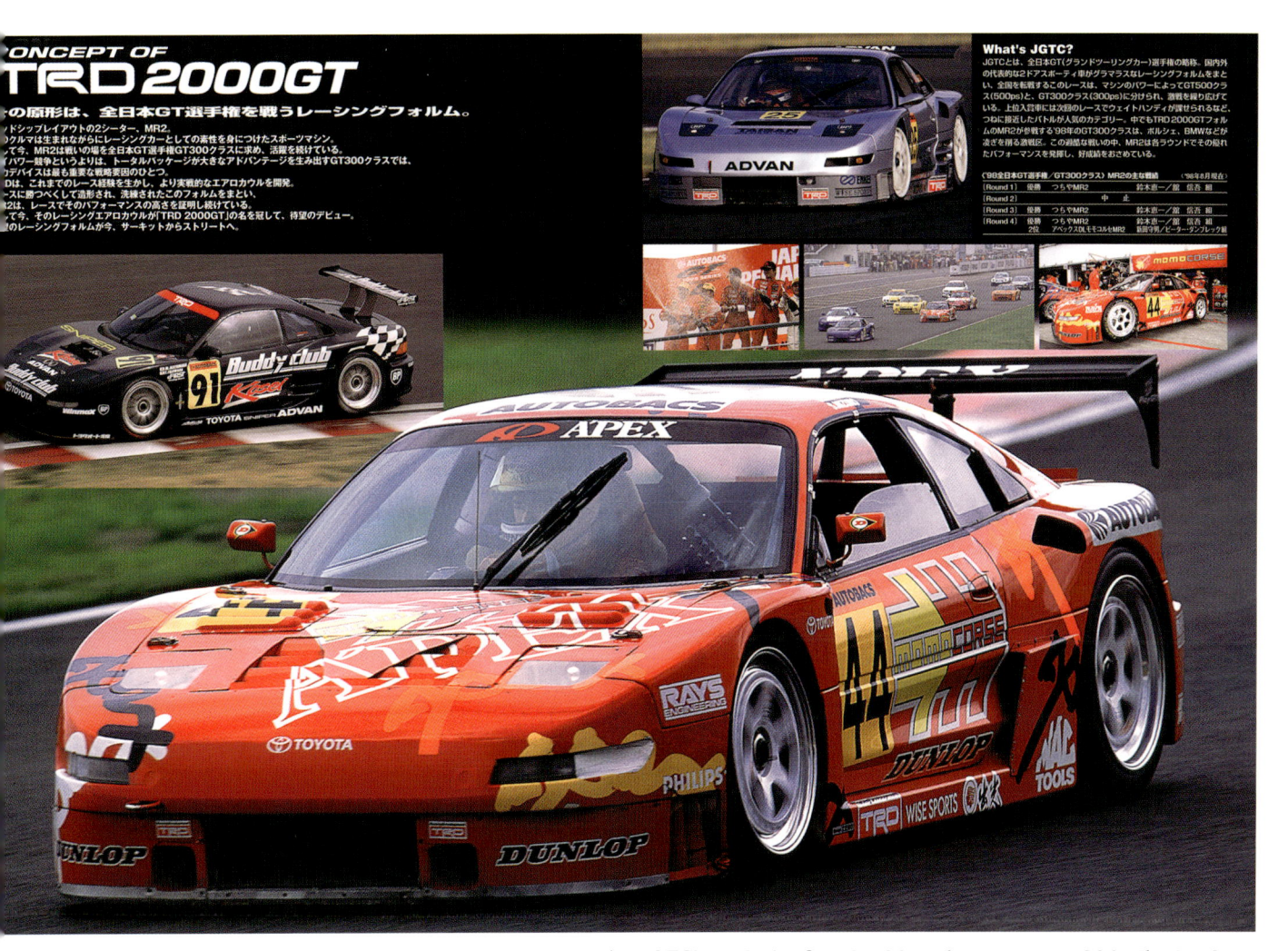

The MR2 in action in the All-Japan GT Championship (or JGTC), with the first SW20s taking part in 1996. The MR2-based SARD MC8-R was campaigned further afield, attempting Le Mans on three occasions, but it failed to make an impression.

cassette. Standard coupé and T-bar models were priced at £20,695 and £22,279 respectively.

Including the 10th Anniversary model, the MR2 recorded 827 sales in the British Isles during 1996, taking total UK sales to a fraction under 30,000 (an impressive figure when one considers that the total for the whole of Europe – including Britain – was only 49,410 units at that time).

By now, though, the MR2 had another two in-house competitors. Celica sales in the UK were given a boost by the addition of a cheaper ST model. 1996 saw a massive leap in Celica popularity, despite the introduction of the new Paseo coupé (or Cynos in Japan) in March, which accounted for around 1400 sales in its first year.

The JGTC

In recent years, the mid-engined machine has competed in the All-Japan GT Championship. 1994 saw the first full year of the JGTC, but it wasn't until 1997 that a second generation MR2 finished in the top five – two Tsuchiya team drivers finished the season in joint-third in the GT300 Class. The specification of the TRD-modified car running in the 1997 JGTC is shown below:

Engine	3S-GE (TRD)
Type	Four-cylinder, dohc, 16v
Bore & stroke	86 x 86mm
Capacity	1998cc
Comp ratio	14.0:1
Max power	290bhp at 8200rpm
Max torque	188lbft at 7600rpm
Fuel delivery	Fuel-injection
Transmission	6SMT
Wheels & tyres (F)	9J alloys with 230/640 R18s
Wheels & tyres (R)	10J alloys with 260/655 R18s
Weight	1000kg (2200lb)

In 1998, a Tsuchiya MR2 took the GT300 title (driven by Keiichi Suzuki and Shingo Tachi), with a Celica second and another MR2 third. The MR2 continued to dominate in the following season, with Morio Nitta (helped by Shinichi Takagi and Yasushi Kikuchi) guiding the Momocorse MR2 to a GT300 Class victory, securing the team title along the way.

133

Pages from a rare Japanese catalogue for the MR Spider. Available in a full range of colours, sadly, this beautiful conversion was not offered outside the Land of the Rising Sun.

オープンカーを
操るという満足。

晴れた日にトップを開けて走る爽快感。季節の移り変わりを空と風で感じる喜び。
数々の制約を抱えてもなお、走りへの欲求を満たすオープンだけの特別なドライビングプレジャーがここにあります。
スポーティなスタイリングにこだわり、幌を簡易式ソフトトップとしたのも、フルオープンへの徹底した想いがあったからこそ。
さらに優れたドライバビリティを実現する、3S-GEスポーツツインカムを搭載。オープンエアモータリングを満喫できる、MR スパイダ
何よりもオープンを愛するドライバーへ、満ち足りた時間をお届けします。

The Technocraft MR Spider

For those who wanted something a little different, in 1996, TRD offered the MR Spider. TRD was established in Yokohama in April 1965, when the Toyopet Service Centre registered a company known as Toyota Racing Development.

The birth of TRD came at a time when the Japanese motorsport scene was starting to come alive, and TRD had a hand in the development of the 2000GT racing models. As with so many Japanese firms, there are a number of branches dealing with different fields of the business, but the main purpose of the company is to develop parts for Toyota racers rather than enter races itself; similar to Nissan Motorsports Department in America. Nevertheless, the company

The prototype TRD 2000GT at the 1997 Tokyo Auto Salon.

134

専用シートファブリック&ドアトリム

着脱式簡易幌 ソフトトップ

幌は着脱式。折り畳んでシートバック後方に収納します。取付けはフロントロック2ヵ所、クォーターピラーロック2ヵ所、ホック15ヵ所で固定。ビニールリヤウインド付き。

本車両はオープン状態で使用することを前提とした簡易幌仕様です。ソフトトップをかけた状態でも一部雨水が浸入することもありますのでご了承願います。

couldn't resist the temptation to offer an attractive soft-top conversion based on the MR2 G Coupé. The hood dropped below a rear deck with twin fairings behind the seats, but the car looked equally good with the top erected or stowed away. Features such as ABS braking, powered steering and an airbag were included in the 3,070,000 yen list price.

Naturally, TRD offered various upgrades, including items such as

continued on page 138

135

TEST DRIVE THE 1993 TOYOTA MR2 TODAY.

Little compares with the sheer thrill of taking to the road in a 4 year old sportscar.

12 Months Toyota Approved Warranty, RAC Approved Quality Check and free 600 mile inspection, Vehicle Mileage Check and RAC Roadside Assistance guarantee a surge of confidence.

Change your mind, and our 14 day Vehicle Exchange lets you choose again from thousands of vehicles in our nationwide Stock Locator System.

So for your nearest dealer and a free information pack, call us on 0800 585 709.

And prepare for the adrenalin rush that only comes with peace of mind.

USED CARS YOU'LL SWEAR ARE NEW CARS.

RAC Auto Assured — FULLY WARRANTED VEHICLES
TOYOTA

NAME................ ADDRESS................
CURRENT CAR. MAKE................ MODEL................
POSTCODE................ TEL NO................
PLEASE CUT OUT AND RETURN COUPON TO: AUTO ASSURED, TOYOTA (GB) LTD, FREEP...

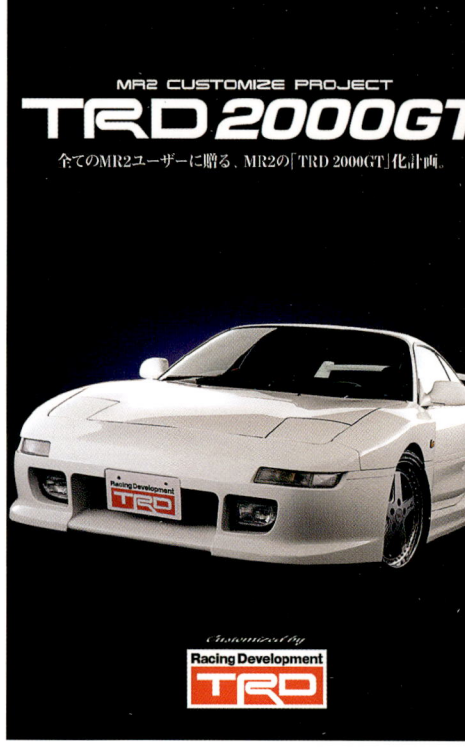

Cover from the TRD 2000GT brochure. The tuning and customizing business is absolutely massive in Japan; it's actually quite rare to see a perfectly standard car on the road.

An MR2 GT for the UK 1997 model year. Note the clear indicator lenses and polished alloy wheels.

British advertising promoted the sale of pre-owned MR2s. With prices up by another £350 on the GT and £375 on the T-bar by the middle of 1997 (when this advert was released), the second-hand market had strong appeal. However, one of the beauties of the later MR2s is the way it can hold its value.

136

The 1998 model year GT T-bar for the UK market. The British Isles provided the third biggest outlet for MR2s, trailing only Japan and North America.

Whilst a number of automakers offered pre-programmed two- or three-step variable valve timing, continuous management of the timing between intake and exhaust valve opening was quite unusual. The VVT-i system selects the optimum intake and exhaust overlap under all operating conditions, thereby ending the traditional compromise between providing standing-start torque or high-speed passing horsepower. At the same time it enhanced fuel economy and reduced emissions so effectively that it eliminated the need for emission control devices like exhaust gas recirculation (EGR). Despite the increase in power, gearing remained the same as it had been in 1989 on all models.

The GT T-bar roof from December 1997. Note the new rear spoiler and alloy wheels – still five-spoke 6J items up front (with 195/55 VR15 rubber), and 7Js shod with 225/50 VR15 tyres at the back. Both turbocharged grades came with Bilstein shock absorbers and a limited-slip differential as standard. Sports ABS came on all cars.

137

its own alloy wheels, sports exhaust system, and so on, but the company also had another MR2-based road car in development. It was duly launched at the 1997 Tokyo Auto Salon held in January.

The TRD 2000GT
Reviving a glorious Toyota name from the past, the 2000GT made its debut at the 1997 Tokyo Auto Salon. During 1994, TRD (of Toyota fame), Mazdaspeed and Nismo (Nissan Motorsports International), joined forces to organise the Tokyo Auto Salon – an alternative motor show purely for tuning and performance companies. In 1997, Mitsubishi Ralliart added its weight to the alliance, and the four adopted the 'Works Tuning' banner.

Apart from promoting the tuning business, Works Tuning also organises motorsport events for owners to give people an opportunity to drive their cars at speed in controlled conditions. This is an extremely responsible attitude, for if a person fits high quality performance parts to their car, it's fair to assume that he or she is going to want to experience the difference they make. The idea is to try and give the likes of the *Zero-Yon* road racers (an illegal run on public roads to cover the standing-quarter in the shortest possible time), a more suitable arena in which to enjoy themselves.

Anyway, based on the 3S-GTE powered MR2 GT, the 2000GT featured Phase I TRD tuning (to give 245bhp), uprated suspension and brakes, wide TRD Alumi-K alloy wheels, and an aerodynamic wide body racing kit modified for the road. Inside, TRD reclining bucket seats were used, along with TRD's own driver's airbag. The price depended on the options chosen, of course, but typically added upwards of 1,000,000 yen to the basic figure.

The UK market for 1997
In August 1996, power output of the two-litre engine was reduced from 173bhp to 168bhp because of revisions to make the MR2 meet stricter emissions regulations introduced at that time. On the plus side, a driver's-side airbag became standard, the audio system was improved, and the electrically-adjusted door mirrors gained a heater element.

From October that year, when the price of the GT went up to £21,605 and the T-bar shot up to £23,225, the two-tone black and silver paintwork first seen in Japan became available in Britain, too. Other changes carried over included the clear front indicator lenses and a polished finish for the alloy wheels.

By mid-1997, a number of magazines from around the world were once again speculating on the new MR2. However, this time the sketches and possible specifications were all starting to look similar; the proposed launch date was the 1997 Tokyo Show. As the Show approached, it was not known whether or not there would be a Third Generation model. Toyota announced that, in the future, the lifespan of passenger cars would be lengthened to nearer five years instead of the traditional four, and that some sports cars could remain unchanged for even longer. The current MR2 had already been in production for almost eight years ...

In October 1997, the buildings at Makuhari Messe hosted the 1997 Tokyo Show and Toyota had a new car on display – the MR-S. This was more of a back-to-basics sports car than the MR2, aimed at a lower price sector of the market. Talking to the staff on the stand, it appeared that the MR-S was definitely going to be put into production, and that both the MR2 and low-volume Supra were soon to be dropped. Only time would tell.

Meanwhile, in the UK, the 1997 Earls Court Show saw a bright red MR2 taking a prominent position high above the Toyota stand. The MR2 GT was priced at £21,955 at this time, with the GT T-bar put at £23,600. Options included air conditioning, a CD player, tailored mats and special paint. Standard coachwork colours for Britain included Sunburst Red and Pure White; a little extra brought Astral Black or the metallic shades of Goodwood Green, Azure Blue and Lucerne Silver (the latter sporting a black roof section). In all cases, interior trim was finished in black.

The MR2 story continues
Despite strong rumours from various sources that the MR2 was due for imminent replacement, in December 1997, Toyota announced yet another minor change for the home market model. The normally-aspirated, two-litre engine now featured continuously variable valve timing (VVT-i), giving increased torque and up to 20 more horses under the bonnet. At the same time, angle adjustment of the rear spoiler became possible, and new five-spoke alloy wheels, a few interior tweaks and three new body colours rounded off the specification changes. Prices now ranged from 2,150,000 to 3,095,000 yen.

Japanese sales figures released for that month confirmed the growing trend towards utility vehicles and MPVs rather than sports cars and coupés. The best-seller in the sporting line-up was

138

The dashboard and interior of the latest GT model. Note the new red stitching on the leather steering wheel cover and gearknob (standard on all cars except the G, as was power-assisted steering), and the stainless steel treadplates fitted to the turbocharged models. Careful inspection will also reveal revised instrument graphics, and red stitching on the GT's standard leather/Escaine trim.

The GT-S of December 1997 vintage. The T-bar roof was still available on all grades.

the Toyota Corolla Levin with 722 units for the month. The Celica managed 464 sales, while the Supra clocked up just 145 – the MR2 recorded a disappointing 91 sales.

Mazda was also struggling, with sales of just 206 Eunos Roadsters (the MX-5) and 202 RX-7s. The 300ZX and the rest of the Fairlady Z range – another car long overdue a replacement – found just 40 customers, although this was still quite a lot compared to the 13 sales of Honda's NSX supercar. By comparison, Honda sold 4230 of its CR-V models, and no less than 11,123 of the StepWgn people mover. In the smaller MPV class, Suzuki sold over 16,000 of its Wagon R models. Even executive cars were outselling sporting machines at a rate of almost ten to one!

Sales abroad were also slowing. At the start of 1998, the exchange rate was roughly 130 yen to the dollar, although currency all around the world was very unstable. (By 1999, the conversion was nearer 100 yen to the dollar). This was obviously not an ideal situation for expensive exports, and could go a long way towards explaining the theory that the MR2's ultimate replacement would definitely be cheaper.

In April 1998, TRD's Spider adopted the more powerful VVT-i engine, and a new colour was added to the paint chart. Sold through the Toyota Auto and Toyota Vista sales channels, it was now available in Super White II, Black, Super Red II, Orange Mica Metallic, Beige Mica Metallic, Dark Purple Mica and, with the S-Package, Silver Metallic.

The changes introduced in Japan in December 1997 were announced in Britain on 1st April 1998. The Toyota GB press release noted: "For 1998, the MR2 wears a new style of five-spoke alloy wheel and adjustable rear spoiler. The latter allows more rear end grip to be generated at high speeds by altering the angle of the rear aerofoil. An Allen key is used to make the adjustments.

"Inside, red stitching on the leather-covered steering wheel and gearknob match the colour of the instrument meter scales which change from white to red. The seat trim in the MR2 GT is also new and a new exterior colour, Cosmos (a metallic dark blue), joins the six body colours already available."

The model's finale

In Australia, the cheaper MR2 Bathurst was introduced for the 1999 model year priced at $50,990, instead of $61,410 for the GT. *Wheels* observed: "Toyota's latest incarnation of its beloved MR2 is little changed from the model it replaces. Fundamentally, the exterior styling remains as is, with alterations limited to a new larger rear deck spoiler and smart looking five-spoke wheels.

"Inside the cabin the same philosophy applies, with change restricted to a new high-grade audio unit accompanied by a restyled gearlever knob and steering wheel.

"While it can't compete against the outrageous [Subaru] WRX or gutsy [Nissan] 200SX, the MR2 has its own individual market. It's still a ball of fun once wound up like a Christmas toy and the Bathurst model now includes anti-lock brakes as standard. The unassisted steering is still a chore at low speed and the glass T-roof can cause grief to the overly tall, but it's still one of the great Sunday drive cars.

Tail of the G-Limited. The spoiler was standard on all cars except the basic G grade, although it could be specified as an option on that model. All Japanese MR2s came with air conditioning, power windows and door locks, electrically-adjusted mirrors and door courtesy lighting included in the price.

Interior of the GT-S, seen here with the optional Recaro seats. These bucket seats were optional on all grades except the G. The GT-S, like the G-Limited, was usually fitted with fabric-covered sports seats, whilst the G had a version with less adjustment.

The basic G grade. The car was available in Super White II, Black, Super Red II, Orange Mica Metallic, Beige Mica Metallic, Dark Purple Mica and, as an option, Sonic Shadow Toning (basically black over silver, as seen here). All interiors were finished in black.

British advertising from June 1998, the month in which another price increase took the GT up to £22,220, and the GT T-bar up to £23,880. However, prices would remain virtually the same (only £5 different) until the model was discontinued.

"But hurry up if you want one. With the Toyota MR-S and Lexus IS200 waiting patiently in the wings the MR2's time may be limited."

Indeed it was. The MR-S was officially announced in October 1999, by which time, all but a handful of the MR2s had been cleared on the home market; the last four were sold in 2000. I know this for sure, as I tried to buy one and couldn't!

The car continued into the spring of 2000 in Europe, however, even though production had long since ceased. Regarding production, 1196 MR2s were built in 1999 (its final year), compared to 4445 of the new open models.

The August 1999 price list for the British market, the last one issued for the Second Generation MR2, saw the GT (with alloy wheels, ABS brakes, a rear spoiler and sunroof as standard) at £22,225 'on the road,' with the T-bar version commanding an extra £1660. Options included air conditioning, mica or metallic paint (at £250), a CD player (£412), tailored mats (£73) and a roof rack.

Incidentally, at the start of 1999, Toyota officially announced its intentions to enter the Formula One arena, stating that a programme had been put in place to enable a team to compete in the 2003 F1 season. Meanwhile, at the 1999 Le Mans 24-hour race, the Toyota team led by Ukyo Katayama finished second overall – the best ever result for the Japanese company. At the end of the year, Toyota won its third World Rally Championship crown.

A UK press photograph of the 1998 MR2 GT. It was said to be able to cover 0-60 in 7.7 seconds before going on to a top speed of 137mph (219kph).

141

British advertising from mid-1999. It wouldn't be long now before both the MR2 and the Celica were superceded. The Chief Engineer on these much-loved cars, and their replacements, was Tadashi Nakagawa.

At the end of 1999, Toyota was once again declared World Rally Champion. However, shortly after, TTE announced its withdrawal from the WRC scene to concentrate on Toyota's F1 efforts, although its aftermarket range of tuned parts continued to be developed.

www.velocebooks.com / www.veloce.co.uk
Details of all current books • New book news • Special offers • Gift vouchers • Forum

TOYOTA
MR2
Coupés & Spyders
1984-2007

4
A NEW DIRECTION

At the 1995 Tokyo Show, the Toyota stand featured a number of interesting concept vehicles, such as the hybrid Prius (now an award-winning production car), and the mid-engined MRJ. With a twin-cam power unit developing 170bhp, an electrically-operated convertible hardtop, and a rather unusual 2+2 seating arrangement, it looked very much as if this advanced machine might make it into the showroom.

The hand-out made interesting reading: "You can have it all with Toyota MRJ: the driving excitement and agility of a mid-engine sports car, the refreshing feel of open-air motoring, and stable handling. This is a midship car like you've never seen: one that offers both a compact exterior and a comfortable interior space. The lively lines of the low, slanted nose and abbreviated overhang, plus the liberating look of the open body, embody the spirit of freedom and quickness.

"The MRJ is powered by a responsive 1.8-litre, 20v dohc engine that delivers plenty of torque in the low-to-medium rpm ranges, where you need it most in everyday driving. The suspension features MacPherson struts in front and

The Toyota MRJ – the result of Tadashi Nakagawa's push for a lighter, more nimble machine, and the car which many thought would be the Third Generation MR2. Here, the electrically-operated top is in the closed position.

Left: For a mid-engined sports car, the MRJ was surprisingly practical. The rear seats (a bonus in itself in a vehicle with this layout) could be folded in a number of ways to give additional luggage space.

Below: The distinctive tail of the MRJ, designed at Toyota's EPOC facility in Belgium. Sadly, it remained a concept vehicle, but did give a clue to the direction the mid-engined project was taking.

Opposite, top: At the touch of a button, the tail section of the car lifted, the top went back and down into the opening, and then the whole thing closed to give the appearance of a full-blooded roadster. This arrangement undoubtedly provided the inspiration for the roof mechanism on the new Soarer (or Lexus SC430).

The MR-S at its public debut on the Toyota stand at the 1997 Tokyo Show. Earlier design proposals had called for a car closely resembling the Sports 800, but the rounded lines were eventually straightened and developed into those of the MR-S. As the proposed replacement for the MR2 – albeit an indirect one – the intention was to sell the car at a very competitive price.

Superstruts in the rear. The car is also equipped with active rear-wheel steering that's linked to vehicle speed and to the turning angle of the steering wheel, of course, and it also gets feedback from the vehicle's yaw rate.

"We made the wheelbase as long as possible within the limits of the car's exterior dimensions. This takes advantage of the lateral force of tyres positioned far from the centre of gravity to increase the vehicle's turning moment. This improves the vehicle's turning response to steering input, which improves stability and makes the ride more enjoyable.

"The instrument panel consists of two LCD monitors and an analogue tachometer. One LCD monitor alternates between displaying the speedometer and a cluster of gauges. The other monitor can be switched between the navigation mode and the audio/air-conditioner mode. Placing the navigational display in the instrument cluster improves its legibility.

"You can arrange the MRJ seats to suit a range of needs. The rear seats fold down or push up and away to reveal an unexpectedly large luggage space. And the regular 2+2 configuration allows room for four passengers."

Was this the much talked about Third Generation MR2? The vast majority of people certainly seemed to think so. Gossip circulating UK dealerships at the time suggested that the new model had a longer wheelbase: sure enough, the MRJ had a 2550mm (100.4in) wheelbase (some 150mm, or 5.9in, longer than that of the MR2). Months passed, but the conviction remained that this was the new mid-engined Toyota. In fact, in March 1997, *Complete Car* predicted that the MRJ would go on sale in 1998, priced in the UK at around £22,000. A couple of years down the line, it had become little more than a memory.

The 32nd Tokyo Show

Although the MR2 started life as the modern interpretation of the Sports 800, due to prevailing market forces, it developed into an expensive Grand Tourer. The MR-S was announced at the 1997 Tokyo Show and was a return to the original concept – lightweight and sporty, and, unlike the MRJ would have been had it entered production, cheap to buy.

In Australia, one of the journalists working for *Wheels* magazine managed to squeeze a rough starting price out of a Toyota official – the 2,000,000 yen quoted was a price intended to compete with that of the Second Generation Mazda MX-5. Despite the glut of lightweight sports cars on the market at that time, it looked as if Toyota could be onto a winner!

The press release stated: "The sportiness of the MR-S is enhanced by greatly shortening the overhang, placing the tyres at the four corners, and adding side air intakes that signify the midship engine design ... The interior of the MR-S produces a feeling of simplicity and gutsy tightness, and provides cargo space behind the seats."

Responsive performance was promised in the specification. In a car weighing only 960kg (2112lb), the 1.8-litre VVT-i engine, linked to a five-speed sequential gearbox, offered lively acceleration, whilst "thanks to the newly-developed lightweight and firm strut-type suspension and long wheelbase, easy handling is at one's fingertips."

In a scoop on the new model, the respected British weekly, the *Autocar*, noted: "Engineers privy to early test results say the new Toyota is a real driver's machine," which seemed to confirm the expectations generated by the company's promotional blurb.

Toyota was hoping for a favourable response from the public at Makuhari Messe. Kunihiro Uchida, Chief Designer on the SW20 MR2, stated: "If people like the MR-S, we would like to mass-produce it, but if this happens we would change some details, like the angle of the A-pillars and the shape of the roll-bars." Fortunately, the reception was good, with some people remarking that the little roadster reminded them of the

These overhead views of the MR-S give a good idea of scale. This car would bring the story of the mid-engined Toyotas full circle, with a return to the lightweight sports concept.

glorious Porsche sports-racers of the late-1950s and early-60s. The future of the MR-S project (MR-S apparently standing for 'Midship Runabout-Sports,' incidentally) was pretty much assured.

The MR-S development story

After the MRJ, design work began on a new small mid-engined car. The Chief Engineer, Tadashi Nakagawa stated that he wanted to break what he termed "the cycle of growth," where each new generation inevitably gets bigger and more powerful than its predecessor. This, in turn, requires a stronger body, leading to more weight, which often means adding yet more power in the future to keep enthusiasts happy.

Nakagawa wanted a return to the LWS (Lightweight Sports) concept. He said: "Our foremost consideration was to let people genuinely experience a good time by buying, riding and driving our car. We wanted to build a sports car that was truly different, geared toward a new generation and a new century. During the process, we established the

continued on page 150

A scale model of the MR-S that appeared on the Toyota stand (the hardtop was not fitted on the prototype displayed at Makuhari Messe, incidentally).

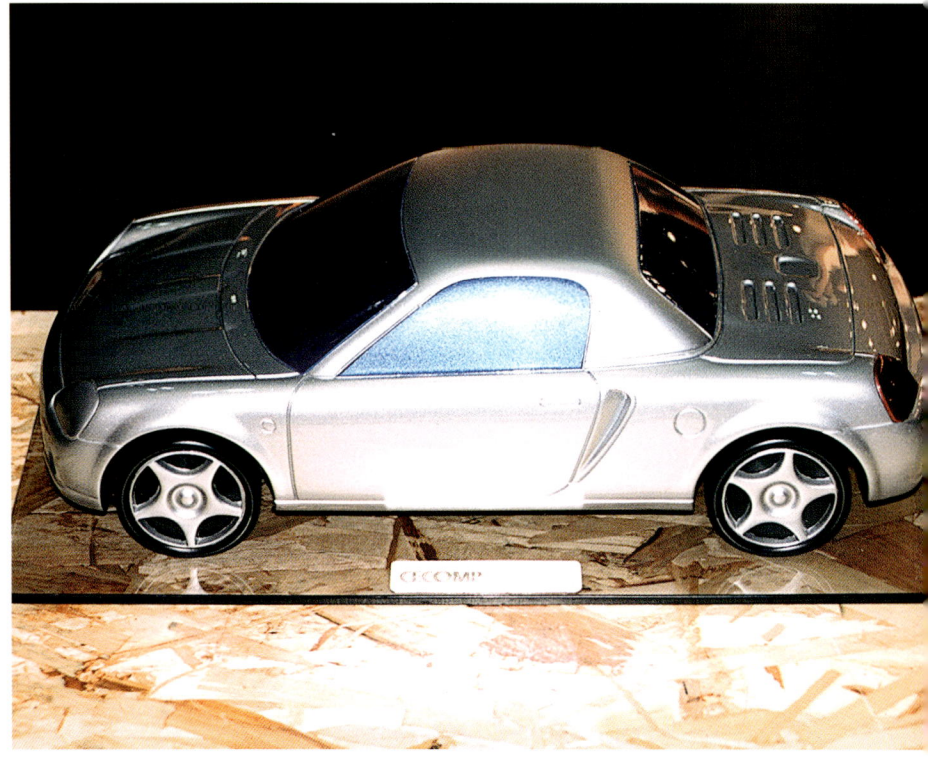

Tadashi Nakagawa, Chief Engineer on the MR-S project, and a number of other important Toyota sports cars through the years.

146

The interior was designed to be simple. As a pure sports car, it was a complete contrast to the relative luxury of the then-current MR2. The five-speed sequential gearbox was not offered on production cars initially, but at least it would eventually find its way onto the specification sheets.

A press photograph showing the chunky frontal aspect of the MR-S – pop-up headlights were never considered for the new model. Only one had been built at the time of the Tokyo Show, although several engineering mules, disguised as SW20 MR2s, were in circulation.

The tail of the prototype. The detailing was delightful, with small touches – such as tiny badges on the front wings – aping those of the great Italian styling houses.

147

A final shot from the 1997 Tokyo Show. Shortly afterwards, a few subtle mechanical and styling revisions were put in motion to enable the car to be launched in 1999. There was talk of a 200bhp engine at this stage but, in reality, it seemed unlikely, given Nakagawa's desire to produce a true lightweight sports model.

This page & opposite: Various key sketches drawn up in the quest to find the ultimate replacement for the SW20 MR2. Note the smaller, open body, and the distinct lack of pop-up headlights in any of the proposals.

149

The key interior design themes were rapidly established.

Right & above: A couple of views of an early interior styling buck. Note the central tachometer – a feature not usually associated with Toyota – and the customary golf bag. Virtually every Japanese company seems to measure luggage space by how many golf bags can be fitted in the car!

catchphrase, 'New Generation Light Sport.'"

Early design proposals submitted by the Tokyo Design Centre called for a car closely resembling the Sports 800. In one-fifth scale, with its sculptured sides, MGF-style front and Sports 800 roofline, it looked stunning, but the stylists rejected it after a full-scale model had been built. The rounded form was duly changed to somewhat straighter, sharper lines, resulting in the true origin of the MR-S.

Like the MRJ before it, Forum of Italy (run by ex-Michelotti man, Tateo Uchida), was involved in building the show car prototype, along with a design development concern called CECOMP. It was built at great expense, but with a reasonably firm intention to put the MR-S into production – depending on reaction, it was a worthwhile exercise.

As we've already noted, the concept was well-received at the 1997 Tokyo

Various shots of the full-sized model produced after the 1997 Tokyo Show concept car. To make the vehicle qualify for crash regulations, modifications to the bodyshell construction meant the front overhang was 65mm (2.5in) greater than on the prototype, whilst the rear overhang was actually 30mm (1.2in) less. Other changes included a slightly different front mask, a new bonnet, revised tail-end styling and a modified A-post. Detailing (such as the fuel filler cover, door handles and lighting) also received the designers' attention.

151

The Toyota team discussing ways of improving the cloth convertible top, released from the top rail by two simple clips. Eventually, as the result of a rather clever piece of engineering, the hood acted as a tonneau cover when folded.

Studies looking at the way the convertible top sits when it is closed. One picture shows a traditional hood with tonneau cover, the other the unique Toyota soft-top arrangement, which not only gives the car clean lines, but means that the owner doesn't have to waste time and effort fitting a separate tonneau.

Show, giving the green light for further development. All of this work was carried out at the Tokyo Design Centre, incidentally, with Yuji Fujiwara the man responsible for the car's distinctive shape (under the watchful gaze of Toshinori Mori).

The interior theme was established very quickly, with an ultra-modern pipe and circle motif chosen from the earliest stages of the design process. The 2+2 seating of the MRJ, despite being practical, sadly, was abandoned in favour of a pure two-seater approach. Simplicity was the keynote, with the Central Motor Company staff pulled in on the project to ensure ease of manufacture.

Meanwhile, the mechanical elements of the vehicle were also being finalised. The all-aluminium, 1.8-litre power unit and transmission were shared with the new Seventh Generation Celica (Tadashi Nakagawa was the Chief Engineer on this project, too) in the interests of standardisation, which would help keeps costs to a minimum.

With a light body, the power-to-weight ratio was 6.9kg (15.2lb)/bhp. This compared favourably with the MX-5, at 7.1kg (15.6lb)/bhp, although the little Mazda was soon to gain some additional horses under the bonnet. The Honda S2000, on the other hand, had to contend with only 4.9kg (10.8lb)/bhp, but this was an altogether more expensive proposition.

It was soon decided that all markets would have a similar specification, but the five-speed sequential gearbox would have to wait; whilst this type of transmission had been employed in MR2 racers, it needed further development for road car use. The manual 'box (automatic ECT was not available) was ultimately given ratios of 3.166:1 on first, 1.904 on second, 1.392 on third, 1.031 on fourth and 0.815 on top; the final-drive ratio was listed at 4.312:1.

Suspension was via MacPherson struts at all four corners with dual-links at the back, while anti-roll bars would be specified for the front and rear for all markets – 20mm (0.79in) and 15mm (0.59in) respectively. To

continued on page 157

152

The next clay model, seen in the foreground in these shots, displaying a number of revised features, including the A-post, air intake, the sill area, tail graphics, the engine cover, hood line, front mask, door handles, fuel filler, side repeater light and heavier wheelarch bulges. The car was also given a more wedge-shaped profile by slightly raising the rear quarters.

The interior which followed that of the 1997 Tokyo Show MR-S. Subtle changes will be noted, but the cockpit was 'right' virtually from the start. Note the white faces on the instruments (with the sporty six o'clock starting point on the needles), and the sequential gearbox (there were hopes for a six-speed version at that time).

154

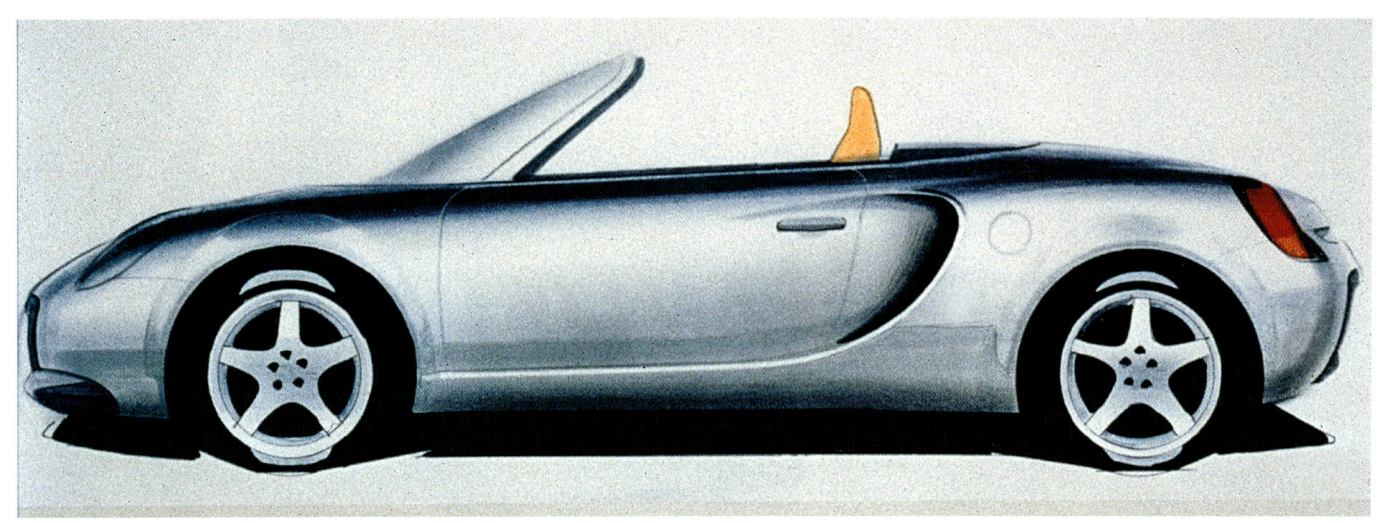

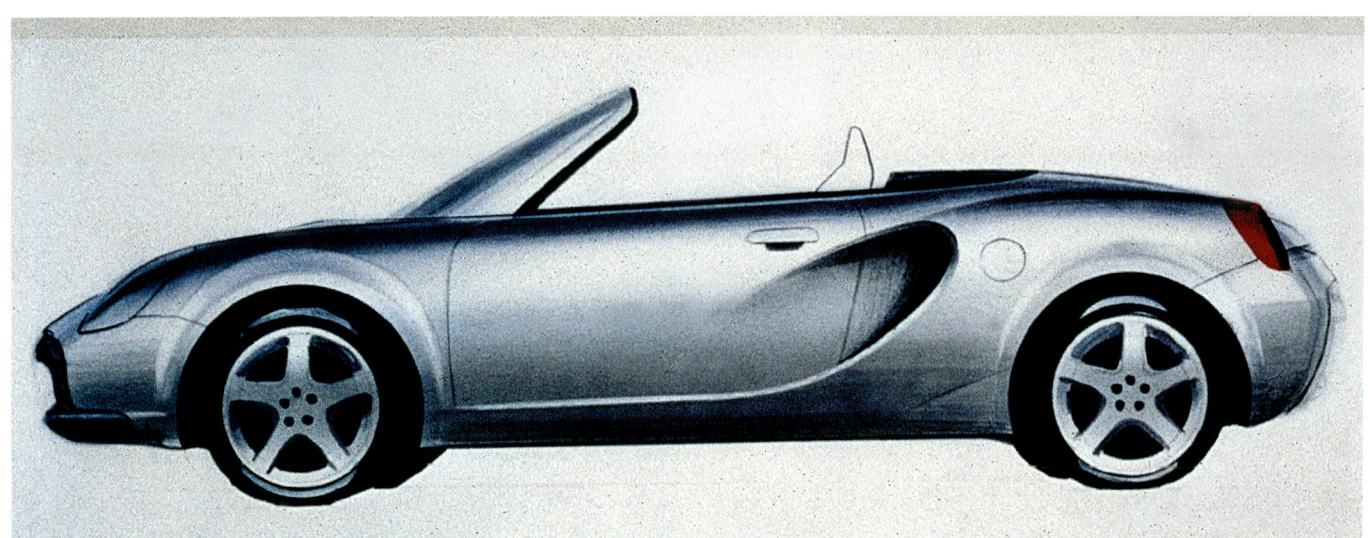

Final design sketches proposing yet more detail changes for the air intakes and nose profile.

Various views of the final prototype, with a few, very subtle, changes in the front airdam area, the tail and the detailing. The car's aerodynamic performance was certainly not as good as the old coupé's but, at 0.35, the Cd figure was more than acceptable for a convertible.

Interior of the final prototype. Once again, the changes were subtle: seating refinements; different heating controls and vents, and a more conventional starting point for the instrument pointers.

million units. The press release read as follows:

Toyota's MR-S – as a Sports Convertible should be

Toyota (TMC) waved the green flag today for sales of its long-awaited, two-seater, soft-top sports car – the MR-S.

Designed to bring out the pleasures of driving in any setting, the lightweight yet rigid, rear-wheel drive MR-S sports a stylish open-top design. Its midship engine and short overhangs provide for reduced yaw inertia moment, and its long wheelbase offers both responsive handling and convergence.

The chief components of the MR-S's new, specially designed open body make up a large cross-section framework, with crossmembers placed effectively throughout to ensure lightness and rigidity. Power pours forth from its high-performance, 1.8-litre, BEAMS 1ZZ-FE engine equipped with VVT-i, while forward cowls and a low centre of gravity emphasise the low stable straddle of the tyres.

The top of the MR-S folds neatly in half for complete storage, opening the way to enjoying the pleasures of a true roadster. A choice of 21 colour combinations – seven exterior colours and three seat colours – helps owners express their individualism, while bolt-on front and rear fenders make for easy detachment for customisation or repair.

The MR-S also boasts class-leading fuel efficiency, helping to cut weight emissions and making it compliant with the new emissions standards set out in Environmental Agency guidelines. And maximum-protection safety features give occupants peace of mind.

The press release went on to describe the car's leading features in more detail:

give the set-up extra rigidity, tower braces were employed above the engine. Power-assisted steering (EHPS) with a tilt-adjustable column and just 2.7 turns lock-to-lock, and ventilated discs all-round (255mm or 10.0in at the front, 263mm or 10.3in at the back) with ABS as standard on all cars, completed the mechanical picture.

Wheels and tyres were 15-inch items, although – with 185/55s up front and 205/50s at the rear – were narrower than those specified on the SW20. A spacesaver spare was fitted under the bonnet, and the car came with a 48-litre (10.6 Imperial gallon) fuel tank.

The dream becomes reality

The press launch was held at the Amlux Building in Tokyo on October 12th 1999, a few days before the Tokyo Show and the month in which Toyota's cumulative passenger car production reached 100

The final prototype with the optional detachable hardtop in place. The hardtop weighed in at 18kg (40lb), but was undoubtedly attractive. It had a subtle double-bubble profile to give additional strength and head clearance, as well as enhanced aerodynamic efficiency.

Midship layout with a long wheelbase
A midship engine with rear-wheel drive gives the MR-S superior handling. Its light weight – 960kg (B Edition) – and reduced yaw moment of inertia, achieved by shortening the front and rear overhangs, ensure very responsive steering.

The MR-S has a relatively long wheelbase (2450mm or 96.5in) compared to overall length (3885mm or 153.0in). This increases the turning force by using the lateral power of the steered front tyres, which are located farther from the vehicle's centre of gravity. The long wheelbase also enhances steering convergence and stabilises the vehicle at high speeds, producing very stable operation overall.

Suspension
The MR-S has a newly-developed, lightweight, four-wheel independent suspension: L-arm MacPherson strut suspension is used in the front, with dual-link MacPherson strut suspension at the rear.

Highly stable operation and a superior ride are ensured by employing the most appropriate geometry, increasing the support rigidity of suspension arms and cutting friction between parts.

The press launch at the Amlux building in Tokyo. A similar car, also in red, was displayed at the 1999 Tokyo Show, along with a red Celica – the Seventh Generation model was another debutant at the event.

Newly-developed EHPS
The steering system employs a small, lightweight, EHPS (Electro-Hydraulic Power Steering) system that is assisted by an electrically-powered hydraulic pump. The resulting highly responsive control makes driving a pleasure at any speed.

Drivetrain and tyres
The five-speed manual transmission offers very smooth shifting, [while the optional] torque-sensitive helical LSD is very responsive to the accelerator pedal.

Different tyres are used in the front and rear – 185/55 VR15 and 205/50 VR15 respectively – corresponding to the rear load ratio of a large midship design. This provides excellent performance in terms of traction and braking.

Fairings have been placed ahead of the front tyres to smooth airflow and to promote stability when [the car is] operating at high speeds.

Light, rigid, exclusive open body
The cross-sections of rockers [sills] and other key framework elements have been enlarged and a crab-shell construction of thick sheeting has been used for the exterior. This minimises the need for reinforcing elements on the framework interior and creates a rigid but light body.

The various framework elements have been placed longitudinally and laterally, and integrated crossmembers have been attached at strategic points as an efficient means of maintaining body rigidity.

The lower section of the front pillar has been enlarged to improve rigidity

The engine bay of the new MR-S. A rear boot was deemed unnecessary as, with an additional bulkhead and heat insulation material, it would have added a lot of weight to the vehicle. Besides, without one, it was possible to give the exhaust more efficient routing. Note the way the hood acts like a tonneau cover when down.

Layout of the MR-S sports car. Weight distribution was 42% front, 58% rear.

in combination with the rocker, and straight pipes have been integrated inside the pillars to put pillar strength on a par with that in closed body vehicles.

The engine

The [140PS] in-line, four-cylinder, 1.8-litre, BEAMS 1ZZ-FE engine with VVT-i, a high compression ratio (10.0:1), and an oblique squish combustion chamber produces ample low- and mid-range torque. An aluminium block and resin intake manifolds help reduce overall weight.

Exterior design

A stylish open sports design has been created featuring a forward cowl and a low centre of gravity. This design emphasises the powerful proportions of the MR-S, and the stable straddle of the tyres on a long wheelbase with short overhangs.

A front grille with low, wide openings gives the vehicle an aggressive profile. Meanwhile, headlamps with simple, functionally-placed round reflectors, and slightly bulging fenders help evoke a sense of energy and motion.

Storage area behind the seats. The choice of a fishing rod as luggage for this publicity shot was a good one, as it made the cubbyhole look bigger! Note the air deflector arrangement immediately above.

A wedge-shaped side view with a full door cross section and side air intakes characteristic of a midship gives the vehicle body a solid sense of mass.

The soft-top can be neatly folded in half for storage, and features a glass rear window with a defogger.

Interior

The instrument panel's novel piped sectioning creates a simple, sporty look, and its layout combines functionality with good form.

In 1999, Hiroshi Okuda (seen here) became Chairman of the company, while Fujio Cho (the former Vice-President) moved up to take his place as the new President.

The silver-faced 'three-eye' combination meter features a tachometer in the centre. Aluminium plating on the accelerator pedal, the brake pedal, the clutch pedal and the surface of the footrest also adds a sense of sportiness. Metallic tone door assist grips and an innovative dimple pattern surface treatment further enhance the sporty feeling of the MR-S.

The seats hold passengers firmly in place even under the lateral G-forces and acceleration/deceleration G-forces experienced during sports driving. Their 3D mesh tone fabric and gleaming surfaces are pleasing to the eye, and harmonise well with the exterior styling when the roof is down.

INDIVIDUALITY AND CUSTOMIZING

A selection of seven exterior colours and three seat colours (black, red and yellow) provides a choice of 21 combinations for individual expression.

Both the front and rear fenders are attached by bolts, making detachment for repairs and customizing easier.

The centre cluster is equipped with knee supports, and features so-called free-rack construction

Memorable Japanese advertising from the time of the car's launch. A big-budget TV commercial featured the same exotic-looking lady dancing to the rhythm of Enrique Iglesias. The MR-S was sold through the Netz and Vista sales channels.

160

that allows the driver to personalise the layout of the AV equipment.

SAFETY
The MR-S's sophisticated midship layout provides highly stable operation and manoeuvrability; stability is further enhanced by the inclusion of ABS as a standard feature and the use of four-wheel ventilated disc brakes.

The MR-S is designed to provide front, side and rear collision protection that easily clears Japanese, US and European legal requirements.

The driver and passenger seats on all models are equipped with seatbelts fitted with pre-tensioners and force limiters as standard items; dual SRS airbags and blinking seatbelt alarms are also standard equipment (the passenger seat in the B Edition is fitted with a pre-tensioner but has no airbag).

Seats are constructed according to the WIL (Whiplash Injury Lessening) concept to absorb the impact on passengers' necks in the event of a rear-end collision.

The brake pedal is designed to limit backward movement in the event of a front-end collision, lessening the impact on the driver's leg.

ENVIRONMENTAL CONSIDERATIONS
Keeping in mind the goal of reducing CO_2 emissions, the MR-S has a class-leading fuel efficiency of 14.2km/litre (in the 10/15 Japanese test mode), made possible by a lightweight body and a highly-efficient engine.

In addition to using VVT-i, independent fuel-injection for each cylinder, and atomisation fuel injectors, a pair of catalytic converters are placed directly below the dual exhaust manifold to enhance their heating properties, with the other catalytic converter in the exhaust pipe, thereby more thoroughly cleaning the exhaust.

The MR-S conforms with the exhaust emission regulations (for vehicles with reduced automobile purchase tax rates) set to go into force in October 2000. The MR-S also meets the Japanese Transitional Low Emission Vehicle (J-TLEV) Exhaust Levels, which call for a 25% reduction in the HC and NOx emission levels stipulated in the new 2000 regulations found in the Environmental Agency's technical guidelines on emissions.

The front and rear bumpers are made of highly-recyclable TSOP (Toyota Super Olefin Polymer) thermoplastic resin, as are internal and external components such as the instrument panel, the door trim and the rear console. The radiator, wire harness insulation, and other parts use materials that do not contain lead, an environmentally hazardous substance. The dashboard silencer and floor silencer are made of high-performance RSPP (Recycled Sound-Proofing Products), which is made of shredder residue from end-of-life vehicles.

ADDITIONAL FEATURES
Luggage space behind the seats comes to 78 litres (according to the VDA measurement method, when the soft-top is closed); a storage box is located beneath the front hood for stowing away small items (S Edition), and the glove compartment comes with a lock.

The upper centre portion of the instrument panel has a small lidded compartment; the centre cluster features an ashtray and two cupholders, and the rear console has a small receptacle which doubles as a cupholder.

A translucent colour acrylic air deflector can be used when the soft-top is down to reduce the wind whipping around from behind, while still allowing a clear view to the rear. The deflector (not available on the B Edition) can be stored away when not needed.

The MR-S is available with a glassfibre detachable top with a moulded lining and trim as a dealer option.

The hazard lights blink in confirmation when locking or unlocking the vehicle doors using the wireless door lock system (S Edition only).

The home market
To begin with, three grades were listed in Japan: the basic 1,880,000 yen MR-S; the S Edition (more expensive by 100,000 yen) and the entry-level B Edition, priced at a more than reasonable 1,680,000 yen.

Tyre and wheel combinations were quoted as 185/55 VR15s on 6J rims at the front, and 205/50 VR15s on 6.5J rims at the back. Pressed steel wheels were the norm, but aluminium alloys came on the S Edition and could be specified as a 60,000 yen option on the MR-S.

All cars came with ABS, a driver's-side airbag, high-mount rear brake light, heated glass rear window with timer, internal boot and fuel flap releases with lock, a map light, door pockets, a footrest, digital clock and resin treadplates.

Moving up to the MR-S brought a leather-trimmed, three-spoke steering wheel and gearknob (the B Edition had a urethane covering), dual airbags, air conditioning, remote control central locking, electric windows, colour-keyed power mirrors and door handles (instead of black), an anti-draught board, and two-speakers pre-installed ready for the 63,000 yen stereo.

The top S Edition model added cast alloy wheels (still 6J x 15 at the front, and 6.5J x 15 at the rear), an uprated central locking system, aluminium pedals, and a front storage box. Even on this top grade though, one still had to hand over 63,000 yen for the four-speaker CD/MD/radio unit, but at least an electric aerial was fitted as standard.

A limited-slip differential was a 30,000 yen option for all grades, while the detachable hardtop was classed as a dealer option (priced at 192,000 yen), as were aluminium pedals for the cheaper models, and air conditioning for the B Edition. Naturally, it being Japan, there were countless audio options to choose from.

Coachwork colours included Super White II, Silver Metallic, Black, Super Red V, Super Bright Yellow, Green Mica Metallic and Blue Mica. Interiors were trimmed in black as standard, although red or yellow seats could be specified as a no-cost option.

To further personalise a vehicle there was the Fun Sports Package (247,000 yen), which included a new front airdam with built-in foglights, side skirts, a rear valance and rear spoiler, the Elegant Sports Package (123,400 yen), containing a front spoiler, side skirts, rear valance, clear repeater lights and 'MR-S' decals for the side of the car, or the Trad Sports Package (135,000 yen), with an aluminium cover for the rearview mirror, a chrome-plated windscreen frame, rear bumper trim, wheelarch extensions, side air intake garnishing pieces and chrome door mirrors. Most

Rear view of the home market's S Edition – the top-of-the-range model.

of the Fun, Elegant and Trad Sports Package components could be bought separately, and the interior could be changed via an Aluminium Item Package, a Wood Item Package or a Colour Item Package.

The MR-S was designed to be fun to drive at slower speeds as well as flat-out along country roads, and, in this respect, it seems the designers succeeded. In addition, most contemporary reports noted the car's excellent stability at high speed, with very little buffeting in the cockpit; the ride was far smoother than that of the old MR2 (doubtless part of the plan to make the new mid-engined model appeal to a wider audience), and the raised front wing profiles helped the driver to place the vehicle more accurately in corners or guide it through a tight gap.

Initial response was very encouraging, but a lack of luggage space was mentioned, and *Car Graphic* raised an interesting point when it questioned the absence of an automatic transmission model as, like Americans, a lot of Japanese drivers prefer two-pedal motoring. However, it will be remembered that the 1997 prototype had a sequential gearbox, and plans were afoot to put one into the production car.

Of the 4054 mid-engined Toyotas sold in Japan during 1999, only 817 were Second Generation models, the remainder of this total was accounted for by the new MR-S. Compared with the initial rush of orders taken for the other two MR vehicles, this could be considered disappointing. However, the specialist nature of the open roadster, in an arena full of strong competition, must be borne in mind, and the figure was perfectly in line with the 1000 units a month forecast by the company.

Incidentally, in a bid to raise the profile of the new model, two cars were entered in the 2000 All-Japan GT Championship. It won the GT300 Class in the seventh and final round of the series, which bode well for the MR-S's chances in the 2001 season.

The new car in the UK
The MR-S made a brief appearance in the UK at the 1998 Motor Show held at the NEC, but stand M8 at the 1999 Earls Court Show (which ran from October 20th to the 31st) had a silver MR2 Roadster and a Seventh Generation Celica finished in the same colour as its main exhibits. Although the press release concentrated on the Celica, it did at least reveal that a hardtop would be available for the open car.

A later piece of publicity material certainly whet the appetite: "The new Toyota MR2 Roadster is an affordable mid-engined, rear-wheel drive roadster designed to excite true sports car enthusiasts. Fun to drive, the two-seater soft-top combines

Fascia of the S Edition. Instruments had black markings on white meter faces, which glowed red on black at night. This arrangement is very effective, and becoming quite popular in Japan. The central tachometer, red-lined at 6800rpm, was very unusual for Toyota. Note the corporate Toyota badge on the steering wheel centre – the only place it was visible on home market cars.

Interior of the 2000 model year S Edition. The highback seats, with four-way adjustment, were very supportive and provided an ideal driving position.

Front three-quarter shot of the S Edition, the only Japanese model to come with alloy wheels as standard at the time of the car's launch. From this angle, in particular, Fujiwara's lines are undeniably pretty.

163

Tail of the standard MR-S grade, seen here with the hood up. This picture was duly used in the first Japanese catalogue.

traditional sports car characteristics with modern engineering for reliability and safety. The light weight of the new MR2 Roadster is the key to its sparkling performance, low fuel consumption, agile handling and stable roadholding.

"Engineers achieved a low weight of 975kg (2145lb) against a target of 1000kg (2200lb). As a result, the new MR2 Roadster has the best power-to-weight ratio in its class at 146bhp/ton, and is one of the most nimble vehicles on the road. Quick and accurate response to driver commands is the name of the game for the new MR2 Roadster."

The Second Generation MR2 was listed in Britain until the 5th April 2000 (370 had been sold in 1999), when it was replaced by the new roadster, introduced at £18,495.

Only one model was listed, with alloy wheels shod with VR-rated tyres, power-assisted steering, ABS brakes, a limited-slip differential, a four-speaker radio/cassette/CD player, remote control central locking, electric windows, colour-keyed power mirrors, a leather-trimmed steering wheel and gearknob, aluminium pedals, an alarm, and dual airbags all coming as standard, along with a three-year mechanical, six-year paint and 12-year anti-perforation warranty.

A colour-keyed detachable hardtop, air conditioning and leather trim could be bought as options, for £1500, £900 and £500 respectively.

Following the press launch in Majorca, *Autocar* carried out a full road test on the new 138bhp machine. It observed: "The MR2 has a couple of impressive tricks of its own, the best of which is its peppy demeanour. Throttle response and deft controls are important in a sports car and the MR2 doesn't disappoint. Some will find the engine noise a little flat, but the way it performs can't be faulted. A broad spread of power and torque leaves it equally happy being revved to the 6900rpm limiter or lugging from just over 1000rpm in fourth gear.

"The sweet engine gives MR2 the pace, but it loses out to its rivals in luggage space. People who care little for practicality will find no problem living with the MR2, but we can't help feeling that, despite the smiles it provides, Toyota has narrowed the appeal of its roadster to a level that makes choosing it over a Mazda MX-5 very difficult indeed."

Having returned an average of 31.8mpg whilst recording a 0-60 time of 7.5 seconds and a top speed of 126mph (202kph), the magazine declared itself pleased with the "lively engine, good performance, grip, brakes and value," but less than amused with the "nervous steering at speed" and the "tiny luggage space."

The Japanese MR-S range finished in each of the seven colours listed for the home market. The three interior choices, and the two different wheel types, can also be seen in this photograph. Note the white car, with its black door handles and mirrors indicating a B Edition grade – all other vehicles had colour-keyed items as standard.

Rear view of the standard MR-S grade, this example finished in Blue Mica combined with red seats. The steel wheels were given a retro look, resembling those found on early Alfa Romeos.

Below left: Kumi Sato, the well-known lady racing driver and journalist, pictured with the MR-S that she campaigned in the 2001 JGTC series. The picture below shows the car in action. (Courtesy Kumi Sato, and Hidenobu Tanaka, Rosso/Neko Publishing)

Dealer's Option

"Fun Sports Package"
- エアロバンパー［交換式］
- サイドマッドガード
- リヤバンパースポイラー
- リヤスポイラー
- フォグランプ［エアロバンパー用］

"Elegant Sports Package"
- フロントスポイラー
- サイドマッドガード
- リヤバンパースポイラー
- クリアサイドターンランプ
- ストライプテープ［タイプ1、ロゴ］

"Trad Sports Package"
- ルームミラーカバー［アルミ］
- フロントピラーガーニッシュ［メッキ］
- リヤバンパーロア［メッキ］
- オーバーフェンダー
- サイドエアインテークガーニッシュ［メッキ］
- メッキドアミラー［ブルーミラー付］

ディタッチャブルトップ

"アルミアイテムPackage"　"ウッドアイテムPackage"　"カラーアイテムPackage"

● "Fun Sports Package" "Elegant Sports Package" "Trad Sports Package" はグレード名称ではありません。
● 販売店装着オプションには、車両・グレード・オプションによって装着できない場合があります。詳しい設定については、販売店におたずねください。
● 上記の各Package車に装着されている装備以外単独装着が可能です。詳しくはMR-S用品パンフレットをご覧ください。
● この他にも数多くの販売店装着オプションをご用意しております。詳しくは販売店におたずねください。
● エアロパーツを装着した場合、稀度など段差によっては路面などと干渉する場合があります。あらかじめご了承ください。

The various packages available in Japan, enabling the buyer to personalise their vehicle. Most of the components, plus a host of others, including such items as a racing-style fuel filler, were available separately. The chances of seeing two cars alike are very remote in the Land of the Rising Sun.

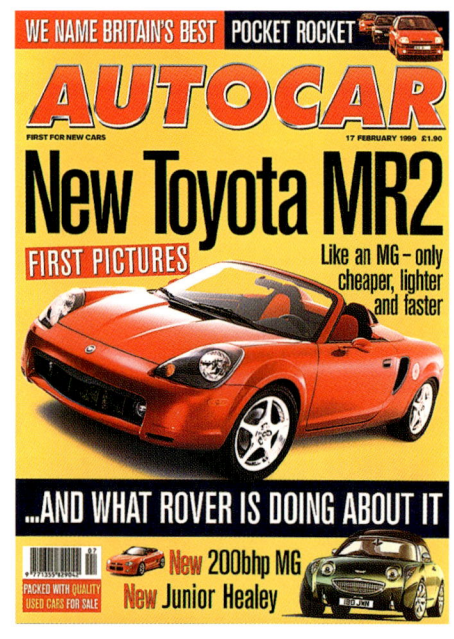

British buyers had a pretty good idea of what to expect from the new mid-engined Toyota. Apart from coverage after the 1997 Tokyo Show, an MR-S prototype appeared at the NEC in 1998 and, for those who missed the event, the Autocar *featured the 1999 Chicago Show model on the cover of its issue dated February 17th 1999. The latest MR2 was expected to reach Britain in spring 2000, priced at around £18,000.*

The MR2's return in America

Following the appearance of the 'MR-Spyder' concept at the Chicago Show in February, Toyota Motor Sales Inc. finally unveiled the MR2 Spyder at the South Florida International Motor Show on October 8th 1999. The MR2 had returned to America.

The model displayed at Chicago had fairings behind the seats, a racing-style fuel filler, sequential transmission and 16-inch wheels and tyres. These were not carried over to the production car, but otherwise it was a pretty good representation of what the public could buy at the end of the year.

Aimed at younger buyers, the MR2 Spyder was due to hit American shores in the spring. Toyota's Don Esmond noted: "The world fell in love with the sports cars of the 1950s, because they were light in weight, light on the road, and light on the wallet. The MR2 Spyder is true to these essential elements. A two-seat, mid-engine, soft-top roadster distilled to its most basic nature, it is simple and functional, and a blast to drive. Most important, it will be surprisingly affordable."

Toyota's Lexus marque was very innovative in the way it reached out to its target audience, and the advertising campaign introduced for the mid-engined model (along with the new Celica and ECHO) was equally

166

inspired, employing the Internet and TV commercials. Sales began in April 2000, with the US expected to take around 5000 MR2 Spyders each year.

Only one grade was available, priced at $23,098 (plus delivery) in basic form. Powered by the familiar 1.8-litre engine (developing 138bhp in American guise) linked to a five-speed manual gearbox, the MR2 Spyder was said to accelerate from 0-60 in a fraction under seven seconds before going on to a top speed approaching 130mph (208kph).

As with home market counterparts, power-assisted steering and ABS was standard, with the US model boasting alloy wheels, air conditioning, dual airbags, a leather-covered steering wheel and gearknob, aluminium pedals, power windows and door locks, a four-speaker radio/cassette/CD combination stereo, colour-keyed door handles and electrically-adjustable mirrors, door pockets, and a retractable wind deflector as part of

continued on page 170

Early publicity shots for the UK market showing front and rear with hood down, and the front with detachable hardtop. Lighting was similar to that in Japan, but the Toyota corporate logo appeared on the nose of European models (instead of a modern interpretation of the trademark MR2 bird), and tail badging was completely different: 'Toyota' appeared on the nearside; 'MR2' was low down in the centre, and 'Roadster' was added on production vehicles just above where home market cars had an 'MR-S' badge. Wheel centres were also different, although the number plates were mounted in the same spot for all markets.

167

As with previous generations, a lot of testing took place in the UK. Changes to the bodyshell and suspension recommended for the European market were duly adopted for all cars.

A press photograph of the UK-specification MR2 Roadster. The wheel and tyre combination was the same as that found on the Japanese S Edition, although the centre caps were of a different design.

British advertising for the MR2 Roadster from the summer of 2000. Toyota GB was hoping to sell 3500 units a year.

Rear three-quarter view of the 2000 model year car. On US cars, the tail featured a 'Toyota' badge on the left (like European models), but a unique 'MR2 Spyder' one on the opposite side. As in Japan, there were no identifying logos lower down on the back panel.

Front three-quarter view of the American-specification MR2 Spyder. Like European models, standard equipment included 185/55 VR15 tyres mounted on 6J five-spoke alloys up front, and 205/50 VR15s on 6.5J rims at the rear. Note the Toyota corporate badge on the nose, and the different side repeaters employed on US cars.

169

The dashboard and interior of the American car. US speedometers were marked up to 150mph, like UK models, while Japanese vehicles had 180kph items, and those bound for Continental Europe had 240kph items.

the package. The only options were dealer-installed accessories, such as an interior tonneau cover, a front mask and wheel locks.

It came in six coachwork colours, with three options for the interior. The body could be finished in Super White, Silver Streak Mica, Solar Yellow, Absolutely Red, Spectra Blue Mica or Black, while the seating could be specified in black, red or yellow.

What did the press think? Sam Mitani stated: "Toyota is definitely back on the sports car scene. The MR2 Spyder is sure to make foreheads sweat in Mazda's corporate boardrooms."

Writing for *Car & Driver*, Barry Winfield noted: "Although the MR2 measures a mere 153 inches long – 2.3 inches shorter than a Miata – its wheelbase stretches 96.5in, 7.3 inches longer than the little Mazda's. This reduces any short-coupled snappishness in the car's handling. Positioning the wheels right at the corners also provides more space for occupants and allows even large drivers to feel comfortably enclosed – unlike their experience in a Miata, where taller ones feel a part of the car's rollover apparatus.

"The footwells are not very roomy, particularly on the passenger side, where ducting impinges on foot space, but there's nonetheless room for six-foot-something drivers to nestle in, and visibility is quite good. Also, the manual soft-top (with glass backlight) turns out to be slightly hump-backed, and it provides surprisingly good headroom.

"Despite its low weight, the Spyder's structure turns out to be extremely stiff and is resistant to the shivers and quakes that afflict many other convertibles."

So how did the new Toyota compare with the Mazda MX-5? *Automobile* magazine plumped for the Hiroshima machine, as did *Car & Driver* (by one point out of 100) in its comparison test, but *Road & Track* thought differently, giving the MR2 Spyder 91.9 points to 87.1. Dennis Simanaitis concluded: "What a quandary! Both of these cars are so much fun. However, I'm opting for the MR2 keys and here's why: the car's handling dynamics are outstanding, yet, like the Miata's, they're utterly approachable in ordinary driving. Its list of standard equipment, of things that I'd want, give it an inherent 10% advantage in price. True, its styling is a bit derivative, but I actually prefer the purity of line of the *original* Miata anyway. The MR2 interior offers a bit more room for two people – and I've got just the duffel bag for our occasional travel."

MR-S Specials

As well as a wealth of tuning firms offering performance parts, including companies like TRD and TOM's, at the

The US market's MR2 Spyder for 2000, seen here finished in Liquid Silver Metallic with red seats. Given the choice, this would be the combination the author would choose.

Right: The glass rear screen, with its integrated heater element, is a great help in bad weather, and, of course, it lasts better, too. The old-style plastic windows in convertible tops often crack and go cloudy with time.

Left: Following its road test of the new Toyota, Car & Driver testers praised the car's "stellar racetrack handling, good mid-range grunt and supportive seats." They called it "maybe the most responsive-handling car made today," but observed there was "barely room for you, a companion and a Snickers bar."

2000 Tokyo Auto Salon, Modellista (a Toyota subsidiary) introduced the limited edition Caserta. Based on the MR-S, this car featured highly-modified bodywork and lighting, a unique interior (in luxury or standard guise), and special lightweight, six-spoke alloy wheels. Finished in Super Red V only, just 150 were built, with prices starting at 3,500,000 yen.

At the following year's Auto Salon, there were more unusual machines based on the MR-S, including the VM180 Zagato, a dramatic piece of automotive sculpture. Carrying the full approval of Andrea Zagato of the world-famous styling house, prices started at 3,980,000 yen. But admirers had to hurry – only 100 units were made available, finished in either Super Red V or Silver Metallic. It wasn't cheap, but did represent a rare chance to own a piece of motoring history from new.

171

Left: American advertising from the summer of 2000. The price shown includes destination charges.

Right: Cover from the TRD tuning brochure for the MR-S. TRD offered uprated suspension components, front and rear tower bars, underbody braces, lightweight 16-inch alloy wheels, a sports exhaust system, high-performance brake pads, filters, spark plugs and oils.

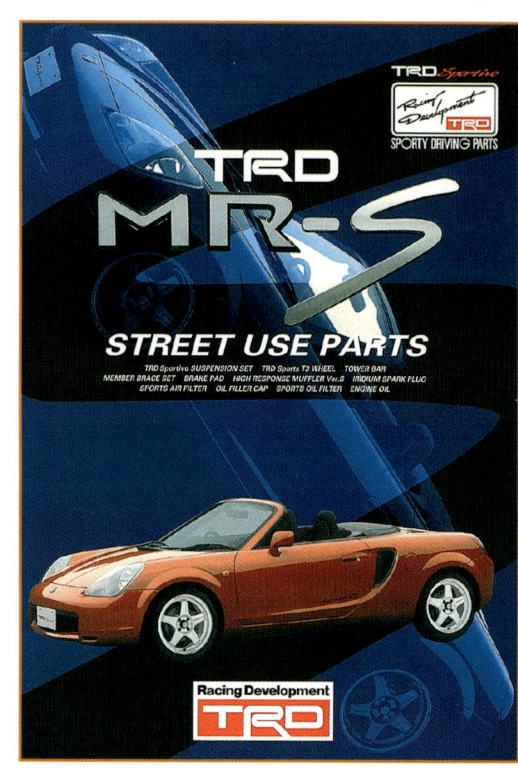

Below: The MR-S-based VM180 Zagato, another highly-interesting vehicle introduced by the Modellista concern. Although only 100 were produced, it featured unique 16-inch, five-spoke alloys, and the cockpit could be specified with a fairly standard level of trim or luxury interior of two-tone leather upholstery. The 5SMT option was added later on.

The Modellista Caserta at the 2000 Tokyo Auto Salon. Only 150 were built.

Another interesting exhibit at the 2001 Tokyo Auto Salon was the TOM's W123. Founded in 1974 by the well-known Toyota contract driver, Nobuhide Tachi, TOM's came to be recognised worldwide through its involvement in Group C racing. TOM's also built the T020 – a fast road or track car based on the SW20 MR2.

A final shot from the 2001 Tokyo Auto Salon, this one showing the DAMD Street Slider MR-S finished in Gulf Oil colours. Mention should also be made of the Monocraft MR-S GT300, the SARD MR-S, the VeilSide conversion and the turbocharged car built by Blitz.

173

Instrument cluster of an SMT-equipped model. Note the gear indicator in the tachometer.

The gearlever for the new sequential transmission. Reverse and neutral were on the left-hand side of the gate, with '+' and '-' on the right. In addition, the driver could execute upshifts via buttons on the back of the steering wheel, and downshifts with buttons on the front of the wheel.

Japanese update

As you will recall, the MR-S prototype was fitted with a five-speed sequential gearbox. At last, from August 2000, it became available on production models, listed for all grades except the basic B Edition, and costing only 75,000 yen extra (prices were otherwise the same as at the car's announcement).

This was the first time a sequential gearbox had been offered on a Toyota road car; indeed, it was a first for Japan, too. Despite its undoubted benefits, this transmission continued to be rare on production models the world over at this time, and was usually restricted to racing machinery.

The SMT gearbox was linked to a new engine management system that controlled throttle settings, meaning that the driver could change gears without having to lift off the accelerator. In addition, if the engine speed dropped below a certain level, first was automatically selected to ensure proper take-off. With a chrome-plated shiftlever and gate, augmented by steering wheel controls, internal and overall gearing was exactly the same as that specified on the manual 'box; a gear indicator was incorporated in the tachometer to keep the driver informed.

At the same time as the new transmission was introduced, a new grade – known as the V Edition – was announced, priced at 2,100,000 yen in

Another view of the V Edition, this time with the hood up.

MR-S "V EDITION"

この"V EDITION"専用に用意された
タンカラー（黄褐色）のソフトトップ。
質感の高い本革のシート&ドアトリム。
そして足元には光沢感のあるアルミホール。
躍動感あふれるスタイリングに、
優雅さや気品をも漂わせている。
ラグジュアリーを身にまとったオープンスポーツ。
MR-Sのもうひとつの表情が、ここにある。

主な標準装備

・フロント15×6JJ、リヤ15×6½JJアルミホイール（光沢）
・タンカラーソフトトップ
・本革シート&ドアトリム表皮
・SUSスカッフプレート
・メッキリング付ツイーター　　　など

The Japanese market's V Edition. The MR2 signature trademark can be seen clearly on the nose of this car, along with the chrome wheels, and tan hood and interior.

manual guise, or 2,175,000 yen with the sequential gearbox. The V Edition was basically the same as the S Edition, except for a polished chrome finish on the alloy wheels, a tan-coloured soft-top (all other cars came with a black hood), leather seats and door trim, special treadplates and four speakers with chrome finishing rings on the door-mounted tweeters.

Whilst standard colours remained the same for the S Edition, MR-S and B Edition, the new V Edition came only in Super White II, Silver Metallic, Black, Super Red V, Blue Mica or a

The VM180 TRD, based on the MR-S S Edition, of which just 100 were built. Available in manual or 5SMT guise, sales started at the end of August 2000.

An MR-S S Edition photographed by the author at Toyota's Mega Web facility in Tokyo, April 2001. Even though the car has been on the market for some time, it still generates a lot of interest. Basic Japanese specifications and RRPs remained unchanged going into the 2002 season, so the seven car line-up ranged in price from 1,680,000 to 2,175,000 yen.

unique Dark Green Mica. In all cases, tan leather trim was the only option; a perfect match for the convertible's hood, and also unique to the new model.

News from Australia

With sales starting in October 2000, Australian specifications were roughly equivalent to those of the UK, although the MR2 Spyder appellation was used. Antipodeans were only able to buy the 2001 car with a sequential gearbox, priced at $44,990, and restricted to 600 units (against 5000 for the US) in the first year. Other than a $1200 price hike, there was no change for the 2002 season.

In December 2000, *Wheels* magazine compared the latest Toyota

The car as it was launched in Australia.

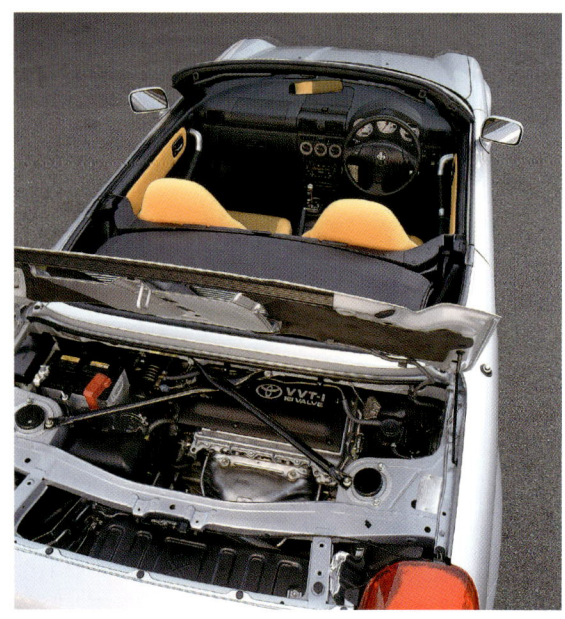

A couple of shots showing the MR2 Roadster fitted with the optional Body Kit offered in the UK during summer 2001. Europe has seen its share of stunning modifications. For example, those who went to the Essen Show at the end of 2001 will have seen a three-litre V6 version of the popular little roadster. There was even talk of the concept vehicle going into limited production.

with the recently-uprated Mazda MX-5. Peter McKay concluded: "The MR2 Spyder is better than the MX-5 in some ways, but lacks the lineage – and the right gearbox – to make it a winner here. Then again, I'm not a PlayStation regular or Gen Xer …"

Europe in 2001

The MR2 Roadster entered the 2001 model year slightly cheaper than before, listed at £17,995. Pricing has always been a problem for foreign markets due to the fluctuation in exchange rates, of course. For instance, in the autumn of 1998, £1 was the equivalent to 240 yen; it then settled back down to around 200 yen to the pound before dropping to 175 just one year later. In early 2001, the rate was fairly stable at 180 yen, but that represents a massive difference compared with the earliest figure quoted here.

Anyway, the biggest change for 2001 was the introduction of the MR2 Roadster SMT. Priced at £19,495, the sequential transmission model came with leather upholstery as standard in the UK. Interestingly, the official 0-60 time was 9.2 seconds, compared with eight seconds dead for the conventional five-speed car.

Car magazine tried a sequential model in its February 2001 issue, and found that "Toyota's decision to put a semi-automatic transmission in the MR2 has one factor in its favour. It works. Brilliantly."

In August 2001, Toyota GB announced the availability of a colour-coded body kit for all MR2 models. Incorporating a front airdam extension, side skirts and pieces to lower the appearance of the car's tail, the £750 Body Kit was basically equivalent to the home market's 'Elegant Sports Package,' although the panels themselves were slightly different.

There was little change for the 2002 season, except for another round of pricing revisions. The manual car now sold for £17,130, while the version with a sequential gearbox was £1500 more – these equated to some serious price cuts, making the MR2 even better value for money.

Options included a package combining a hardtop and air conditioning (priced at £2400), air conditioning on its own, leather trim (standard on the semi-automatic model), metallic paint, a CD autochanger, mudflaps, a rear spoiler, or the full body kit introduced a couple of months earlier.

Interestingly, the long-running *Autocar* weekly pitched the new MG TF against the MR2 and Mazda MX-5 in February 2002, and its writer, Steve Sutcliffe, found the MG to be the best of the bunch in his eyes. Although the Toyota possessed "sweet handling" and agility, he stated that it lacked the focus of something like a Lotus Elise, and definitely lagged behind the MG in the practicality stakes. The Vauxhall VX220 was another new and worthy rival, in a marketplace suddenly flooded with open cars.

But Toyota could at least take pride in the result of a similar shoot-out arranged by *Top Gear* ("the Toyota MR2 is just too much fun not to come out on top"), and another by *Evo* magazine that brought together the MR2, MG TF and Peugeot 206CC. In this test, the mid-engined car from Japan refused to budge. The testers noted: "The more we drive the Toyota, the more we admire

Publicity shot of a lhd car for the mainland European market, along with a dash of a similar car, this one equipped with the semi-automatic gearbox. Note the 240kph speedo.

The MR2 Spyder pages from the American 2001 model year Toyota range catalogue.

178

American advertising from spring 2001 (left), and from the early part of the 2002 model year.

it. It is an exceptionally sensitive and rewarding device – a car that teaches you more about driving than anything else for the money."

The US 2001 & 2002 model years

In the February 2001 issue of *Motor Trend*, the mid-engined Toyota came up against its old foe again, the Mazda Miata (MX-5); this time with the latter sporting its recently revamped engine. Matt Stone concluded: "The Miata and MR2 Spyder are the types of cars real enthusiasts spend their weekends driving around in – just because. The driving sophisticate will get more out of the MR2 Spyder, but the Miata wins in the giggle department." An honourable draw, perhaps?

From the early part of 2001, American models could also be specified with the five-speed sequential gearbox. Other features were exactly the same as at the time of the car's introduction, with the exception of a new coachwork colour – Electric Green Mica – being added to the list. Even the $23,098 price tag was carried over.

For 2002, the cost of MR2 motoring increased slightly – the manual car costing $24,220, with the sequential gearbox model (complete with cruise control on US-spec cars) listed at $25,000. However, the most important specifications remained unchanged from the previous season.

The seven coachwork colours were also carried over, although the yellow, blue and red shades could be specified with a black interior only, whilst the green came with tan leather trim and a matching hood. The white, black and silver hues were available with black or red cloth seats, or with the optional Leather Package (including a tan interior and tan hood).

In addition to the aforementioned Leather Package, the owner could opt for a number of extras, such as a remote keyless entry system, floormats, a front mask, wheel locks, number plate frames and carbonfibre dash trim.

A minor change

Following the introduction of the sequential gearbox in August 2000, other than new pistons, fresh oil and water pumps, and a revised harmonic balancer for the engine, there were no real changes in Japan until the 2003 season. This is when, in August 2002, Toyota announced a minor change (MC) for the MR2, giving it a fresher appearance and friendlier handling.

The biggest change was the option of six-speed transmissions, both for the manual and semi-automatic versions of the car. The manual shift layout was that of a 'double-H' with reverse up and to the left, and ratios were listed at 3.166, 1.904, 1.392, 1.031, 0.815 and 0.725; a 4.31:1 final-drive was specified. As it happens, the driver's view of the SMT transmission was the same as before (tuning of the ECU made

179

it respond quicker and allow automatic downchanges at low speeds, though, to ensure decent progress when rolling up to traffic lights, and so on), and the ratios were the same as those of the 6MT gearbox. This modification, with overdriven gearing on the top two ratios, whilst adding a small amount of weight, helped improve fuel consumption, and reduced noise, at cruising speeds.

In response to calls to reduce the car's natural oversteer tendency, which was frankly never a problem for those with a modicum of driving feel anyway, the rear wheel and tyre combination was changed to 215/45 W16s on a 7J rim. All home market cars now had alloy wheels to save weight, although the basic wheel design was carried over from earlier the models, and those on the V Edition continued to sport a polished finish. Combined with a few tweaks to the steering, spring and damper rates, some of the subtle control quality was lost, but the limit could be explored a lot more easily, that's for sure; a helical LSD was listed as a 30,000 yen option. Despite these changes, and the addition of new underbody bracing pieces, at the front and rear, to tighten things up, the new models were only 10kg (22b) heavier than the original vehicles introduced in 1999.

In keeping with a minor change scenario, there were subtle revisions to the bodywork and interior, too. As well as the adoption of projector-style headlights across the board, the front bumper assembly was changed to include front foglights as a standard fitting on all cars, the side air intakes were made more attractive, and the combination lights and bumper blade were changed at the rear, with the latter gaining a new cut-out area surrounding the number plate (incidentally, only the S Edition and V Edition came with chrome exhaust trim as standard).

Inside, the seat design was slightly different, with a vent added in the head restraint area, a new stereo was introduced, the optional navi system was upgraded (being nicely integrated into the top roll cubby space), and there were revised markings on some of the gauges and HVAC controls.

Japan had the same basic line-up as before, with the manual-only B Edition costing 1,780,000 yen (up a fraction), and the strict MR-S, S Edition and V Edition completing the range, all three coming with a manual or SMT transmission option. Green Mica Metallic had been dropped from the colour palette back in August 2001, although Grey Mica Metallic and Light Blue Mica were added at this time as late replacements, while the 2,180,000 yen (or 2,260,000 yen, with a semi-automatic gearbox) V Edition continued to boast its unique dark green paint option. Black fabric seats were still the

This page and opposite: Cover and selected pages from the Netz catalogue from August 2002. The Vista one had a different cover, but the contents were exactly the same.

norm, although the optional colours were now red or grey, rather than red or yellow. Again, the V Edition sported tan leather seats and door inserts. As for packages, the Fun Sports Package was renamed the Aero Sports Package, and the Elegant Sports Package and Trad Sports Package were adjusted to allow for the new bumper arrangements.

181

The WedsSport MR-S pictured at the 2002 Tokyo Auto Salon, in the livery it campaigned the 2001 and 2002 JGTC seasons in.

American advertising for the 2003 model year MR2.

In the background, whilst riding high in the US CART Indycar series, Toyota lived up to its promise of fielding an F1 team, with the Cologne-based team making its debut at the 2002 Australian Grand Prix. The Formula One arena was not kind to Toyota, however, and the company ended its campaign at the end of 2009. It was sad that Toyota had left rallying and sports car racing behind to support this programme, which was somewhat at odds with the 'green' image presented by cars like the Prius anyway. And it's not like the Japanese giant needed the publicity either! Like many moths drawn to the bright lights beforehand, wings got burnt for very little benefit – beyond filling the coffers of those behind the series ...

Closer to home, no less than five MR-S models had been running in the 2001 JGTC series, but they were unable to touch the mighty Porsche GT3R, and the season was rather disappointing until the last round, when the Sigma car restored Toyota pride. There were five cars in the 2002 edition, too, but it was much the same story, with Porsche domination, although the ARTA MR-S piloted by Nitta and Takagi managed to finish the season in third, the pair claiming the drivers' title along the way. Five cars were present again in 2003, but, despite a few strong performances, there was no real joy for the Toyota guys.

The US market

The North American market vehicles inherited the new headlights and foglight arrangement introduced in Japan, along with the styling changes, but only some of the mechanical ones. Other items added for the 2003 US season included a keyless remote control locking system, and an automatic aerial to go with the three-in-one stereo unit.

182

The US-spec MR2 for the 2003 season.

183

Exterior and interior shots of the face-lifted MR2 for the UK market. Available from November 2002, the manual car was priced at £16,995, with the semi-automatic model commanding £18,495.

In addition to the standard lighting differences (such as the requirement for daytime running lights), there were a few other things that set the US cars apart from their home market cousins, such as the paint and trim options, the odd decision to stick with a five-speed manual transmission (still with first through fourth in a conventional 'H' pattern, fifth up and to the right, and reverse below that), the use of a full-size spare wheel (new for 2003), and cruise control for the newly-introduced six-speed semi-automatic machines.

On the colour front, Paradise Blue Metallic augmented the existing seven paint hues, the red cloth seat option was replaced by a grey one, and the tan Leather Package was joined by a black version at this time (featuring black leather trim and a black hood); otherwise, the option list remained unchanged.

Rhd export markets
As per the domestic machines, the UK-spec cars received a number of cosmetic and mechanical changes for the 2003 model year, following Japan's lead in most respects, except for the standard fitment of a limited-slip differential. As such, in addition to the updated bodywork, a six-speed manual and six-speed SMT transmission were listed; traction and stability control systems were added on the semi-automatic grade, although most British buyers plumped for the £16,995 driver-focused manual model anyway.

Writing for *Evo*, Richard Meaden noted: "Though not as ultra-pointy as the original, the revised MR2's front-end is addicted to apexes, clinging resolutely to your chosen line without a hint of

Striking publicity shot showing a 2003 MR2 for mainland Europe.

The body kit launched in the UK on 1 July 2003.

The CS&S concept car that first appeared at the 2003 Frankfurt Show, employing a hybrid 4WD setup that used electric motors for powering the front wheels, and another set of electric motors, combined with a small mid-mounted 1.5-litre petrol engine, for driving the rear wheels.

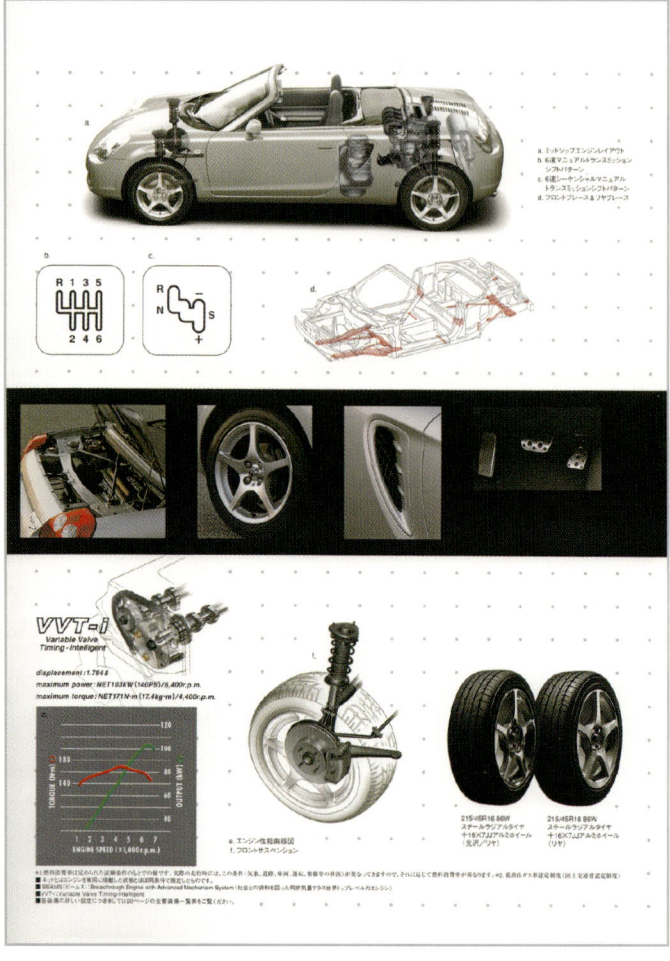

understeer. There's plenty of feel, too, and the rack is perfectly judged, with half a turn of lock sufficient for all but the tightest corners.

"The tail is better controlled than the original car, feeling less prone to roll-induced oversteer. In fact, it generates terrific grip and traction, only beginning to slide when deliberately provoked.

"On balance, the added stability, predictability and control at higher speeds is worth the loss of low-speed comfort and refinement, but city dwellers won't find the MR2 quite as pliant as before."

A new body kit became available during the summer of 2003, priced at £850 including colour matching. The three-piece kit consisted of front spoiler extensions, side skirts, and a different rear valance, but it was a subtle kit that actually helped enhance the car's looks – so many kits, sadly, manage to do the opposite by going OTT.

Cover and a couple of significant pages from the MR-S catalogue released after the 2004 minor change. Other than these, most of the catalogue was the same as the one before.

186

Right: One of the last MR2s for the US market: this one finished in Phantom Grey with a red hood and interior trim package.

Below right: The MR2 Roadster Red Collection model for the UK market.

In the southern hemisphere, Australian buyers were offered the six-speed, semi-automatic model from October 2002, priced at $48,990. As before, the Aussies had to do without a manual gearbox option.

Another change
In February 2004, a new, much heavier underbody brace was added up front, along with several gussets around the B-post area, and a couple of strengthening pieces where the rear bumper blade attached to the main frame. These modifications added 30kg (66lb) to the car's kerb weight and around 100,000 yen to the RRP, but were deemed necessary to keep up with regulations. The B Edition disappeared from price lists at the same time, leaving only the strict MR-S, the S Edition, and V Edition in the Japanese catalogue.

On the subject of catalogues, in May that year, the Vista sales network merged with the Netz one, so only one brochure was produced from this point.

2004 wasn't kind to the Toyota MR-S drivers in the JGTC, but when the championship changed its title to the Super GT Series the following year, things improved no end. The two MR-S teams claimed one GT300 Class victory apiece, with Kota Sasaki and Tetsuya Yamano picking up enough points along the way to take the GT300 title at the end of the season, both for themselves and Team Reckless.

Looking abroad, there was no change in the States for 2004, other than availability of a limited-slip differential. The 5MT car was priced at $24,645 (a fraction more than a Mazda Miata, but significantly less than a Honda S2000), with the six-speed sequential gearbox adding $1000 to the invoice.

However, July 2004 saw the announcement that MR2 (and Celica) sales would end in the USA at the close of the 2005 season. With withdrawal of the Celica and MR2 from the US market, American buyers would have to wait several years, until the launch of the new 86, before the opportunity to buy a lightweight, fun-to-drive Toyota arose again.

As it happens, US cars for 2005 (with a base price of $25,145) came with a new six-disc CD/radio unit to replace the old, three-in-one stereo, and a new Red Leather Trim Package, which featured a red leather interior combined with a red hood (both the tan and black leather packages continued alongside this new one). Tasteful Phantom Grey Pearl paintwork was added at this time for those who chose the red trim package: otherwise, the colour palette was carried over for this run-out year.

A wide range of accessories allowed owners to personalise their vehicle, though, with registration number

187

The UK's 2005 model year MR2 was offered with the £900 Chrome Collection, which brought together three separate accessories in one package. It included a chrome styling bar across the back of the cockpit, a bright fuel filler cap surround and twin exhaust finishers.

Opposite page: The colour variations available for the V Edition 'Final Version.' A dedicated accessory catalogue was also produced for the model (bottom left), along with a six-page brochure outlining the history of the MR2 (bottom right).

frames in different colours still listed alongside a front mask, various sporty gearknobs, a carbonfibre-style dash appliqué, and colour co-ordinated floormats.

In the meantime, in the UK, April 2004 saw the launch of the so-called MR2 Roadster Red Collection model, which came with Sable (dark grey) paintwork, a red hood, a red leather interior, and special badging. Priced at £17,995, it was sold in manual guise only.

There was also a lot of development work going into a retrofit turbocharger package for the MR2. This was being undertaken by TTE (under the auspices of Toyota Motorsport), with a Garrett blower and an air-to-air intercooler boosting maximum power up to 195bhp, and peak torque up to 210lbft. Lag was negligible, although the extra horses meant that some additional bracing was required to strengthen the bodyshell. The turbocharged car put in a low-key appearance at the 2005 Tokyo Auto Salon, but sales were basically restricted to Europe, the conversions being done by a handful of authorised outlets. In the UK, for instance, the turbo cost around £4000, while a stainless free-flow exhaust added another £800. Few would have stopped there, of course, with tuned suspensions and larger wheel and tyre packages being commonplace amongst those willing to spend four or five grand on car that only cost 17K in the first place!

In Australia, the base car continued unchanged except for a $740 price hike, although there was a limited edition TTR (TTR standing for Toyota Team Racing) model launched in 2004, and that retained the $48,990 sticker price, despite having extra equipment, including air conditioning, leather seats and TTR badges.

For 2005, the Aussies were able to secure a semi-automatic car (still no manual models) for $47,710, with air conditioning adding $2530 to the invoice, and leather trim a further $940. A full range of eight coachwork colours was listed, but the mid-engined machine fell silently by the wayside in March 2006, bringing the MR2 series run to an end Down Under.

Christmas present

In December 2005, all cars gained an indicator on the foglight switch to warn when they were on, and, while the unit looks the same at first glance, the positions of the taillight and brake light sections were swapped over inside the rear combination lamp. There were no other changes, and even the domestic colour schemes (for both exterior and interior) were carried over from the 2003 season.

Not long after, following the retirement of Hiroshi Okuda, Fujio Cho became the Chairman of Toyota in mid-2006; Cho's place as President was duly taken by Katsuaki Watanabe. By this time, Toyota was still fielding an F1 team, but the change from CART to IRL Indycar racing didn't work out, and the company switched its attention to NASCAR racing instead.

An MR-S taking part in the 2008 Super GT Series. (Courtesy Wikimedia Commons/Morio)

188

Color Variation

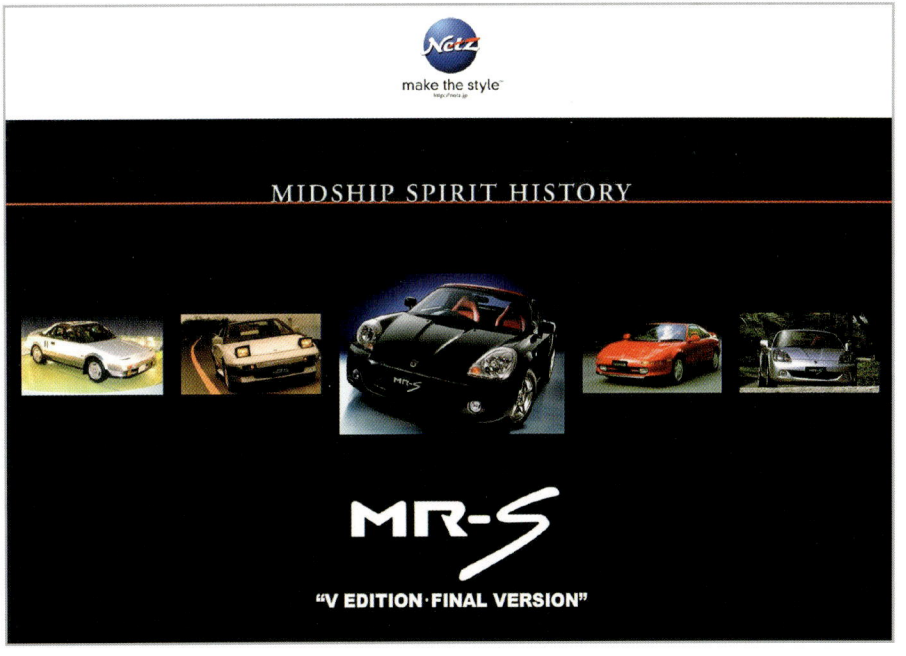

MIDSHIP SPIRIT HISTORY

MR-S
"V EDITION·FINAL VERSION"

The MR2 Roadster TF300, on sale in the UK from the summer of 2006, with an on-the-road price of £18,015. The number on the seatback is the production run number, which ran from 001 to 300.

On the domestic front, Toyota was represented by two MR-S runners in the 2006 Super GT Series (what used to be the JGTC), but they had to settle for a lowly fifth and 15th at the end of the season. There was only one team for 2007, although it ran two cars under the 'apr' banner. The one machine claimed two Class victories, handing Kazuya Oshima and Hiroaki Ishiura the drivers' crown, despite a draw on points with another pairing. 2008 was nothing to write home about, though, and that signalled the end of the line for the mid-engined car.

In the meantime, in November 2006, Toyota announced its 1000-off MR-S 'Final Version' model, based on the V Edition. Priced at 2,320,000 yen in manual guise, or 2,400,000 yen with the sequential gearbox, it was available in silver, grey, red or black, and came with a red (or black) hood instead of a tan one, silver inserts in the side intakes and rear valance, red or black leather trim, silver dash and gear selector accent pieces, and special badges.

The UK had its own final version of the MR2, incidentally, known as the TF300. Priced at £18,015 and limited to just 300 vehicles, the TF300 featured a special leather and Alcantara trim package, and a TTE sports exhaust system. For the record, silver, black and grey cars came with a red leather interior, while red and blue machines had a grey interior. By July 2007, though, the mid-engined Toyota had passed into the history books ...

TOYOTA MR2
Coupés & Spyders
1984-2007

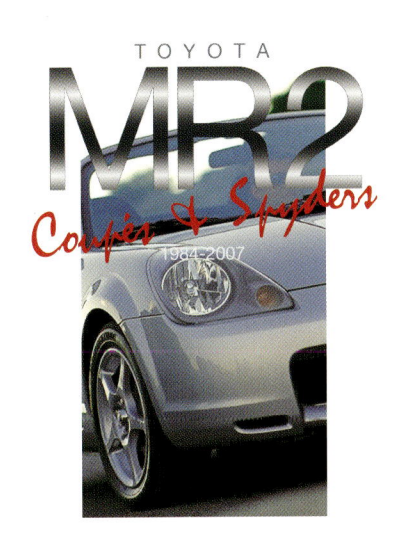

APPENDIX I
SPECIFICATIONS

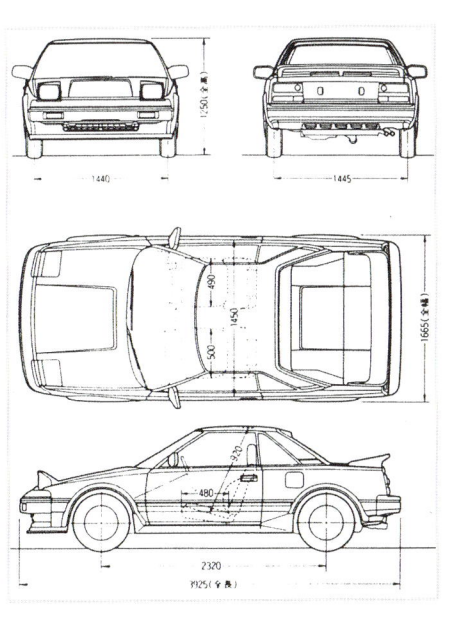

This appendix outlines the basic specifications for each of the three generations of Toyota mid-engined sports cars (the weight entry reflects the lightest version available). The power unit section refers to mainstream models for the American, Japanese and European markets, with the years referring to model years (see text for some of the odd designations, like the US 1993 range, introduced in early 1992). Important production changes are included in the notes for each engine.

First Generation models
Dimensions:
Length 3925mm (154.5in)
Wheelbase 2320mm (91.3in)
Width 1665mm (65.5in)
Height................. 1250mm (49.2in)
Front track 1440mm (56.7in)
Rear track........... 1440mm (56.7in)
Ground clearance 140mm (5.5in)
Weight 920kg (2024lb)
Chassis code........ AW10

Engine specifications:

4A-GELU
Main market .... Japan
Years 1984-1989
Type .... Four-cylinder, dohc, 16v
Bore & stroke ...... 81 x 77mm
Capacity 1587cc
Comp ratio........... 9.4:1
Max power .... 130bhp at 6600rpm
Max torque .... 110lbft at 5200rpm
Fuel delivery .... Fuel-injection
Transmission .... 5MT or 4ECT
Notes: For 1988, engine uprated to 4A-GELU (4A-II) specification to comply with emissions regulations. Power reduced to 120bhp at 6600rpm, and torque to 105lbft at 5200rpm.

3A-LU (3A-II)
Main market .... Japan
Years 1984-1989
Type .... Four-cylinder, sohc, 8v
Bore & stroke ...... 77.5 x 77mm
Capacity 1452cc
Comp ratio........... 9.3:1
Max power .... 83bhp at 5600rpm
Max torque .... 87lbft at 3600rpm
Fuel delivery .... Carburettor
Transmission .... 5MT or 4AT

4A-GE
Main market .... America
Years 1985-1989
Type .... Four-cylinder, dohc, 16v
Bore & stroke ...... 81 x 77mm
Capacity 1587cc
Comp ratio........... 9.4:1
Max power .... 112bhp at 6600rpm
Max torque .... 97lbft at 4800rpm
Fuel delivery .... Fuel-injection
Transmission .... 5MT or 4ECT
Notes: Automatic available from 1986. Subtle modifications for 1988 saw power rise to 115bhp at 6600rpm, and torque increase to 100lbft at 4800rpm.

4A-GE
Main market .... Europe
Years 1985-1989
Type .... Four-cylinder, dohc, 16v
Bore & stroke ...... 81 x 77mm
Capacity 1587cc
Comp ratio........... 10.0:1
Max power .... 122bhp at 6600rpm
Max torque .... 105lbft at 5000rpm
Fuel delivery .... Fuel-injection
Transmission 5MT
Notes: Subtle modifications for 1988 saw power rise to 123bhp at 6600rpm, and torque increase to 107lbft at 5000rpm.

191

The 4A-GE engine in cutaway form.

The supercharged 4A-GZE power unit.

The 4A-GE power unit.

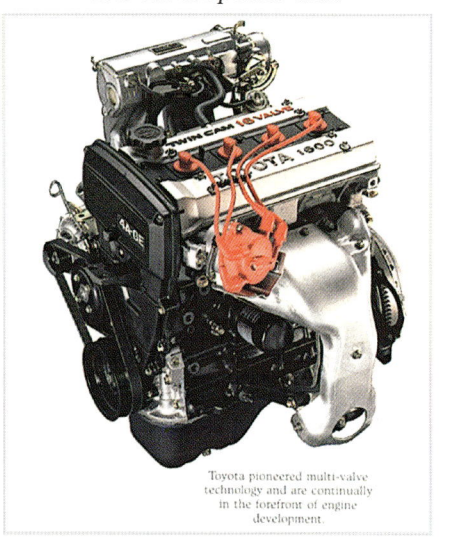

Toyota pioneered multi-valve technology and are continually in the forefront of engine development.

4A-GZE

Main market .... Japan
Years 1987-1989
Type .... Four-cylinder, dohc, 16v
Bore & stroke ...... 81 x 77mm
Capacity 1587cc
Comp ratio 8.0:1
Max power .... 145bhp at 6400rpm
Max torque .... 137lbft at 4400rpm
Fuel delivery .... Fuel-injection with supercharger
Transmission ...... 5MT or 4ECT

4A-GZE

Main market .... America
Years 1988-1989
Type .... Four-cylinder, dohc, 16v
Bore & stroke ...... 81 x 77mm
Capacity 1587cc
Comp ratio 8.0:1
Max power .... 145bhp at 6400rpm
Max torque .... 140lbft at 4000rpm
Fuel delivery .... Fuel-injection with supercharger
Transmission ...... 5MT or 4ECT

The 3S-GE power unit.

The turbocharged 3S-GTE power unit.

Second Generation models

Dimensions:

Length	4170mm (164.2in)
Wheelbase	2400mm (94.5in)
Width	1695mm (66.7in)
Height	1240mm (48.8in)
Front track	1470mm (57.9in)
Rear track	1450mm (57.1in)
Ground clearance	135mm (5.3in)
Weight	1160kg (2552lb)
Chassis code	SW20

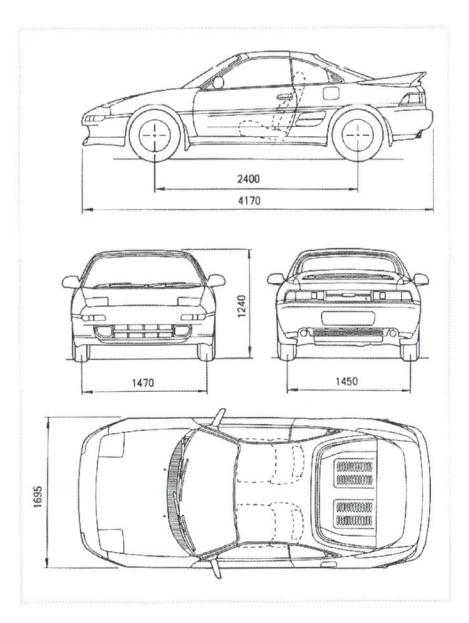

Engine specifications:

3S-GE

Main market	Japan
Years	1990-1999
Type	Four-cylinder, dohc, 16v
Bore & stroke	86 x 86mm
Capacity	1998cc
Comp ratio	10.1:1
Max power	165bhp at 6800rpm
Max torque	141lbft at 4800rpm
Fuel delivery	Fuel-injection
Transmission	5MT or 4ECT

Notes: Power increased to 180bhp at 7000rpm for 1994 model year (or 170bhp at 6600rpm for automatic versions) after adding ACIS and change in Comp ratio to 10.3:1. For 1998, the VVT-i system was adopted, along with an 11.0:1 c/r, boosting power to 200bhp at 7000rpm, with maximum torque output going up to 152lbft at 6000rpm.

193

3S-GTE
Main market .... Japan
Years 1990-1999
Type .... Four-cylinder, dohc, 16v
Bore & stroke ...... 86 x 86mm
Capacity 1998cc
Comp ratio........... 8.8:1
Max power .... 225bhp at 6000rpm
Max torque .... 224lbft at 3200rpm
Fuel delivery .... Fuel-injection with turbocharger
Transmission 5MT

Notes: Power increased to 245bhp at 6000rpm for 1994 model year, despite a drop in Comp ratio to 8.5:1. torque output unchanged, but now developed at 4000rpm.

The 3S-GE engine in cutaway form.

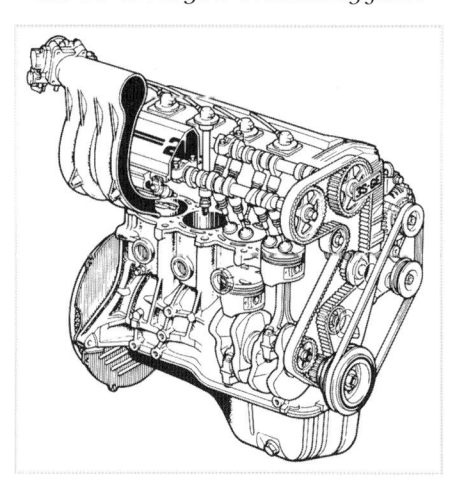

3S-FE
Main market .... Europe
Years 1990-1992
Type .... Four-cylinder, dohc, 16v
Bore & stroke ...... 86 x 86mm
Capacity 1998cc
Comp ratio........... 9.8:1
Max power .... 119bhp at 5600rpm
Max torque .... 130lbft at 4400rpm
Fuel delivery .... Fuel-injection
Transmission .... 5MT or 4ECT

Notes: For UK only. Automatic not available for 1992.

3S-GE
Main market .... Europe
Years 1990-1999
Type .... Four-cylinder, dohc, 16v
Bore & stroke ...... 86 x 86mm
Capacity 1998cc
Comp ratio........... 10.0:1
Max power .... 158bhp at 6600rpm
Max torque .... 140lbft at 4800rpm
Fuel delivery .... Fuel-injection
Transmission 5MT

Notes: Catalytic converter reduced power slightly for 1992 (154bhp and 137lbft at same engine speeds). Increase in Comp ratio, to 10.3:1, and addition of ACIS saw output rise to 173bhp at 7000rpm in 1994, although from late-1996, power reduced again to 168bhp at 7000rpm. Throughout these changes, the maximum torque figure remained the same.

5S-FE
Main market .... America
Years 1991-1995
Type .... Four-cylinder, dohc, 16v
Bore & stroke ...... 87 x 91mm
Capacity 2164cc
Comp ratio........... 9.5:1
Max power .... 130bhp at 5400rpm
Max torque .... 140lbft at 4400rpm
Fuel delivery .... Fuel-injection
Transmission .... 5MT or 4ECT

Notes: Changes in early 1992 for the 1993 model year saw power up to 135bhp for most cars (except those for California, which remained at 130bhp), although all American 2.2-litre engines gained 145lbft of torque (at 4400rpm) at this time.

3S-GTE
Main market .... America
Years 1991-1995
Type .... Four-cylinder, dohc, 16v
Bore & stroke ...... 86 x 86mm
Capacity 1998cc
Comp ratio........... 8.8:1
Max power .... 200bhp at 6000rpm
Max torque .... 200lbft at 3200rpm
Fuel delivery .... Fuel-injection with turbocharger
Transmission 5MT

Notes: This unit not available with the California emissions package for the 1995 model year.

The 1ZZ-FE power unit.

Third Generation models
Dimensions:
Length 3885mm (153.0in)
Wheelbase 2450mm (96.5in)
Width 1695mm (66.7in)
Height 1235mm (48.6in)
Front track 1475mm (58.1in)
Rear track 1460mm (57.5in)
Ground clearance 135mm (5.3in)
Weight 960kg (2112lb)
Chassis code ZZW30

Engine specifications:

1ZZ-FE
Main market .... Japan
Years 2000-2007
Type .... Four-cylinder,
                          dohc, 16v
Bore & stroke ...... 79 x 91.5mm
Capacity 1794cc
Comp ratio 10.0:1
Max power .... 140bhp at 6400rpm
Max torque .... 126lbft at 4400rpm
Fuel delivery .... Fuel-injection
Transmission ...... 5MT or 5SMT
Notes: Sequential gearbox available for 2001.

1ZZ-FE
Main market .... America
Years 2000-2005
Type .... Four-cylinder,
                          dohc, 16v
Bore & stroke ...... 79 x 91.5mm
Capacity 1794cc
Comp ratio 10.0:1
Max power .... 138bhp at 6400rpm
Max torque .... 125lbft at 4400rpm
Fuel delivery .... Fuel-injection
Transmission ...... 5MT or 5SMT
Notes: Sequential gearbox available for 2001.

1ZZ-FE
Main market .... Europe
Years 2000-2007
Type .... Four-cylinder,
                          dohc, 16v
Bore & stroke ...... 79 x 91.5mm
Capacity 1794cc
Comp ratio 10.0:1
Max power .... 138bhp at 6400rpm
Max torque .... 125lbft at 4400rpm
Fuel delivery .... Fuel-injection
Transmission ...... 5MT or 5SMT
Notes: sequential gearbox available for 2001.

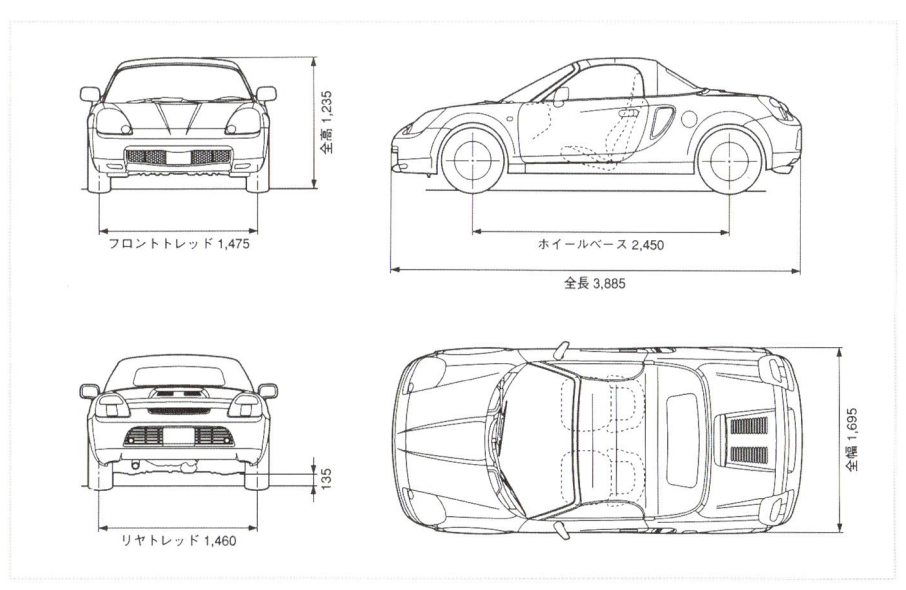

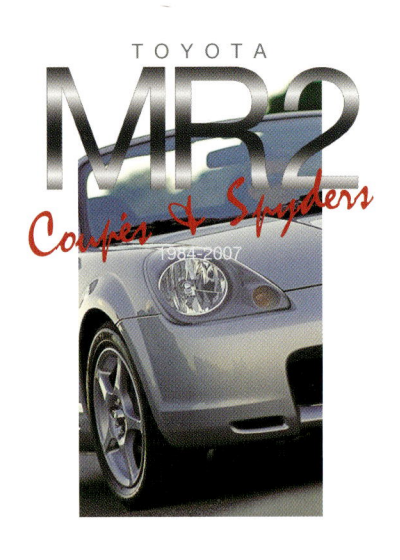

APPENDIX II
PRODUCTION FIGURES

Year	Production	Home sales	USA sales	Total exports	Cumulative prod total
1984	14,677	10,533	0	548	14,677
1985	51,271	7852	32,309	44,676	65,948
1986	42,506	6087	27,841	36,955	108,454
1987	26,368	6041	15,847	20,828	134,822
1988	18,129	5808	8044	12,421	152,951
1989	13,153	5473	5205	7321	166,104
1990	45,424	19,022	14,257	25,131	211,528
1991	31,603	10,805	9676	20,024	243,131
1992	19,897	11,964	5292	9686	263,028
1993	11,981	7452	2917	4918	275,009
1994	10,039	7909	908	2609	285,048
1995	5477	4317	387	1324	290,525
1996	3309	2487	37	991	293,834
1997	2466	1413	9	1089	296,300
1998	2481	1614	0	860	298,781
1999	5641	4054	0	441	304,422
2000	27,368	5520	7233	16,525	331,790
2001	13,268	3113	6254	13,570	345,058
2002	11,041	2132	4705	9909	356,099
2003	8893	1743	2934	6863	364,992
2004	6458	1402	2621	5747	371,450
2005	3883	1368	780	3035	375,333
2006	1328	1324	5	1215	376,661
2007	1156	1203	0	8	377,817

Total first generation cars	Approx 163,000
Total second generation cars	Approx 137,000
Total third generation cars	Approx 78,000

196

ALSO BY VELOCE PUBLISHING LTD —

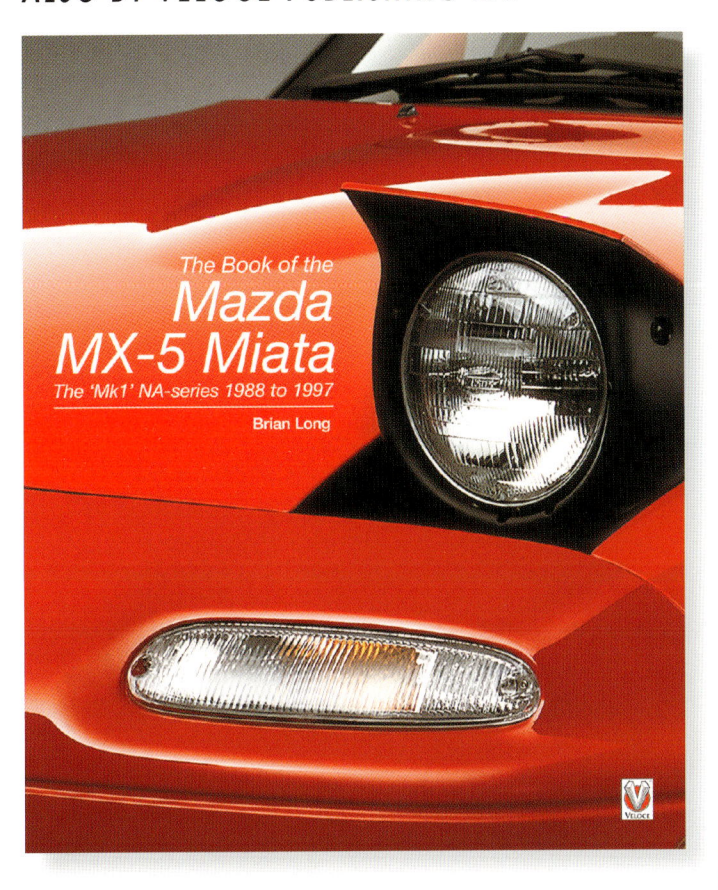

This is the definitive history of the first generation Mazda MX-5 – also known as the Miata or Eunos Roadster. A fully revised version of an old favourite, now focusing on the original NA series, this book covers all major markets, and includes stunning contemporary photography gathered from all over the world.

ISBN: 978-1-845847-78-4
Hardback • 25x20.7cm • £30* UK/$50* USA
• 144 pages • 221 pictures

For more info on Veloce titles, visit our website at www.veloce.co.uk • email: info@veloce.co.uk
• Tel: +44(0)1305 260068
* prices subject to change, p&p extra

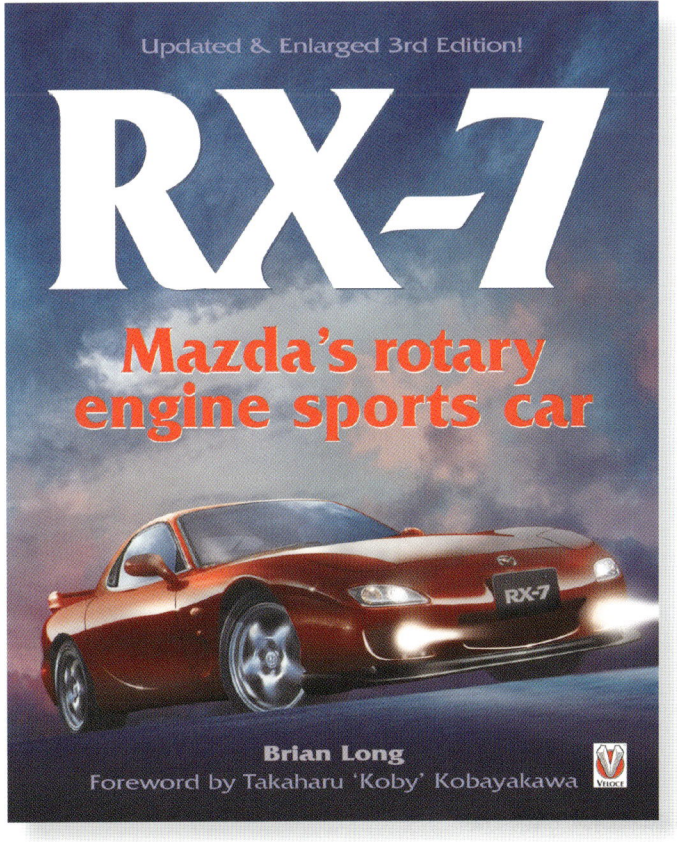

New edition of the definitive international history of Mazda's extraordinarily successful Wankel-engined coupés and roadsters, up to the end of production and the introduction of the RX-8. Advice on buying your own RX-7, plus coverage of the RX-7 in motorsport, and production figures. Heavily illustrated in colour.

ISBN: 978-1-845840-47-1
Paperback • 25x20.7cm • £35* UK/$60* USA
• 216 pages • 425 colour and b&w pictures

For more info on Veloce titles, visit our website at www.veloce.co.uk • email: info@veloce.co.uk
• Tel: +44(0)1305 260068
* prices subject to change, p&p extra

Datsun Fairlady Roadster to 280ZX
The Z-car story

Foreword by Yutaka Katayama - 'Father of the Z-car'
Brian Long

The Datsun 240Z inspired a generation of enthusiasts, outselling and outperforming almost all of its contemporaries. This book covers the full story of the Datsun sports cars, from the Fairlady roadsters through to the final 280ZX production model, illustrated throughout with contemporary material.

ISBN: 978-1-845840-31-0
Paperback • 25x20.7cm • £19.99* UK/$39.95* USA • 208 pages • 304 pictures

For more info on Veloce titles, visit our website at www.veloce.co.uk • email: info@veloce.co.uk • Tel: +44(0)1305 260068
* prices subject to change, p&p extra

Nissan 300ZX 350Z
The Z-car story

Brian Long

The definitive history of Nissan's Z-cars.
From concept to the end of production, covers all versions of the Nissan 300ZX and 350Z.
The 300ZX model enjoyed much success and is very highly-regarded by enthusiasts.
The stunning new 350Z has taken the Z-car back to its Datsun 240Z sports car roots.

eBook ISBN: 978-1-845847-18-0
£24.99* UK • 320 pictures

For more info on Veloce titles, visit our website at www.veloce.co.uk • email: info@veloce.co.uk • Tel: +44(0)1305 260068
* prices subject to change

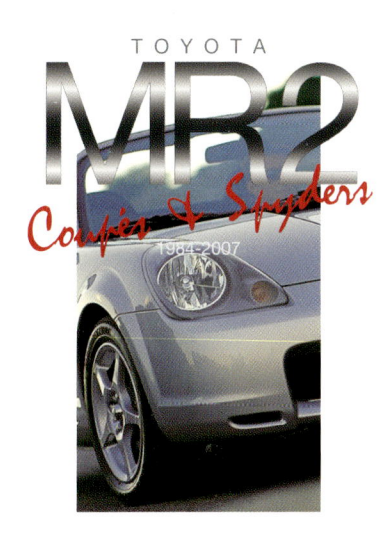

INDEX

Acropolis Rally 55
AHF 125
Alfa Romeo 165, 185
Alpine Rally 55
Andersson, Ove 17, 55
Aoki, Hideo 22, 25, 34, 35, 90, 92
apr 190
Arctic Rally 17
Arima, Kazutoshi 29, 72
ARTA 182
Assenza, Tony 49
Audi 57
Auriol, Didier 118
Australian GP 182
Auto Express 132
Autocar (& Motor) 46, 59, 68, 97, 98, 112, 124, 145, 164, 166, 177
Automobile 50, 170

Banks, Mike 69
Bell, Roger 60
Bertone 19, 65
Blitz 173
BMW 47, 105
Bremner, Richard 52
BTCC (BSCC) 17

Calamia, L 116
Car (GB) 98, 177
Car (Japan) 96, 126
Car & Driver 49, 50, 64, 65, 103, 115, 116, 125, 126, 170, 171
Car Graphic 166
CECOMP 150
Chevrolet 10, 126
Chicago Show 49, 166
Cho, Fujio 164, 188
Chrysler 9, 10, 16
Classic Cars 15, 46, 106
Complete Car 145
Copeland, Mike 39, 41
Coulter, Jeremy 46, 56

Daihatsu 16
DAMD 173
Dixon, Mark 106
Durig, J 116

Earls Court Show 100, 118, 138, 166
Esmond, Don 166
Essen Show 177

Evo 177, 184

F1 141, 142, 182, 188
Fast Lane 46
Ferrari 17, 36, 81, 97, 102, 104, 116, 117, 125, 126
Fiat 19, 20, 22, 45-47, 50, 65
Financial Times 116
Ford 9-12, 16, 47, 55
Forum 150
Frankfurt Show 185
Frere, Paul 17
Frey, Donald 12
Fujiwara, Yuji 152, 163

Galati, Michael 66
General Motors (GM) 9, 16, 47
Geneva Show 19
Gurney, Dan 102, 103

Hartley, John 37
Hashimoto, Masujiro 9
Hertz, Arne 55
Hino 12, 16
HKS Fritzinger M/sport 106
Honda 14, 37, 65, 67, 106, 139, 152, 187
Honda, Soichiro 125
Horning, Craig 66
Hosoya, Shiomi 13, 23

Iglesias, Enrique 160
IMSA 54, 55, 65, 66
Indycar 182, 188
Inomoto, Yoshihiro 30
Ishida, Taizo 11
Ishikawajima 9
Ishiura, Hiroaki 190
Isuzu 9, 10

Jaguar World 96
Japanese Grand Prix 15, 23
JGTC 133, 165, 182, 187, 188, 190
Jordan, Dave 16
Jordan, Michael 49

Kaishinsha 9
Kamiya, Shotaro 12
Katayama, Ukyo 141
Katayama, Yutaka 141
Kawano, Jiro 15

199

Kikuchi, Yasushi 133

Lamborghini 36, 126
Lancia 19, 57
Le Mans 133, 141
Lotus 19, 26, 36, 45, 100, 126, 177
Luthi, A. 116

Maling, Robert 126
Matra 19
Matsumoto, Kiyoshi 21
Mazda 17, 30, 48, 64, 71, 100, 102, 105, 106, 139, 145, 152, 164, 170, 177, 179, 187
Mazdaspeed 138
McCarthy, Mike 42
McCurry, Bob 104
McKay, Peter 177
McLaren 27
Meaden, Richard 184
MG 26, 41, 150, 177
Michelotti 55, 150
Mikkola, Hannu 17
Misono, Hideichi 72
Mitsubishi (Colt) 9, 17, 105
Mitsubishi Ralliart 138
Monocraft 173
Monte Carlo Rally 55
Mori, Toshinori 152
Morimoto, Masao 11, 12
Misono, Hideichi 72
Mitani, Sam 170
Motor (GB) 17, 30, 35, 45, 52, 57, 58, 60
Motor (Japan) 96
Motor Style 62, 64
Motor Trend 50, 69, 102, 104, 105, 125, 126, 179
MotorSport 46, 59, 96, 98, 105, 106, 116

Nakagawa, Tadashi 118, 142, 143, 146, 148, 150, 152
NASCAR 188
National Geographic 117
NEC Motor Show 40, 41, 63, 162, 166
Nismo 138
Nissan (Datsun) 9, 10, 12, 14, 15, 17-19, 37, 53, 67, 102, 135, 138, 139
Nitta, Morio 133, 182

OECOD 14
Ohno, Taiichi 12
Ohta 9
Okuda, Hiroshi 164, 188
Okuma-Nippon Sharyo 9
Ono, Sumio 26
Oshima, Kazuya 190
Otomo 9

Panther 75
Patrick, Scooter 16
Penske, Roger 104
Percy, Win 17
Performance Car 61
Peugeot 47, 57, 177
Philipp, K. 116
Plymouth 104
Pontiac 19, 23, 47, 48, 65
Porsche 19, 36, 64, 104, 106, 115, 146, 182
Portugal, Rally of (TAP) 17
Prince 16

RAC Rally 17, 55
Radley, Kevin 35, 58
Renault 12, 52
Road & Track 48, 52, 56, 65, 102, 104, 106, 170
Road Test 16

Safari Rally 41
Saito, Shoichi 11
San Remo Rally 55
SARD 133, 173
Sasaki, Kota 187
Sasaki, Shiro 20
Sato, Kiyondo 96
Sato, Kumi 165
Sato, Shozo 14
SCCA 16, 55, 118
Schwan Cabrio Co. 62
SE Asian Supercars Champs 116
Shelby, Carroll 16
Sigma 182
Simanaitis, Dennis 170
Smith 9
South Florida Motor Show 166
Sports & GT Cars 50
Stone, Matt 179
Strasser, J 116
Subaru 139
Suphot, Kasikam 116
Sutcliffe, Steve 177
Suzuki 139
Suzuki, Keiichi 133
Swiss Touring Car Champs. 116

Tachi, Nobuhide 173
Tachi, Shingo 133
Taguchi, Genichi 125
Takagi, Shinichi 133, 182
Tanaka, Hidenobu 165
Team Reckless 187
Thailand GP Champs. 116
Tokyo Auto Salon 134, 138, 171, 173, 182, 188
Tokyo Automobile Works 9

Tokyo Show 14, 15, 17-19, 23, 25, 26, 71, 89, 126, 138, 143, 145, 147, 148, 151, 152, 154, 157, 158, 166
TOM'S 170
Top Gear 177
Townsend, Brian 46
Toyoda, Eiji 11, 125
Toyoda, Kiichiro 9, 11, 18, 31
Toyoda, Sakichi 9
Toyoda, Shoichiro Dr 18, 31
Toyota Atlantic Champs. 68
Toyota Automobile Museum 22
Toyota Grand Prix 54
Toyota Team Europe (TTE) 55-57, 103, 142, 188
Toyota Today 100, 126
TRD 133, 134, 136, 138, 139, 172, 176
Triumph 19, 49
Turin Show 55
TVR 71, 105

Uchida, Kunihiro 72, 88, 145
Uchida, Tateo 150
Ukiya, Togiro 13

Vauxhall 177
VeilSide 173
Vogue 132
Volkswagen 14, 16, 19, 47, 67, 105
Volvo 10

Wada, Akihiro 18
Watanabe, Katsuaki 188
WedsSport 182
What Car? 19, 41, 47, 56, 67, 71, 100, 184, 185
Wheels 66, 104, 119, 120, 139, 145, 176
Winfield, Barry 116, 170
Works Tuning 138
WRC 17, 18, 55, 56, 71, 103, 119, 141, 142

Yamaha 15
Yamano, Tetsuya 187
Yamauchi, Seiichi 19-23, 27
Yates, Brock 115
Yoshida ('Takuri') 9
Yoshida, Akio 19, 25, 26
Yoshida, Shintaro 9

Zagato 171, 172
Zagato, Andrea 171

The Toyota Motor Corporation, its subsidiaries and products are mentioned throughout the book.